THE
OTHER
LOYALISTS

THE
OTHER
LOYALISTS

Ordinary People, Royalism, and the
Revolution in the Middle Colonies, 1763–1787

Edited by

Joseph S. Tiedemann,
Eugene R. Fingerhut,
and Robert W. Venables

"A map of Pensilvania, New-Jersey, New-York, and the three Delaware counties. 1749," By Lewis Evans. Courtesy Library of Congress, Geography and Map Division.

Published by
State University of New York Press, Albany

For information, contact State University of New York Press, Albany, NY
www.sunypress.edu

Production by Eileen Meehan
Marketing by Anne M. Valentine

Library of Congress Cataloging-in-Publication Data

The other loyalists : ordinary people, royalism, and the revolution in the
   middle colonies, 1763–1787 / edited by Joseph S. Tiedemann, Eugene R.
   Fingerhut, and Robert W. Venables.
      p. cm.
   Includes bibliographical references and index.
   ISBN 978-1-4384-2589-4 (hardcover : alk. paper)
      1. American loyalists—Middle Atlantic States.   2. Middle Atlantic States—
History—Revolution, 1775–1783.   I. Tiedemann, Joseph S.   II. Fingerhut,
Eugene R.   III. Venables, Robert W.

E277.O84 2009
973.3—dc22   2009005423

10 9 8 7 6 5 4 3 2 1

Contents

List of Figures

Acknowledgments

Gene Fingerhut and Joe Tiedemann began this project over two years ago. We both had had a long-term interest in Loyalism as a field of research, and we both believed that Loyalists of the ordinary sort in the Middle Colonies had never received sufficient attention. Unfortunately, Gene died in 2006 before the project was completed. Joe would like to take this opportunity to note how much he has appreciated Gene's friendship and colleagueship over the past thirty years. He also wants to express his special thanks to Bob Venables, who graciously stepped into the breach as an editor and made completion of this manuscript possible.

The map of New Jersey in chapter 2 is by John P. Snyder. It is used by permission of the New Jersey State Archives, Trenton, New Jersey, and has been adapted for this chapter by Timothy Corlis and Valerie Addonizio of Special Collections and University Archives, Rutgers University Libraries, New Brunswick, New Jersey. The Van Bergen Overmantel that appears in chapter 3 was photographed by Richard Walker and is used here courtesy of the New York State Historical Association, Cooperstown, New York. The scene, which is attributed to John Heaten, includes three African American slaves; two American Indians appear in the foreground and were perhaps there to trade. The painting was originally over the mantel in the home of Dutch farmer Marten Van Bergen in Greene County, New York. The map on the Quakers in chapter 4 is from Lester J. Cappon, ATLAS OF EARLY AMERICAN HISTORY, ©1976, Princeton University Press, and is reproduced here with the permission of Princeton University Press. The Map of the Country of the VI Nations, 1771, in chapter 5 is from Thomas Donaldson, Henry B. Carrington, and T. W. Jackson, Extra Census Bulletin: The Six Nations of New York (Washington, DC: U.S. Census Printing Office, 1892). The image, reportedly, of John Connolly, used in chapter 6, has a questionable provenance. It is most likely an early-twentieth-century creation, commissioned by Louisville historian Reuben Durrett. It is used here with permission of the Filson Historical Society, Louisville, Kentucky.

  Finally, we wish to thank Fredricka Rene Davis for her fine map of the Delmarva Peninsula, which was made especially for this study, and to Brant Venables for his skill in scanning the illustrations.

  All three editors wish to extend our thanks to the authors who contributed chapters to *The Other Loyalists*. They all cooperated fully in the endeavor and made our task of editing a very pleasant one. We also express our deep appreciation to our own families. To our wives, Lyn Fingerhut, Barbara Tiedemann, and Sherene Baugher, for amiably sacrificing family time. To Terry, Mindy, Gady, Shiri, Talia, Karin, Zachary, and Haley for being there. To Scott, Erika, Michael, Colleen, Hannah, Emma, and Annie Tiedemann, who bring constant joy and who good-naturedly and unfailingly put the study of history in the proper perspective. To Brant Venables, the best son parents could have, whose views of archaeology and history are always helpful; to my mother, Florence, who at ninety-five and, along with my late father, Charles, did so much to inspire my love of history; and to Chief Irving Powless Jr. of the Onondaga Nation, whose close friendship since 1970 has meant so much to me personally and professionally.

Introduction

Joseph S. Tiedemann and Eugene R. Fingerhut

Americans living in the Middle Colonies—Pennsylvania, Delaware, New Jersey, and New York—were demonstrably loyal to Great Britain throughout the French and Indian War (1756–1763). Praised by the government for their contribution to the war effort, their patriotism soared following the spectacular victory over France. Only when the British government attempted to balance its budget, pay off its war debts, and increase its grip over its North American colonies by taxing them and by rigorously enforcing and tightening its trade laws did urban residents in the Middle Colonies begin to question whether the government's policies were threatening their liberty and economic well-being. A postwar depression, which many colonists blamed on the government's stern policies, only worsened tempers and the economic climate.

Most Americans nonetheless initially refused to see villainy in Britain's behavior. For British Americans, it was the mother country. For other European Americans, including the Dutch in New York and the Germans in Pennsylvania, it was the country that allowed them great religious and political freedom. Surely when the government understood how its policies were hurting Americans, it would change course. Moreover, Middle Colony residents, who lived in rural areas and who were consequently not immediately affected by the government's new economic policies, did not earnestly participate in the protest movement until 1774.[1]

Government policies were only one source of tension that Americans in the Middle Colonies experienced in the postwar period; local issues also divided them. Anglicans and Presbyterians clashed repeatedly for religious and political advantage.[2] The Dutch Reformed were bitterly split over how their church should be organized and over what language should be used in religious services.[3] New Englanders and New Yorkers clashed over land titles in what would eventually become the state of Vermont.[4] Landlords

1

and tenants came to blows over land tenure in the Hudson Valley, where Loyalism and neutrality would become major forces during the Revolution.[5] Pennsylvanians and alleged intruders from Connecticut fought over possession of the Wyoming Valley in Pennsylvania.[6] Scots-Irish Presbyterians on the Pennsylvania frontier and Benjamin Franklin's Quaker Party fought over Indian policy and whether the province should become a royal colony.[7] The East Jersey proprietors and the settlers of Newark and Elizabethtown, Essex County, New Jersey, clashed, sometimes violently, over landownership.[8] In short, in the 1760s and 1770s, the Middle Colonies were a cauldron of religious, ethnic, economic, and social tensions. As British-American relations turned violent, these internal strains helped determine the side individuals and groups supported in the imperial conflict.

Despite the considerable efforts historians have made to uncover and examine these tensions, their understanding of the American Revolution in the Middle Colonies is uneven and incomplete. Scholars know much about the victors but much less about the Loyalists; those Royalists, with whom they are familiar, were usually from the elite rather than from the common sort.[9] Books have been written about Loyalism as it existed in each of the Middle Colonies.[10] Others have delved into Loyalist intellectuals, who ideologically justified their cause, or into prominent Royalist leaders, such as Joseph Galloway.[11] However, no study has focused on the Loyalists of the lower and middle sort who constituted the muscle and sinew of their cause.

The Other Loyalists: Ordinary People, Royalism, and the Revolution in the Middle States, 1763–1787 seeks to remedy this situation. It aims to uncover how these long-ignored, ordinary people of the Middle Colonies chose the side they did; to illustrate the ways in which they participated in and endured the Revolution; and to determine what happened to them because of their defeat. It offers a collection of chapters written by scholars of the Middle States who have focused their research on the experiences of the American Loyalists. In addition, a chapter on the Haudenosaunee (Iroquois) explores why most of these Indians eventually sided with Britain and remained loyal to their long-standing treaty obligations with the Crown.

The "other Loyalists" were a complicated medley of individuals escaping attention primarily because of the paucity of evidence. Most remained faithful to the Crown throughout the conflict because of their political beliefs, religious convictions, or self-interest. Some had started as Patriots but later converted to Loyalism. For example, Ross Curry of Philadelphia abandoned the Patriot cause to become a lieutenant in a unit of Pennsylvania Loyalists. He was attainted for treason, had his property confiscated, and became an exile in Parrtown (St. John), New Brunswick, Canada.[12] Gilbert Giberson, a Monmouth County, New Jersey, farmer, resigned his captaincy in a Patriot militia unit when the Declaration of Independence was promulgated.[13] Ellis

Barron of Woodbridge, New Jersey, served on the Patriot Committee of Observation for Middlesex County in 1775 but joined the Loyalists when British troops entered New Jersey in 1776.[14]

Others returned to Loyalism for reasons that had little to do with political independence. Nicholas Housecker, who was allegedly a mercenary, fought first as a major under Whig General Anthony Wayne but then switched over to the other side.[15] Some individuals found themselves labeled and mistreated as Tories, even though they did not consider themselves Loyalists. The predominately neutral Quakers, for example, had initially tried to remain aloof from the contest because of their religious commitment to pacifism. However, their refusal to aid the American Patriots, who needed all the help they could get, led to Friends being labeled Tories. New Jersey Whigs seized the property of Joseph Peddle, a Quaker farmer residing in Burlington County, who had refused to bear arms for either side because of his religious beliefs. Delaware Patriots denounced Quaker John Cowgill of Duck Creek Hundred as an enemy of his country and carted him through the streets for declining for religious reasons to use Continental money.[16]

Once the military conflict commenced, many Loyalists signed pro-British loyalty oaths, supplied provisions, and worked as civilian auxiliaries in support of the Crown. They performed militia service in places that the British controlled. For example, James Burwell of Morris County, New Jersey, enlisted in the British military in 1776 and fought at Yorktown in 1781.[17] Loyalists also joined the irregular forces that harassed the American forces in areas that were in dispute.[18] Evan Thomas became a commander in the Bucks County Volunteers, engaged in predatory warfare against the Whigs around Philadelphia, and finally settled in New Brunswick, Canada. Lewis Fenton and Jake Fagan, both of Monmouth County, raided out of the New Jersey pine barrens.[19] Some adherents of the Crown suffered imprisonment or gave their lives for the cause. Elizabeth Vandyne was jailed in New Jersey in 1776 for counterfeiting Continental currency. Fagan was killed in 1778, and Fenton the next year. Lawrence Marr of New Jersey was captured attempting to carry off the books and papers of the Continental Congress. The state of Pennsylvania tried him as a spy and executed him in Philadelphia in 1781. John Connel and David Dawson of Chester County, Pennsylvania, joined the British army during its stay in Philadelphia (1777–1778) and removed with the troops to New York. Connel eventually served on a British privateer, was captured in 1779, and was subsequently imprisoned. Dawson was caught passing counterfeit Continental money, for which he was put to death. Abraham Carlisle, a Philadelphia Quaker, also aided the British, when they occupied that city. After they withdrew, Pennsylvania prosecuted him in 1778 for assisting the enemy. He was consequently put to death, and his property was confiscated.[20]

Ultimately, many of the active Loyalists, who had virulently opposed the Revolution, fled from the new nation to settle elsewhere in the empire. They became the founders of Upper Canada (Ontario), the solidifiers of British control of Arcadia (Nova Scotia), and the creators of New Brunswick as the Loyalist province.[21] Isaac Allen, a Trenton, New Jersey, attorney and a lieutenant colonel in the New Jersey (Loyalist) Volunteers, suffered a disability while fighting in the South and went to New Brunswick, where he eventually became a Supreme Court justice. Thomas Francis, an African American slave, fled New Jersey for New York in 1782 and subsequently went to Canada.[22] Other Crown adherents went to Great Britain, Bermuda, or the British West Indies. However, many Loyalists, especially those who had refrained from displays of demonstrative support for the Crown or who had not alienated their American neighbors, remained in the new nation after the war and sought to reintegrate themselves into their communities.[23] William Debnam, an English shoemaker, became a Loyalist but remained in Burlington County, New Jersey.[24]

The imperial policies that Britain pursued following the French and Indian War eventually persuaded many Middle Colony residents that George III was engaging in a conspiracy against liberty and that American independence was the only option. It is consequently advisable to outline the key British actions that led to civil war and revolution in the thirteen North American mainland colonies that became the United States.[25] To start, the king issued the Proclamation of 1763 in October of that year. It forbade colonists from settling west of the Appalachian Mountains. At first, westward-looking colonials believed that this prohibition injured their economic prospects by restricting their ability to acquire land, but over time loopholes enabled investors and settlers to ignore the line and to move beyond the mountains. However, the proclamation included another important provision. Land that the Crown controlled, and for which no land grants had been made, was to be allotted to veterans of the war. This provision led to the establishment in New York of large pockets of veterans on the northern frontier, near Canada. These settlements placed experienced soldiers, who had fought for the empire, in a strategic location in case of a future war that involved the former French colony. Many former soldiers here and elsewhere in the Middle Colonies were either indifferent to the Revolutionary cause or eventually became Loyalists, for they would not accept the destruction of the empire for which they had fought.[26]

Richard Robert Crow, who served with the British army at Quebec, Louisburg, Martinique, and Havana, was granted land in New York but settled in Perth Amboy, New Jersey. At the time of the Revolution he turned down an offer to serve as a high-ranking officer in the American army and fled to Nova Scotia at war's end.[27] Philip Skene, who had been wounded at the Battle of Ticonderoga (1758), received a land patent in 1765, in what became the township of Skenesborough (presently Whitehall, New York). He served with the British army until he was captured at the Battle of Saratoga (1777). In 1779, the state of New York confiscated his property because of his Loyalism. William Gilliland, a British veteran, received a grant of land north of Crown Point on the west side of Lake Champlain. Whigs arrested him early in the war for his pro-British activities. His finances consequently suffered, and he was imprisoned for debt from 1786 until 1791. In 1771, another British veteran, Adolphus Benzell, received a land grant for over 1,000 acres at Crown Point, New York. Although he died in 1775, he had favored the British before the war, and most members of his family were Royalists in the Revolution.[28] A few veterans did transfer allegiance to the revolutionaries, however. Richard Montgomery, for example, served as a general in the Continental Army and in 1775 gave his life for the cause.[29]

The Revenue (or Sugar) Act of April 1764 was designed to help pay for the British troops stationed in America, in part to keep the colonists in check. The act cut in half the duty on foreign molasses in the belief that the lower rate would inhibit smuggling; banned the importation of foreign rum into the colonies; doubled the duties on foreign products shipped from England to the colonies; and extended the list of enumerated goods, which colonists could transport only within the empire. The act also authorized creation of a new vice admiralty court in Halifax, Nova Scotia. At a prosecutor's discretion, any colonial maritime or civil case falling within the jurisdiction of a vice admiralty court could now be filed at the new site. The cabinet hoped this step would improve the chance of conviction, enhance compliance with the act, and increase revenues. Because rural people were little affected by this act, they remained quiet. However, aggrieved urban colonials, especially those such as Isaac Sears, a future Whig, who favored free trade, did protest.[30] Over time, as Parliament enacted other measures to regulate and tax trade, urban merchants in the Middle Colonies would be forced to calculate whether or not the advantages they reaped from the Acts of Trade and Navigation outweighed the cost of the legislation enacted after 1763. The conclusions that individuals reached about this matter in turn often influenced how they sided during the Revolution.[31]

The Quartering Act of March 1765 required colonial governments to supply and house British troops sent into their provinces. These troops were supposed to protect the empire from attacks by a revived French military or by aggrieved Native Americans. Protesting colonists argued that the measure was really taxation without representation, for Parliament was attempting to compel provincial assemblies to allocate money for specific purposes. Urban Americans claimed too that these troops were being kept in or near the major cities along the Atlantic coast to enforce Britain's postwar policies and to intimidate residents. The presence of these troops on American soil inescapably became a sore point. In 1770, the "Battle of Golden Hill" pitted British regulars against New York City's Sons of Liberty and neighborhood civilians.[32] However, De Lancey party leaders, many of whom eventually became Loyalists, saw the army as a counterweight to the Liberty Boys and were pleased that local militants had gotten a drubbing in the fracas.[33]

Heedless of the negative (although predictable) consequences of its actions, Parliament also passed the Stamp Act (March 1765), the first direct tax Britain ever levied on its North American colonies. The measure taxed most printed material, including newspapers, broadsides, and many commercial and legal documents. The tax was to be used to support the army stationed in America. Infractions of the law could be tried, at the prosecutor's discretion, in either the juryless vice admiralty courts or the local common law courts. The tax antagonized many economic constituencies in the Middle Colonies. Merchants were incensed because the need for stamps on commercial documents would increase costs and complicate business transactions. The requirement that the tax be paid in specie threatened (following the Currency Act) to kill the very commerce upon which the measure aimed to raise revenue. Land speculators were vexed by the taxes that were now to be levied on their deals. Lawyers were upset, for stamps would have to be affixed to court documents. Printers were appalled, because the statute inflated the cost of what they printed, threatened to undermine freedom of the press, and could wreck their business. Clergymen feared that baptisms, marriages, and funeral services would not be performed, for the certifying documents would be taxed.

The Stamp Act consequently managed to offend all of the key interest groups in the Middle Colonies. Thomas Jones, a staunch Loyalist who would finish his life as an exile in England, believed that "all parties, all denominations, and all ranks of people appeared unanimous in opposing its [the Stamp Act's] execution." Joseph Galloway, a future Pennsylvania Loyalist, argued that "one Half of the Americans will die rather than submit to it. The Fermentation is almost general to the Eastward, and does not seem much less to the Westward."[34] Not all colonists, of course, opposed this legislation. James McEvers, a New York City Anglican merchant and future Loyalist, accepted appointment as a stamp officer only to resign when he was threatened with violence against his person and possessions.[35] William Coxe, a Philadelphia merchant who had been appointed New Jersey's stamp distributor, had initially expected provincial residents to comply with the act and had even executed the 3,000-pound sterling bond required by the Stamp Commission. However, after the *New York Gazette; or the Weekly Post-Boy* reported on August 22 that someone had refused to rent him a home "unless he would insure the House from being pulled down, or Damaged," Coxe resigned and pledged to a large crowd that he would not implement the measure.[36] John Hughes, Pennsylvania's stamp distributor, was not so easily intimidated. He recommended to the Stamp Commissioners that his son Hugh be appointed Coxe's replacement. In mid-September, with the help of about 800 "White Oaks," Hughes even withstood a mob that wanted to demolish his house because he would not resign his commission. However, it was all to no avail. In early October he pledged before a crowd that he would not execute the Stamp Act. What is unknown is what this stubborn man thought, in the midst of his tribulations, about the fact that his brother Hugh was a prominent New York City Liberty Boy. An embittered man, John Hughes died in 1772 in Charleston, South Carolina, where he had been serving since July 1771 as Collector of the Customs.[37]

More than self-interest was involved in the opposition to the Stamp Act. As early as the 1752, William Livingston, a future Whig and the first governor of the state of New Jersey, had argued: "It is a standing Maxim of *English Liberty*, 'that no Man shall be taxed, but with his own Consent.' "[38] This argument was repeated in rebuttal to the postwar British imperial policies. One writer neatly summarized the American constitutional position: "Since we are agreed in the *Right* of the Colonies, *to be taxed only by their own Consent given by their Representatives*; It follows, that if they are not so represented in Parliament, [then] they have not given, nor can they possibly give their Consent to be there taxed, consequently . . . such a Tax must be arbitrary illegal and oppressive." "Freeman" avowed that it was "not the Tax itself" but "the unconstitutional Manner of imposing it, that is the great Subject of Uneasyness to the Colonies. Whatever Justice there may be in their bearing a proportional Charge of the War, they apprehend, that Manner of levying the Money upon them, *without their own Consent*, by which they are deprived of one of the most valuable Rights of British Subjects, *never can be right*." A third writer, "A. B. C.," insisted that Americans could be "taxed only by our Legal constitutional Representatives."[39] However, future Loyalist Joseph Galloway took a different approach: "If then it be reasonable that America should be taxed towards her own safety, and her safety depends on her enabling the Crown to secure it; if without this she may be lost to the mother country, and deprived of her civil as well as religious rights, if she has been thus negligent of her duty, and perversely obstinate," is it not undeniable that it "becomes the indispensable duty of a British parliament to interfere and compel he to do what is reasonable and necessary" and tax the colonies.[40]

Although the protest movement against the mother country led by 1765 to a significant amount of violence, most colonial farmers were largely unaffected by the laws passed between 1762 and 1765 and did not perceive the ruckus against the new British policies to be important in their lives. They continued to support the government, if for no other reason than that they rarely trusted urban merchants and their machinations. Although there were exceptions, most assemblymen and government officials from the rural areas of the Middle Colonies never became leaders of the protest movement in the 1760s. In Dutchess County, New York, many tenant farmers of Patriot landowners turned Loyalist, not because they favored Britain but because they resented their landlords. On the other hand, many Loyalist landlords, such as the Johnson family, which held vast acreage in the Mohawk Valley and which had retained the fidelity of its tenants, often took them into the pro-British camp.[41]

Although the ministry had backed down in the face of urban riots and repealed the Stamp Act in March 1766, the government's general policy remained the same. Immediately after the repeal, Parliament passed the Declaratory Act, which proclaimed its supremacy over the colonies "in all cases whatsoever."[42] The continued need for revenue led George Townshend, chancellor of the Exchequer, to persuade Parliament in 1767 to pass the Townshend Act, which levied duties on glass, lead, paint, paper, and tea imported into the colonies. The proceeds were to be spent for colonial defense and for defraying the cost of government. A companion measure created an American Board of Customs at Boston that had power over all colonial customs officials. Urban colonists responded with a boycott of British goods, and in 1770 Parliament again backed down, this time by repealing all of the Townshend duties except the one on tea, which was to remain a symbol of parliamentary sovereignty. The De Lancey party, which favored close economic ties with the empire, consequently persuaded New York City residents to lift their boycott against all items except tea, and the other Middle Colonies reluctantly followed suit. Relations with the mother country improved.[43]

In 1773, Parliament enacted the Tea Act, mainly because the East India Company faced bankruptcy and needed to sell the vast amounts of tea overflowing its warehouses. The Tea Act remitted all British duties on tea exported to the colonies and allowed the company to sell directly to consignees there instead of at public auction in Britain. Company tea would thus be cheaper than the tea British Americans smuggled into the colonies to avoid paying the Townshend duty. The ministry failed to consider how colonists would react to a law that overturned established patterns of trade, that ruined a few influential businesses by granting the East India Company a monopoly in America, and that would set a precedent for Parliament's creating similar monopolies over other commodities on the American market. It also reopened the question of whether Parliament could tax the colonies.[44] Many Americans considered the Boston Tea Party (December 1773) and the corresponding events that prevented the marketing of tea in other cities, including Philadelphia and New York, virtuous resistance to a program that would ultimately harm all Americans. The resulting tea parties split colonial public opinion between those who supported the protests against this monopoly and those who may have lamented the act but who detested even more the mass public actions that violated the laws.[45]

Parliament responded to the Boston Tea Party with the Coercive (or Intolerable) Acts, which aimed to punish Massachusetts for its insubordination and to intimidate colonists elsewhere from following that province's lead. But the altering of the Massachusetts charter, the tampering with the administration of justice in the province, and closing the port of Boston only awakened colonists throughout America, in both urban and rural areas, to the imperial dangers that menaced them. If Parliament could unilaterally change the Massachusetts charter and mistreat that colony, then it could do the same to them.[46]

Both rural and urban communities in the Middle Colonies sent food and money to support Boston in its crisis. This was the first time many agrarian areas became active in the protest movement.[47] The fear of violence was so great that the pro-government response to the crisis was muted. For example, in November, "Cassius" informed New York City that William Kelly, a retired merchant who was living in London, had told officials of the East India Company that "there was no danger from the Resentment of the People of New York" over the Tea Act, for New York's "Governor [William] Tryon, (a Military Man) who . . . would cram the Tea down their Throats." Kelly's effigy was consequently carted around town and burned at the Coffee House before thousands of spectators."[48]

In the wake of the Coercive Acts, most of the colonies agreed to send representatives to Philadelphia in September 1774 for what became the First Continental Congress. In October, that body adopted the Continental Association, which called for the cessation of all British imports beginning on December 1, 1774, and for an embargo on all exports to Britain, Ireland, and the British West Indies starting on September 1, 1775. Most important, Congress called for the creation of committees in every town, city, and county to enforce the association and to punish violators. In time, these extralegal bodies became the de facto governing bodies in each colony.[49] They enforced boycotts and made sure that local residents supported the protest movement. To do this each committee circulated the Continental Association and demanded that everyone living in the community sign it. Even more pressure was now put on those who remained loyal to the Crown. If they did not sign, they might be ostracized, tarred and feathered, or run out of town on a rail.[50] Many people signed under protest to save their lives, health, and property.[51] After the Cumberland

County, New Jersey, committee forced Silas Newcomb to confess that his family had consumed tea, he was compelled to sign a recantation rather than be denied all contact with his neighbors.[52] In effect, the associations became law enforcement agencies, maintaining obedience to congressional and state committees' policies.

When the North Ministry and General Thomas Gage responded with military force against the protesters in Massachusetts and shed American blood at Lexington and Concord (April 1775), many Americans rose to meet the challenge.[53] It was now almost inevitable that only a clash of arms could settle the conflict.

As American Patriots in the Middle Colonies moved from protest to rebellion, other Americans, who opposed independence, joined the Royalist camp. John Alsop, who was representing New York in the Continental Congress, resigned his position over independence and consequently was labeled a Tory.[54] Some of these Loyalists, such as Governor William Franklin of New Jersey and Thomas Jones, a justice of the New York Supreme Court, had objected to at least a few of the new imperial policies that followed the French and Indian War, but they now stopped short and refused to make a complete break with the mother country.[55] Others were involved in groups of people that were much more Loyalist in sentiment than they themselves were, but because of friendship these lukewarm persons were cemented to Loyalism. What follows in these pages are the stories of ordinary people who for various reasons withstood the hostility of their neighbors to remain faithful to the Crown.

Middle Colony Loyalists, for the most part, were disorganized, because they relied heavily on government officials to enforce colonial ordinances. This dependence was their great weakness. As the associations in the local communities and the committees that they spawned grew in strength and became de facto governments, the official royal colonial governments, on which the Loyalists depended for their safety and security, were rapidly wasting away, for British power in America had really rested on the consent of the governed. Hence, in many communities, officials such as sheriffs, who were responsible for enforcing laws, either shirked their duty or were not obeyed. The associations were becoming the new political powers, and the Loyalists were forced to obey, suffer punishment, or leave.[56]

The reasons individuals chose to support the Crown are varied and complicated. As the following chapters will demonstrate, many colonials did so for reasons that were personal or local rather than imperial in nature. The causes for allegiance to the Crown often involved religion, ethnicity, relations with neighbors, crime, and revenge for perceived wrongs. The horse thief, William Clarke of New Jersey, for example, had self-interest rather than principle in mind when he stole and then sold more than 100 horses to the British for profit before he was killed in 1782.[57] Some Royalists resented the newly emerging Whig leaders, especially those who did not come from an elite background. Still other Loyalists were clearly motivated by the imperial crisis. Throughout this period of imperial reorganization, many Loyalists had agreed with the protesters that the acts passed by Parliament were undesirable, did not meet the needs of the empire, and were destructive of patriotism. However, these critics differed from the Patriots in that they did not perceive these acts as a suitable justification for either violence or independence. Some Crown supporters were pacifists who opposed violence and war. Other Loyalists blamed the adoption of Britain's policies on evil ministers and misguided parliamentarians. They anticipated that when "good" King George saw through the plans of these ministers, he would correct the problem. The Crown was sovereign and would right all evils. This misunderstanding was their undoing. They did not realize that the king and Parliament were allied in pursuing this policy. Loyalists maintained their belief that the Patriots were misguided, ill informed, and more destructive of liberties and freedoms than was the British Crown.

Notes

1. For the situation in the rural areas, see John B. Frantz and William Pencak, eds., *Beyond Philadelphia: The American Revolution in the Pennsylvania Hinterland* (University Park, PA: Pennsylvania State University Press, 1998), and Joseph S. Tiedemann and Eugene R. Fingerhut, eds., *The Other New York: The American Revolution beyond New York City, 1763–1787* (Albany: State University of New York Presss, 2005).

2. See Joseph S. Tiedemann, "Presbyterianism and the American Revolution in the Middle Colonies," *Church History* 74 (2005): 306–44.

3. Arthur J. Wall, "The Controversy in the Dutch Church in New York concerning Preaching in English, 1754–1768," *New-York Historical Society Quarterly* 12 (1928): 39–58; John W. Beardslee, "The Dutch Reformed Church and the American Revolution," *Journal of Presbyterian History* 54 (1976): 165–81; Randall Balmer, *A Perfect Babel of Confusion: Dutch Religion and English Culture in the Middle Colonies* (New York: Oxford University Press, 1989), viii–ix, 38–39, 106–108, 141–56.

4. Michael A. Bellesiles, *Revolutionary Outlaws: Ethan Allen and the Struggle for Independence on the Early American Frontier* (Charlottesville, VA: University Press of Virginia, 1993); Paul R. Huey, "Charlotte County," in *The Other New York*, ed. Joseph Tiedemann and Eugene Fingerhut, 199–222.

5. Sung Bok Kim, *Landlord and Tenant in Colonial New York: Manorial Society, 1664–1775* (Chapel Hill, NC: University of North Carolina Press, 1978), chs. 7, 8.

6. William Smith, *An Examination of the Connecticut Claim to Lands in Pennsylvania. With an Appendix, Containing Extracts and Copies Taken from Original Papers* (Philadelphia, PA: Joseph Crukshank, 1774), in *Early American Imprints,*

1639–1800, ed. American Antiquarian Society (New York: American Antiquarian Society, 1981–1982), no. 13629 (hereafter cited as *Early American Imprints*); Lorett Treese, *The Storm Gathering: The Penn Family and the American Revolution* (University Park, PA: Pennsylvania State University Press, 1992), ch. 9.

    7. William S. Hanna, *Benjamin Franklin and Pennsylvania Politics* (Stanford, CA: Stanford University Press, 1964); James H. Hutson, *Pennsylvania Politics, 1746–1770: The Movement for Royal Government and Its Consequences* (Princeton, NJ: Princeton University Press, 1972).

    8. John E. Pomfret, *Colonial New Jersey: A History* (New York: Charles Scribner's Sons, 1973), 158–59; 161–63; Nicholas Murray, *Notes Historical and Biographical concerning Elizabeth-town, Its Eminent Men, Churches, and Ministers* (New York: Columbia University Press, 1941), 1–12; Brendan McConville, *These Daring Disturbers of the Public Peace: The Struggle for Property and Power in Early New Jersey* (Ithaca, NY: Cornell University Press, 1999).

    9. The terms *Loyalist* and *Royalist* are used interchangeably in the text for stylistic reasons. Whigs often used the pejorative term *Tory* to refer to a Loyalist, for in Britain a Tory was a person who had supported James II during the Exclusion Crisis (1678–1681) and the Glorious Revolution (1688) or who in the eighteenth century championed the Church of England and upheld the prerogatives of the Crown over the rights of Parliament; see "Whig and Tory," in *Encyclopædia Britannica*, retrieved September 12, 2007, from *Encyclopædia Britannica Online*, http://0-www.search.eb.com.linus.lmu.edu:80/eb/article-9076766.

    10. Alexander C. Flick, *Loyalism in New York during the American Revolution* (New York: Arms Press, 1901); Philip Ranlet, *The New York Loyalists* (Knoxville, TN: University of Tennessee Press, 1986); Anne M. Ousterhout, *A State Divided: Opposition in Pennsylvania to the American Revolution* (New York: Greenwood Press, 1987); Harold Bell Hancock, *The Loyalists of Revolutionary Delaware* (Newark, DE: University of Delaware Press, 1977); E. Alfred Jones, *The Loyalists of New Jersey: Their Memorials, Petitions, Claims, Etc., from English Records* (Newark, NJ: New Jersey Historical Society, 1927; reprint, New York: Gregg, 1972).

    11. Janice Potter, *The Liberty We Seek: Loyalist Ideology in Colonial New York and Massachusetts* (Cambridge, MA: Harvard University Press, 1983); John E. Furling, *The Loyalist Mind: Joseph Gaslloway and the American Revolution* (University Park, PA: Pennsylvania State University Press, 1977); Eugene R. Fingerhut, *Survivor: Cadwallader Colden II in Revolutionary America* (Washington, DC: University Press of America, 1983).

    12. Lorenzo Sabine, *Biographical Sketches of Loyalists of the American Revolution with an Historical Essay*, 2 vols. (Port Washington, NY: Kennikat Press, 1966), 1: 353. Wilbur Henry Siebert, *The Loyalists of Pennsylvania* (Boston, MA: Little, Brown, 1864; reprint; Boston: Gregg, 1972), 105.

    13. Jones, *Loyalists of New Jersey*, 81–82.

    14. Ibid., 21.

    15. Sabine, *Biographical Sketches of Loyalists*, 1: 545.

    16. Jones, *Loyalists of New Jersey*, 170; Hancock, *The Loyalists of Revolutionary Delaware*, 23, 74.

    17. Sabine, *Biographical Sketches of Loyalists*, 1: 277; Jones, *Loyalists of New Jersey*, 264.

18. The literature on the American Loyalists is extensive. For a start, see William H. Nelson, *The American Tory* (Oxford: Clarendon Press, 1961); Wallace Brown, *The Good Americans: The Loyalists in the American Revolution* (New York: Morrow, 1969); Robert M. Calhoon, *The Loyalists in Revolutionary America, 1760–1781* (New York: Harcourt, Brace, Jovanovich, 1973). For an estimate of the number of Loyalists in the colonies, see Paul H. Smith, "The American Loyalists: Notes on Their Organization and Numerical Strength," *WMQ*, 3rd ser., 25 (1968): 259–77.

19. Sabine, *Biographical Sketches of Loyalists*, 2: 353; 1: 420, 408; Jones, *Loyalists of New Jersey*, 275.

20. Sabine, *Biographical Sketches of Loyalists*, 2: 451, 48; 1: 331, 361, 296; Jones, *Loyalists of New Jersey*, 275, 293; Siebert, *Loyalists of Pennsylvania*, 69, 77.

21. For Canada see A. G. Bradley, *The United Empire Loyalists: Founders of British Canada* (London: Thornton Butterworth, 1932); Robert M. Calhoon, Timothy M. Barnes, and George A. Rawlyk, eds., *Loyalists and Community in North America* (Westport, CT: Greenwood Press, 1994), Part 3.

22. Sabine, *Biographical Sketches of Loyalists*, 1: 159, 435; Jones, *Loyalists of New Jersey*, 9–10.

23. Mary Beth Norton, *The British Americans: The Loyalists Exiles in England, 1774–1789* (Boston: Little, Brown, 1972); Wilbur Henry Siebert, *The Legacy of the American Revolution to the British West Indies and the Bahamas: A Chapter Out of the History of the American Loyalists* (Columbus, OH: Ohio State University, 1913).

24. Jones, *Loyalists of New Jersey*, 59.

25. Jack P. Greene, "The Seven Years War," in *The British-Atlantic Empire before the American Revolution*, ed. Peter Marshall and Glyn Williams, 90, 94 (London: Cass, 1980); Lawrence Henry Gipson, *Triumphant Empire: Thunder-Clouds in the West*, vol. 10 of his *The British Empire before the American Revolution*, 15 vols. (New York: Caxton Printers, 1936–1970), 202–207; Jack M. Sosin, *Agents and Merchants: British Colonial Policy and the Origins of the American Revolution, 1763–1775* (Lincoln, NE: University of Nebraska Press, 1965), 39; Bernhard Knollenberg, *Origins of the American Revolution, 1759–1766* (New York: Macmillan, 1960), 134–35.

26. For this issue, see Eugene R. Fingerhut, "Assimilation of Immigrants on the Frontier of New York, 1764–1776," PhD diss., Columbia University, 1962.

27. Jones, *Loyalists of New Jersey*, 56–57.

28. Horace S. Mazet, "Skene, Philip (1725–1780)," in *The American Revolution, 1775–1783: An Encyclopedia*, 2 vols., ed. Richard L. Blanco, 2: 1526–27 (New York: Garland, 1993); Huey, "Charlotte County," in *The Other New York*, 200–205, 207, 209, 214. The editors of this volume wish to thank Paul Huey for his assistance concerning this issue.

29. Hal T. Shelton, "Montgomery, Richard (1738–1775)," in *The American Revolution*, 2: 1091–94.

20. Joseph S. Tiedemann, *Reluctant Revolutionaries: New York City and the Road to Independence, 1763–1776* (Ithaca, NY: Cornell University Press, 1997), 39, 160.

31. Gipson, *Triumphant Empire*, 228–31; Knollenberg, *Origins of the American Revolution*, 166–68.

32. Lee R. Boyer, "Lobster Backs, Liberty Boys, and Laborers in the Streets: New York's Golden Hill and Nassau Street Riots," *New-York Historical Society Quarterly* 57 (1973): 281–308; Sosin, *Agents and Merchants*, 34–36; John Shy, *Toward Lexington:*

The Role of the British Army in the Coming of the American Revolution (Princeton, NJ: Princeton University Press, 1965), 178–90; Tiedemann, *Reluctant Revolutionaries*, 108–12, 147–49.

33. William Smith, *Historical Memoirs of William Smith, Historian of the Province of New York, Member of the Governor's Council*, 2 vols., ed. William H. W. Sabine, (New York: Ayer Publishing, 1956–1958), 1: 172–73.

34. Jones, *History of New York during the Revolutionary War and of the Leading Events in the Other Colonies at That Period*, vol. 1 (New York: Printed for the New-York Historical Society, 1879), 18; Extract of a Letter from Joseph Galloway, September 20, 1765, in "Intelligence from the Colonies Relating to the Stamp Act," House of Lords Manuscripts, no. 209, Library of Congress, Washington, DC.

35. James McEvers to Cadwallader Colden [August 1765], *The Letters and Papers of Cadwallader Colden*, 9 vols. (New-York Historical Society, *Collections*, vols. 50–56, 67–68 [New York: Printed for the New-York Historical Society, 1918–1923, 1937–1938]), 7: 56–57; Tiedemann, *Reluctant Revolutionaries*, 66, 68, 72–74.

36. *New York Gazette, or the Weekly Post-Boy*, August 22, 1765; William Coxe to the Stamp Office, August 24, 1765, Coxe to William Franklin, September 3, 1765, Treasury 1/442, Treasury 1/455, Library of Congress.

37. Extracts of Letters from John Hughes, September 8, 12, 1765, in "Intelligence from the Colonies Relating to the Stamp Act," House of Lords Manuscripts, no. 209, Library of Congress; Edmund S. Morgan and Helen M. Morgan, *The Stamp Act Crisis: Prologue to Revolution*, rev. ed. (New York: Collier Books, 1963), 314–16; *The Massachusetts Spy*, September 3, 1771; *Boston Evening-Post*, March 9, 1772.

38. William Livingston et al., *The Independent Reflector or Weekly Essays on Sundry Important Subjects More Particularly Adapted to the Province of New York*, ed. Milton M. Klein (Cambridge, MA: Harvard University Press, 1963), 62, emphasis in original.

39. *New York Gazette, or the Weekly Post-Boy*, May 16, June 13, July 11, 1765.

40. "Americanus" [Joseph Galloway] to Mr. Bradford, *Pennsylvania Journal and Weekly Advertiser*, August 29, 1765.

41. For political sentiment in the rural areas, see Frantz and Pencak, eds., *Beyond Philadelphia*, and Tiedemann and Fingerhut, eds., *The Other New York*. For Dutchess County, see John Shy, "Armed Loyalism: The Case of the Lower Hudson Valley," in *A People Numerous and Armed: Reflections on the Military Struggle for American Independence*, ed. John Shy, 181–92 (Oxford: Oxford University Press, 1976).

42. Morgan and Morgan, *Stamp Act Crisis*, 347–48.

43. Thomas C. Barrow, *Trade and Empire: The British Customs Service in Colonial America, 1660–1775* (Cambridge, MA: Harvard University Press, 1967), 226; Robert Middlekauff, *The Glorious Cause: The American Revolution, 1763–1789* (New York: Oxford University Press, 1982), 146–52; Tiedemann, *Reluctant Revolutionaries*, 121–24, 153–54.

44. For a Royalist's defense of Parliament's right to pass the Tea Act, see "Z" to Mr. Rivington, New Jersey, August 23, 1774, *Rivington's New-York Gazetteer*, September 8, 1774.

45. Benjamin W. Labaree, *The Boston Tea Party* (New York: Oxford University Press, 1964). For a Loyalist condemnation of the Boston Tea Party and the

support that American Whigs gave to Boston, see Benjamin Booth to Mr. Charles Thomson of Philadelphia, New York, July 6, 1774, *Rivington's New-York Gazetteer*, July 7, 1774.

46. David Ammerman, *In the Common Cause: American Response to the Coercive Acts of 1774* (Charlottesville, VA: University Press of Virginia, 1974). For the text of these acts, see Merrill Jensen, ed., *American Colonial Documents to 1776* (London: Oxford University Press, 1955), 779–85.

47. See, for example, Philadelphia, July 25 [1774], "At a Provincial Meeting of Deputies chosen by the several counties in Pennsylvania; held at Philadelphia, July 15, 1774," *Rivington's New-York Gazetteer*, July 28, 1774.

48. *New York Journal*, November 18, 1773; Smith, *Historical Memoirs*, 1: 156; Robert J. Christen, *King Sears: Politician and Patriot in a Decade of Revolution* (New York: Arno Press, 1982), 280–81.

49. Jensen, *American Colonial Documents to 1776*, 813–16. For a Loyalist challenge to the Continental Congress and the committees it created, see "An Englishman," *Rivington's New-York Gazetteer*, March 30, 1775.

50. For a defense of Parliament's actions, see "The following DIALOGUE . . . ," *Rivington's New-York Gazetteer*, May 26, 1774.

51. For one example of individuals who signed the Continental Association under pressure, see Letter to Mr. Rivington from the precinct of Newburgh in Ulster County, July 14, 1775, *Rivington's New-York Gazetteer*, July 21, 1775.

52. Sabine, *Biographical Sketches of Loyalists*, 2: 120.

53. Tiedemann, *Reluctant Revolutionaries*, 220–25.

54. Ranlet, *The New York Loyalists*, 7.

55. Sheila L. Skemp, *Benjamin and William Franklin: Father and Son, Patriot and Loyalist* (Boston: Bedford Books, 1994), 51: Jones, *History of New York*, 1: 18.

56. On the importance of this process for American victory, see John Shy, "The Military Conflict Considered as a Revolutionary War," in *A People Numerous and Armed*, 199–200.

57. Sabine, *Biographical Sketches of Loyalists*, 1: 317.

PART 1

Places

CHAPTER 1

"The Ghost of Clow"

Loyalist Insurgency in the Delmarva Peninsula

Wayne Bodle

Americans have not taken Loyalism very seriously as a historical subject. This was especially true during the "Whiggish" middle decades of the nineteenth century, when a celebratorial *national* identity emerged to support state building. Despite occasional pulses of modest academic interest in Loyalist studies, the "King's friends" always seem to be one big book away from popular critical mass, or at least historiographical redemption.[1] At the *local* level, however, members of small communities during the century after 1783 recalled the agonized political choices their Loyalist ancestors had been forced to make and the high price they had paid for their convictions in violence, exile, and sacrificed fortunes. Romantic narratives emerged about "bandit" Loyalists who repaid intolerance with resistance or who sought revenge for acts of Patriotic coercion. Such accounts suggest how radical the Revolution really was. Legends about James De Lancey's "Cowboys" in Westchester County, New York, or about the Claudius Smith family across the Hudson River, or about the "Pine Robbers" of coastal New Jersey, or about the Doane Gang of Bucks County, Pennsylvania, reveal the internal conflict of the Revolutionary years in some measure of its true intensity and even horror.[2]

Early in the twenty-first century, when American leaders find it easier to topple rogue regimes than to replace them with viable national governments, the study of small insurgencies—and an appreciation of the energy that they drain from conventional struggles—offers more than merely an inclusive understanding of the past. One locally celebrated but otherwise obscure episode of counterrevolutionary resistance during the Revolution was the "insurrection" led by China Clow on the Delmarva Peninsula during

1778. Erupting in a "marginal" and isolated locality, the event caused more noise than it did harm, but it forced both sides to confront the dangers inherent in autonomous violence. The decade that the affair took to resolve as a political and criminal matter also reminds us of the difficulty contemporaries had in extracting modern statehood from the scattered debris of a Revolutionary conflagration.[3]

We have few analytical models with which to compare these apparently similar, but often idiosyncratic, episodes that took place during the Revolution. A cursory look at them suggests that motives of raw criminality and preexisting ethno-religious or social antipathy helped initiate and sustain rebellions against the Revolution. Systematic comparative investigations, however, are rare. In *Between the Lines*, Harry M. Ward has offered a framework organized around the concept of military "lines." Wherever two or more institutionalized armed bodies establish control over defined territories near each other and project force into the intervening areas, whether to contain their adversaries or to organize their supporters, he argues, opportunistic private military activities are likely to erupt nearby.

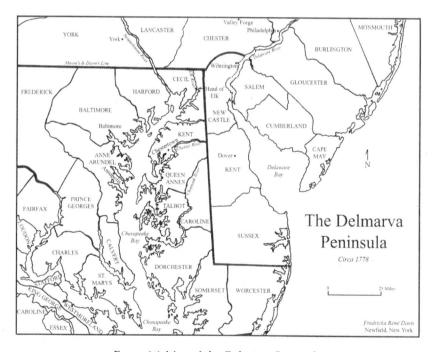

Figure 1.1 Map of the Delmarva Peninsula

Ward probes a dozen such episodes in a wide range of diverse localities to find their common meaning.[4]

Ward's project is a useful beginning, but in many arenas of Revolutionary conflict, stable military *lines* were hard to find. As violence dragged on for seven long years and civilians tired of it, control became harder to maintain, and distinctions between civil and military spheres blurred. Below Pennsylvania, complex overlapping geographies, longer distances between the coast and the frontier, tangled Indian alliances, and a lack of urban areas to anchor headquarters garrisons all complicated the military situation. This was especially true on the "Delmarva" Peninsula, which was located between the Chesapeake and Delaware River estuaries. Few places sustained a greater range or intensity of internal clashes during the war. Where there *were* any "lines" in this region, they were not often military, they were seldom very clear, and they were almost never congruent with each other. Conflicts *straddled* diverse and opaque boundaries rather than occurring *between* them and generated different dynamics from those to the north.[5]

This phenomenon began with the landscape itself. Viewed from outer space, the Delmarva Peninsula looks like a crumb of land that might have been flung from the continent with one more tectonic convulsion. Its bounding estuaries had rich marine resources, but they were quickly dismissed by explorers looking for "Northwest" passages through the continent. European settlement of the central Atlantic coast occurred south of the Chesapeake and east of the Delaware and only slowly encroached onto the peninsula. Virginians assumed that the Chesapeake Bay was part of their domain, but Charles II's 1632 grant to the Calvert family of "Maryland" above the Potomac River frustrated that design.[6]

New Netherlanders focused on the Hudson River and made only token settlements on the east bank of the Delaware. The resulting vacuum encouraged renegade Dutch investors and Scandinavian settlers after 1638 to carve out a "New Sweden," but that colony never had more than a few hundred Europeans.[7] Native American "lines" of operation were even more complex. The Susquehanna Valley directed a prong of Iroquoian power southeast into a complex coastal web of Algonquian agricultural and migratory hunter-gatherer bands. Pressed from above after 1600 by the aggressive "Five Nations" Iroquois confederacy, the Susquehannocks reanchored their domain near the neck of the Delmarva Peninsula. They made war on or forged alliances with Algonquian peoples as opportunity dictated and traded with diverse Europeans.[8]

The Dutch seized the South (or Delaware) River from the Swedes in 1655, only to be swallowed up by Englishmen nine years later. The restored Stuart king, Charles II, tried to close the territorial gap between New England and Virginia by seizing New Netherland in 1664, but his brother, the Duke of York, gave the area between the Hudson and Delaware rivers to two of his own retainers. Those men established "New Jersey," but that colony soon crumbled into two separate colonies, while the proprietary bodies governing each one fragmented continuously. Virginia gained economic sway over Maryland, but it never eliminated its rival. Royal governors of New York after 1680 tried to reverse the fragmentation of New Netherland, but proprietary interests resisted them. York claimed the west bank of the Delaware River as an implicit fruit of New Netherland. When Charles in 1681 gave William Penn a large grant west of the Delaware River, the Duke sold Penn his suspect claim to allow his friend to control access to the river.

The Penn family then began a generations-long struggle with the Calverts over not just the north-south boundary between Pennsylvania and Maryland but also the east-west division of the Delmarva Peninsula. Penn found the settlers in his three "Lower Counties on the Delaware" resistant to Quaker rule. In 1701, he gave those counties their own legislature, but they shared an appointed governor with Pennsylvania. What emerged along the lower Delaware was less than a real colony, and it only became an embryonic state at the start of the Revolution. The Penn-Calvert border was under negotiation or in litigation from the 1680s through the 1750s. When "Mason's and Dixon's Line" was surveyed in the 1760s, the "Tangent Line" that divided the peninsula shifted territories long administered by Maryland into Delaware's jurisdiction.[9]

If geophysics and geopolitics failed to consolidate the Middle Atlantic's estuarine coast, then socioeconomic development was no more effective. By 1700, the Delmarva Peninsula was an integral part of a Chesapeake Bay tobacco dominion. Then, beginning in the mid-eighteenth century, some Eastern Shore planters began shifting their crops from tobacco to cereal grains.[10] This transition gave small Delmarva planters a more stable but much more modest external source of income than tobacco markets had. The marketing structure of grain tied the northern peninsula to Philadelphia's export merchant community and gradually drew it into that city's trade hinterland. This changed, if it did not weaken, the political, economic, and social relationships between small planters and local elites in affected Chesapeake counties.[11] As Delaware Valley farmers learned after 1680, large investments in enslaved African labor were incompatible with the economic dynamics of grain-based mixed farming. The unfree, racialized labor system to which Chesapeake planters had become wed came under increased pressure.[12]

There also was a religious dimension to Delmarva's emergence as a dynamic if an eccentric place. Maryland was a Catholic colony, but after 1650 it became more like Virginia in its social composition, political style, and dominance by Anglican planters. The cultural model to the north in Pennsylvania, toward which Delmarva was trending, embraced religious pluralism. The Great Awakening of the 1740s was an explosive event best known for boisterous, urban-centered revival tours led by men such as George Whitefield, who landed in America in 1739 at New Castle. The spiritual stirring of the counties around the head of the Chesapeake Bay helped launch some important Revolutionary political careers.[13] Whitefield's English life was a chapter in the emergence of "Methodism" as a reform movement within the Church of England. Methodism came much later to America, but the Delmarva Peninsula was its colonial "cradle." It was a vigorously proselytizing sect spread by missionaries and circuit-riding lay preachers. It attracted diverse colonists but especially the smaller planters who were likeliest to be displaced or threatened by the agricultural transition occurring in the same period. It also appealed to African slaves and to the many freed blacks whose unstable social status was partly a product of the same phenomenon. Both before and during the Revolution, its leaders struggled to disentangle themselves from the imputation of having pro-English political sympathies.[14]

All of these factors shaped Delmarva's reputation as an incubator of individualistic tumult as the imperial crisis began. Insurrections, however, are led by *actors*, not factors, and we need to locate China Clow against this mosaic of institutional structures and cultural processes. This is no easy task. The same circumstances that promoted upheaval on the peninsula kept agents likeliest to record it at a distance. "Delaware's" three counties managed their own affairs, and Patriot forces dominated only New Castle County in the north. Maryland became almost *two* colonies after 1632, known as the Eastern and Western Shores. When the Revolution began, the pro-Independence forces were secure only west of the bay. That area had the state's capital, Annapolis, and the seaport of Baltimore, which emerged after 1740 as a grain exporting center.[15]

The Revolution forced Patriots to defend their sovereignty everywhere, but that job was difficult between the Chesapeake and the Delaware, and Continental and state leaders embraced it cautiously. George Washington took his army to Wilmington in September 1777 to block the British invasion of Pennsylvania through the Chesapeake; he then retreated to defend Philadelphia. After settling at Valley Forge, he sent Maryland troops back to Wilmington to protect his southern supply lines. The British were frequently tempted to meddle in Delmarva to exploit Continental weaknesses, but their leaders usually resisted those temptations.[16]

I

China Clow was born in the 1730s into a small planter family from the Chesapeake side of the Delmarva Peninsula. His parents, Nathaniel and Susannah Clough, in 1748 owned two tracts of fifty acres each in Queen Anne's County, Maryland. With three boys and nine children to support, this made them very small planters. The earliest record specific to him shows the 1758 enlistment of "Cheaney" Clow in a company that Captain Benjamin Noxon had raised to serve in the Seven Years' War from the "Lower Counties." Clow either gave his age or was estimated by the recruiter to be twenty-four years old, and he was described in the return as a "lab[orer]."[17]

Local historians assume that Clow remained in the British army after the war and became an officer, but this is doubtful.[18] Enlistment in Noxon's unit would not have made him a member of the "British army" but rather of the "provincial forces" that colonies raised to support regular royal troops and their own militias. Tensions between British and local forces were deep, and they were only partially relieved by political compromise or financial incentives. Even Washington coveted but failed to win a commission as a regular, and there is no reason to believe that Clow fared better. Poor laborers were caricatured targets for the scorn that British officers poured on "*Americans*," who first heard themselves called by that name in the 1750s. Washington's army swarmed after 1775 with yeomen whose consciousness was forged in the derogatory crucible of Seven Years' War service. If China Clow's Toryism—to say nothing of the crimson uniform that he supposedly pulled from a closet in 1782 to save his life—stems from the 1750s, it would be surprising.[19]

Noxon's company took part in General John Forbes's expedition in 1758 across Pennsylvania from Carlisle to the Monongahela River and Fort Duquesne.[20] After 1760, as the war wound down on the North American continent, poor men such as Clow were discharged in droves onto a shrinking colonial economy. In addition to the economic transitions that the upper Chesapeake experienced from a staple to a mixed-farming regime, wealth in most colonies became more concentrated, land prices rose in coastal and urban areas, intergenerational relations were strained by resulting inheritance anxieties, and a proto-class structure began to replace the more flexible existing systems of social hierarchy. The social strains that these changes produced everywhere undoubtedly affected political allegiances as the Revolution loomed, but scholars do not agree about their specific effects.[21]

China Clow apparently avoided landlessness, tenancy, and continuation in the precarious status of a laborer.[22] He may not have inherited land, but how he otherwise acquired any is hard to know. It mattered greatly where his property was and how well he developed it and managed its integration into the new market structures emerging on the peninsula. The family's hearth was in the upper part of Queen Anne's County, Maryland, above where the Choptank River forked into the Tuckahoe and the Choptank proper, near an imperceptible line between that drainage system and one running into the Chesapeake through the Chester River. These watersheds participated differently in the transition from tobacco to grain cultivation. The "Oxford" port hinterland of the Choptank shifted earlier but less fully than did the "Chestertown" district on the Chester River. The specific crop mix ran more to corn in the Oxford area and to wheat in the Chester system. These circumstances shaped the role of local versus outside merchants in organizing the export of commodities, and the area's North American or Atlantic commercial and cultural connections. Kent County, Maryland, and its port, Chestertown, were drawn into an Atlantic grain trading world. Lower Queen Anne's farmers sold their corn surpluses to planters along the tobacco coast of the Chesapeake Bay.[23]

China Clow's life was affected by a much more tangible external factor in the 1760s. Those years saw the resolution of the long dispute between the Penn and Calvert families over the boundary between their colonies. Two English surveyors, Charles Mason and Jeremiah Dixon, came to America to plot a line on the ground reflecting this compromise. That line is famed mostly for its east-west segment that formed a symbolic marker during the Civil War era. Their survey, however, also fashioned the distinctive circular boundary around Wilmington that separated the "Lower Counties" of Delaware from Pennsylvania, and a "Tangent Line" running from the juncture of the two former lines to the southwestern corner of Delaware. The latter's determination was largely a technical process, but one that had inevitable political dimensions.[24] China Clow's land wound up in Little Creek Hundred, in Kent County, Delaware, west of modern Kenton. The only marks he left on the public record before 1778 were criminal in nature. In the spring of 1774 a Kent County grand jury accused Clow, who it described as a "yeoman," and his accomplice, of being "persons of evil fame and name, and of conversation, and not caring to get their livelihood by honest labour, but by fraud and deceit, maintaining their idle course of life." The grand jury alleged that they had won more than twenty-eight pounds cheating a man in a card game. Both men were convicted and fined three pounds each. This was not the kind of conduct that would win them many friends in a society that was already plummeting toward political disorder.[25]

Both halves of the peninsula were galvanized when fighting broke out near Boston in the spring of 1775, and the situation began to unravel when Independence was declared just over a year later. Maryland's Whig government had difficulty maintaining a grip on the Eastern Shore counties, which had no obvious urban subadministrative community centers. The overburdened governor, council, and legislature managed that place through two-way communication with elite Patriots living there. Many of the latter, however, took refuge near Baltimore or Annapolis, or accepted Continental political, military, and diplomatic appointments. Clashes between radical and moderate Whig forces on the Western Shore provoked a bitter struggle over Maryland's postindependence state constitution, which drew attention from the situation across the Bay.[26]

Delaware's even weaker government had opposite problems. Its political seat or capital, at Dover, was *embedded in* an area of doubtful political allegiance. Its leaders were cautious moderates who took their cues during the late imperial crisis from elites in nearby states such as Pennsylvania. They united in 1775 to topple the old proprietary government under John Penn, but they could not commit to Independence. Their efforts to suppress a Loyalist uprising in Sussex County almost kept Delaware from even being *represented* on July 2, 1776, when the Continental Congress embraced separation. Delaware, like Maryland, also focused its attention between 1776 and mid-1777 on the contentious problem of drafting a state constitution. Messier issues about relations on the ground between population groups and economic interests, especially in the bitterly divided counties of Kent and Sussex, had to wait for serious attention.[27]

This situation changed in mid-1777, when the military conflict veered toward Delmarva. British Commander in Chief General William Howe sought to sever the rebellion along Mason's and Dixon's Line by subduing Pennsylvania and bringing its supposedly loyal residents back into the empire. In July he decided to attack Philadelphia by sea rather than by marching across New Jersey. His fleet appeared in the mouth of the Delaware Bay in early August; it then headed up the Chesapeake Bay later that month. Threatened with intervention from both sides, Delmarva erupted. This situation might have created a "between-the-lines" scenario such as the one Harry M. Ward described in analyzing the dynamics of bandit Loyalism.[28] The contest soon moved, however, back into Pennsylvania. As Howe's men landed at the head of the Elk River, the Continental army advanced to Wilmington but then shadowed the enemy north toward the open countryside of the Brandywine Valley. A sharp but indecisive skirmish at Cooch's Bridge in New Castle County on September 3 ended general action in Delaware. Left behind in a world of swamps, cedar stands, small farms, and sharply incised but navigable tributary rivers, especially on the Chesapeake side, the peninsula resumed its role as a sideshow or even a backwater of the Revolution.[29]

Delaware appeared ready to crumble. After Howe's troops defeated the Americans at Brandywine Creek in Chester County, on September 11, 1777, he seized Philadelphia and sent troops to Wilmington, where they captured John McKinley, the "president" of that state. The redcoats held Wilmington until mid-October. By then, Admiral Richard Lord Howe's fleet of transport vessels had come around from the Chesapeake to the Delaware side of the peninsula to resupply his brother's army. While Lord Howe tried to clear the defensive obstructions in the river below Philadelphia, he used the New Castle coastline as an anchoring point for these operations.[30]

This situation made New Castle unsafe as a seat of government. October elections for the legislature in the county had to be moved inland. The legislature had agreed to meet that fall in Dover as a concession to conservative political forces in the central and southern parts of the state. Washington's decision in December to send Maryland General William Smallwood to garrison Wilmington with 1,800 Maryland and Delaware troops blocked Delaware's government from returning to the north. It thus had to govern the state from within a hearth of popular disaffection. While the state's elected chief executive remained a prisoner of war, the legislature met in concert with two acting governors, Thomas McKean and then George Read. A successor willing to take President McKinley's place permanently was not found until March 1778.[31]

Caesar Rodney accepted that office on March 31 in circumstances that appeared grim. Two weeks earlier, he had lamented to McKean that it would be necessary to "rouse this little Branch of the Union from its heretofore Torpid State." Rodney summarized the plight of "those in this Peninsula who Openly profess friendship to the American Cause, a narrow neck of Land liable to the incusions of the Enemy, by water, in small parties."[32] On the Maryland side of the peninsula, meanwhile, Colonel George Dashiell of that state's militia warned his governor from Somerset County about "Loyalist activities" in his district. Dashiell enclosed depositions from his officers describing their efforts to round up American deserters. They met aggressive resistance that led to personal injuries and an attack by some deserters on the home of one of the state's officers.[33] Back on the Delaware coastline, Colonel Charles Pope, a Continental officer stationed at Wilmington under Smallwood, warned Rodney that thirty or forty British "mereens" had landed near the mouth of Little Duck Creek and carried off a herd of cattle grazing in the salt marshes.[34] The Delaware Council was soon "convinced that some of the disaffected inhabitants of Sussex County have taken up arms, much to the terror of the good people of said county and the encouragement of the British forces to land and make excursions there." It asked acting President McKean to order General Dagworthy to disarm any disloyal residents in the area.[35]

It is unclear why this insurgency erupted suddenly on the peninsula in March and April. One possibility is an awkward intrusion by Continental forces into Delmarva in late February on a scale substantial enough to provoke the region but far too weak to overawe its population. The American army, camped at Valley Forge sixty miles to the north, had experienced its most sustained and dangerous period of material hardship of that famous winter between February 12 and 20. Constant rain washed out regional roads and made river transportation impossible, and the army's logistical systems collapsed. Washington reluctantly exercised the draconian martial powers Congress had given him to impress food, clothing, and wagons from local civilians.[36]

After exhausting the hope of seizures near his camp and sending General Anthony Wayne on an expedition into New Jersey, Washington looked to Delmarva's granary in the south to restock the commissary stores at Valley Forge while shielding Continental supply lines from the southern states through Head of Elk. To lead this mission, Washington chose Captain Henry Lee, a Virginian who had shown great sensitivity in dealing with civilians while overseeing Washington's intelligence-gathering service in Chester County early in the winter.[37] The gravity of the crisis at camp, however, impaired Lee's ability to protect civilians from the ravages of an official plundering expedition. Lee remained in Delaware until early March. The eruption of Loyalist disorders there shortly after he returned north suggests that the intrusion of Continental military force was one catalyst for popular resistance.[38]

Lee's initial impression of the area in late February was that "very little discontent prevails among the inhabitants" except for the "notoriously disaffected." He found Delaware "void of government," a situation that turned the area into a haven for deserters. Lee believed that there were at least 500 of them, and that their defiance had been encouraged by "men of power and influence." He carried out a methodical foraging operation in which his men visited "each and every farm," and he worried that if the farmers were not paid, as he had promised, their acquiescence would end. He said that disaffected persons were "by far the most numerous in this state," but that by a combination of strength and leniency he had kept them "sullen" rather than actively hostile. Less than a month later, the peninsula was in chaos.[39]

China Clow emerged suddenly at the center of this insurrection in mid-April 1778. Although it is clear that he was active in this episode, Clow also may have provided Continental authorities with the necessary human face in an otherwise abstract crisis that they were desperately trying to contain from afar. The first indications that the disturbances even *had* a leader came from Maryland. Lieutenant Colonel William Henry of that state's militia wrote from George Town on April 13 to his superior Colonel William Bordley, requesting orders about suppressing "an insurrection." A day later he described an operation in progress to capture China Clow.[40] By the 15th, Henry reported that his cavalry was retreating from "Loyalist insurgents."[41] On April 17, the Maryland Council sent Bordley a company of artillery. If the wind allowed, they were ordered to sail up the Chester River to Chestertown in Kent County, Maryland. If not, they should land at Queens Town, in lower Queen Anne's County, and march toward the site of the trouble. The councillors told Bordley that if, with these reinforcements, he "should prove too hard for the Insurgents, we would not have you stop short at the Line of our own State, but follow them 'til they are entirely broke up." In other words, he should push them into Delaware.[42]

That state's authorities were aware of Clow's presence in the area, and they fully intended to keep the rebels in Maryland. Militia Colonel Samuel Patterson wrote to General Smallwood that the " 'old disorder' [was] still reigning in this state." Between 600 and 700 Tories had "assembled in arms on Jordan's Island at the Head of Chester River near Edward Tilghman's plantation." They were "commanded by China Clow, Mr. Tilghman, and others; they are obliging persons to go with them and taking arms of those who refuse." "Some believe," he wrote, "that they expect to be joined by British forces landing in Delaware in a few days."[43]

Smallwood had been warned the day before by Colonel Pope, whom he had sent to Kent County, Delaware, to assess the situation, that "China Clow and others have collected a body of Tories and raised a fort." That structure was probably located on Clow's land, immediately on the Delaware side of the line, twelve miles northwest of Dover. Pope gathered a group of militia and cautiously approached the site to investigate, when a hot skirmish erupted. About 150 of the enemy, he wrote, "sallied out" from the fort, and "a smart fire began." Pope withdrew with one casualty on each side. He believed that Clow had more than 200 men, and that they had armed themselves by coercing their neighbors. He asked Smallwood for "40 or 50 good men" and an artillery piece.[44] Pope wrote to Governor Rodney on the same day that he could not assail the fort without reinforcements and confirmed that his forces had killed one of Clow's men.[45]

Reporting to political leaders from two states that uneasily shared the peninsula and groping across the complex topography of central Delmarva, Pope, Bordley, Dagworthy, Henry, and others seemingly had China Clow surrounded. Smallwood, at Wilmington, with access to Continental resources in Pennsylvania, came closest to being a coordinating "hinge" for this operation. On April 17 he wrote to the president of the Continental Congress, Henry Laurens, in York, Pennsylvania, and enclosed copies of his recent correspondence but judged that while the insurrection "appeared to be powerful . . . there is more smoke than fire."[46]

Smallwood, having sent Pope to lead the enterprise, left it to the states to supply additional manpower. Grudgingly, and with difficulty, they did, and the situation began to resolve itself. On April 16, Pope "ordered the Militia from Head of Chester to Join me . . . within one mile and a half of their fortress." The fact that the headwaters of the Chester River were in Maryland suggests that—with Smallwood's blessing and the tacit acquiescence of normally jealous state political authorities—Pope as a Continental officer was leading an informal two-state combined operation. On April

16 or 17, Pope's men attacked Clow's position and dispersed its occupants
with relative ease. The state leaders were soon congratulating each other
and reassuring colleagues at greater distances that the danger had at least
temporarily subsided.[47]

II

Because angry echoes of this event still reverberated in both states fourteen
years later, we can achieve a modest glimpse into its dynamics from a closer
range than the "armchair" perspective that most of the rest of the extant
documentation offers. In 1792, James Tilghman, who may have been the
son of the aforementioned Edward Tilghman, collected depositions from
leaders of the Maryland militia forces who had tried to rout China Clow.
Donaldson Yeates, a Kent County, Maryland, planter who described himself
as "the eldest officer called on the emergency," led Maryland's militia on the
spot that week. Yeates remembered that the "insurrection" had begun "in the
Forrest of Queen Anns County headed by China Clows." James Tilghman
was a young man who "resided at his Father's farm in the neighbourhood of
the insurgents." When asked, Tilghman "gave me every information that I
believe he was possessed of." Yeates sent Tilghman and several other locals
"out on the business of making discoveries."[48]

When they returned, several militiamen furiously claimed that Tilghman was one of Clow's men, and that he had been in his "fort." Trying to
maintain order in his own ranks, Yeates arrested Tilghman and challenged
anyone in camp to show proof of his guilt. No one came forward with evidence, and Yeates concluded that Tilghman was not a Loyalist. The episode
scarred Tilghman's reputation in Maryland for years. Its chief interest for
our purpose is its disclosure of the precarious degree of military order on
the Whig side in 1778. Yeates elaborated on his testimonial in two other
letters in 1792, describing his need to protect Tilghman from "insult" and
to maintain order among his own men. He recalled that "at this time there
was no Court Martials Established and the militia [was] unorganized by
government to laws of discipline." The depositions show how uncertain the
situation was after Pope's assault on Clow's fort. Tilghman and his friends
were sent to find where "China's next lodgement" was. They failed, but
Yeates recalled that Clow had "left a number of his poor adherents to shift
for themselves." "These became prisoners," he noted, "and were separately
examined in order to make discovery if any carracters of more weight and
influence than China was connected."[49]

President Rodney smugly informed his predecessor, Thomas McKean,
that Pope had attacked the "Refugees" on "the Western Borders of this
County, and verry [sic] soon routed Mr. Clow & his army, and burnt the

fort." He notified President Laurens that "Mr Clow and his gang" had, on "hearing of their approach, fled." Reveling in the story and his own growing part in it, Rodney said, "I then fitted out a number of Horse-men, Since when many of them have been taken and others Surrendered to the number, all in all, of about fifty." Rodney gave another hint that an informal joint operation between two states had been mounted under the pressure of the crisis. "With what the Maryland Militia have done," he exulted, "this infernal set are, I believe, broke up, and I hope to hear in a few days that the Villain Clow is taken."[50]

He would hear no such thing. By April 20, Colonel Bordley had arrived in Chestertown, Maryland, from the southern tip of the Eastern Shore. His subordinates gathered testimony from "the prisoners brought in" during Clow's operation. His troops failed to capture Clow, but Bordley told Governor Thomas Johnson that he hoped that a reward just offered would achieve that end. He released two companies of Maryland militia to go to Head of Elk to protect the supply depots there. The artillery company that the state had loaned was "of no use here," he observed, so it was returned to the Western Shore.[51] Thomas McKean, a delegate to the Continental Congress in York, wrote to congratulate Rodney on "the success of Lieutt. Colo. Pope," but it was clear that China Clow had eluded the net strung around his "fort" by forces from two adjacent states.[52] He had—as a modern theoretician of guerilla warfare taught his followers to do—slipped back into a sea of fishes, where he was invisible to the state. Colonel Pope admitted that one of his own "relations" had become "so lost to Virtue" as to join a Loyalist party. He blasted civil authorities, saying that Rodney could "not Expect anything else whilse the Executive Power of your State is so Relax (sic), and nothing but Public Examples will put a stop to that Evil Practice of Trade."[53]

Clow may have disappeared from the sight of Whig authorities, but he had embedded himself in the imagination of the local populace. British military leaders in Philadelphia were tempted by the inability of their enemies to restore order in Delmarva to intervene with force to worsen that situation. On April 21, Hessian Captain Friedrich Muenchhausen, an aide to General Howe, proposed leading a raid into Delaware. Hearing that "two gentlemen of Congress and 22 sub-delegates with other men of the topmost rebels, were staying at Dover," Muenchhausen offered to take 100 Hessian Grenadiers and two schooners to "seize those gentlemen during the night." Howe rebuffed the proposal but then reconsidered a few days later. However, according to Muenchhausen, bad weather and a dispersal of his targets foiled the plan.[54]

Even without formal approval from Howe, British forces made disruptive probes into Delaware. On May 8, 1778, President Rodney lamented to McKean that "We are constantly alarmed in [Dover] by the enemy and

Refugees, and seldom a day passes but Some man in this and the Neighbouring Counties is taken off by these Villians, so that many, near the Bay, Who I know to be hearty in the Cause, dare neither Act nor Speak least they should be taken away."[55] On May 23, a group of residents from "the upper part of [Queen Anne's] County" petitioned the governor of Maryland that "Clow and his party" had the night before tried to kidnap one of their neighbors. The Maryland Council attributed the event to "Cheney Clow and his Parties" and voted to authorize a "scouting party" of up to forty militiamen to protect the neighborhood.[56]

Edward Tilghman, the planter from the Eastern Shore in lower Queen Anne's County, portrayed himself as a well-meaning citizen caught in the middle. He complained to Governor Johnson that his tenants could not pay their rents because they had been "plundered by China . . . Clow" *and* requisitioned by Captain Henry Lee's February expedition from Valley Forge. He asked the governor's permission to go "home," which he said was actually in Kent County, Delaware, over the "stone line." This would make Tilghman Clow's neighbor.[57]

Like an exposed class truant, China Clow became both an easy mark when anything untoward happened or was even suspected, and a measuring rod by which to judge others' sins. His religious affiliation is unclear, but he was known to some residents as "a backsliding Methodist."[58] In September 1778, an itinerant Methodist preacher, Freeborn Garrettson, rode into Dover, expecting to preach. He considered the community "a proverb for wickedness" that he had long wanted to "attack" ecclesiologically, so he agreed to go there despite the risks. On alighting from his horse, he said, "I was surrounded by hundreds; some cried one thing, some another; some said, he is a good man, others said nay, he deceiveth the people." "I was also accused of being a friend to King George," he noted, and his tormentors shouted, " 'He is one of Clowe's men—hang him—hang him.' " "I know not what the event would have been, had not the Lord interposed," Garrettson wrote. "I had no possible chance to speak for myself; and to all human appearance, was in a fair way to be torn in pieces every moment: I was, however, rescued by several gentlemen of the town, who hearing the uproar, ran to my assistance."[59]

Less than three weeks later, a miscreant received an opportunity to *save* his life because of a presumed comparison between himself and Clow. In Queen Anne's County, Maryland, John Tims was sentenced to hang for treason. The county sheriff, William Wright, however, sent Tims's wife to plead for his life with Governor Johnson. Wright noted that Tims was the father of two children who had shown remorse, but the main reason for his support for clemency was his wry observation that he "would be sorry to hang this one out of a neighborhood infested by China Clough and his gang, where two thirds of the people are Tories in spirit if not in action."[60]

Clow's rebellion—and Loyalist insurgent activity generally—may have declined when the "seat of war" moved from the Delaware Valley toward New York City and then into the South. Any faintly polar military "lines" of the sort that, according to Harry Ward, sparked banditry that may have existed while Philadelphia was occupied and the Continental Army guarded its hinterland disappeared. By June 1778, Caesar Rodney congratulated Thomas McKean that "affairs now wear a different complection" in Delmarva.[61] But the nature of aggressive disaffection may have merely changed now that the attention of the outer world had faded but internal tensions continued to fester. The Delaware Assembly, which had feared an armed assault on its own session at Dover before China Clow was routed in April 1778, passed a bill to divide the Loyalist community by offering conditional pardons to many of its members. It pointedly exempted persons considered irredeemably corrupted, including China Clow.[62] Deprived of any reason to amend his ways, Clow fled Delaware and did not test Rodney's hope that, with Congress's help, "Civil Government . . . will soon be in such force as to cause those who have offended to tremble."[63] He probably fled west from Colonel Pope's forces and slipped through the mesh of Maryland militia parties trying to seal the border. In the somewhat more permissive climate of that state's Eastern Shore, he would be safer than he was in Delaware.

III

China Clow was not heard from for four years. By early 1782, there was a general sense in America that royal government and the war itself were about finished. The British surrender at Yorktown, Virginia, in the fall of 1781, an event that brought large numbers of Continental forces back into the Chesapeake for the first time since 1778, demoralized partisans of the King from Whitehall to the alehouses of New York City. Defeatism also spread on the peninsula.[64] At some point Clow slipped back to his plantation, accompanied by his wife Elizabeth. What looked to Colonel Pope four years earlier like a formidable "fort" was now a ruined farmhouse. When authorities in Kent County discovered his presence, a grand jury indicted him for various acts of treason. From then on, parts of Clow's story become almost a question of folklore. With Continental authorities indifferent to how their local counterparts resolved an abortive, half-forgotten insurgency, and with even Maryland's government a bystander to the process, one's vision of the endgame depends on local legal proceedings that probably were only informally recorded.

The indictment spared Clow nothing that legal invective could articulate, and it suggests the bitter aftermath of years of civil conflict on the Delmarva Peninsula. A man who eight years earlier was legally described as

no worse than a person "of evil fame and name and of dishonest conversation" had become one who "not having the fear of God before his Eyes [had
been] . . . seduced by the instigations of the Devil." The bill alleged several
overt acts that Clow had committed, including gathering confederates, arm-
ing "in a warlike and hostile manner," and "levy[ing] war" against a state to
which he owed unquestioned allegiance. The legal narrative revealed that
under pressure of an emergency, two states *had* combined their militia forces
under the field command of a Continental officer and the broad oversight
of General Smallwood. The state of Delaware, having the victor's proverbial
last word, preferred to remember that Clow had "attack[ed] and repuls[ed] a
party of militia coming from Maryland to the aid and assistance of the militia
of the said Delaware State," before Pope's Delawareans won the day.[65]

Indictments without swords to enforce them are merely scraps of paper.
It fell to Kent County's sheriff, John Clayton, to serve the writ and bring in
the body. Assembling a posse on November 21, 1782, he rode toward the
Maryland line, where he faced the daunting prospect of having to repeat
Colonel Pope's 1778 coup of reducing Clow's "fort." A demand for surren-
der was met with a hail of gunfire. One attacker fell dead in the dooryard.
The final approach to the house was made with axes, crowbars, and gun
butts, and the firing continued as the door was smashed in and barricading
household furniture was pushed aside. When the noise stopped, Clayton
and his men were amazed to find themselves facing not a small army of
Tories but only a well-armed, middle-age man and his badly wounded wife.
As the story entered print in the 1830s, it could have described an action
anywhere from the Jacksonian Tennessee frontier to the Republic of Texas
to a wagon train in the Rocky Mountain west. Ma Clow, a bullet lodged
in her breast, was loading guns and passing them to her husband, who kept
up the hail of gunfire. A pot of melting lead over the fireplace suggested
that she was also making bullets as fast as he could discharge them. Beaten
fair and square, Clow surrendered and asked only for permission to change
his clothes before he was led away to face justice. This small dignity "Mr.
Clayton readily granted," according to the earliest historian of this episode,
and Clow "put on a full suit of British uniform, such as was then worn by
captains in their army." He then mounted a horse and rode off with his
captors toward Dover. Mr. Moore, the fallen member of the posse, and the
only casualty of the day besides Elizabeth Clow, was probably taken home
for private burial. Whoever may have cared for Mrs. Clow, the annalist does
not say. One almost imagines that she scraped lead from the pot, boiled
water in it, dug out the slug, and patched up her own wound.[66]

On the way to Dover the posse was accosted by an embittered group
of local militia, who demanded the prisoner for summary execution. But
according to a historian of the episode, Clayton refused to surrender his

charge. Clow was tried for treason in December. He supposedly produced a copy of his British captain's commission and "placed himself upon the footing of a prisoner of war." If a court accepted this evidence, it would have had to acquit the defendant, which tradition claims it did. The reasons to doubt that Clow held such a commission, pursuant to his service in the Seven Years' War, have already been discussed. Any claim of protection under the Articles of War would have led to the involvement of Continental military authorities and the defendant's British superiors. It is possible, of course, that with the war "winding down," such procedural formalities would have been dispensed with.[67]

Acquittal or not, an angry crowd surrounding the courthouse demanded that Clow not be released. The court ordered him to enter bail of 10,000 pounds for his "good behaviour during the continuance of the war." He was unable to do this, so he was bound over indefinitely. During the winter Clow's enemies pressed for his indictment for the murder of the posseman, Joseph Moore. One was returned in May 1783, and Clow was tried for his life a second time.[68] The antiquarian historian who first reconstructed the case used court records that a later scholar claimed no longer existed by the early twentieth century.[69] The trial was held in circumstances as charged as those of the previous fall. Colonel Pope himself, Clow's old nemesis, supposedly "officiously drew up a troop of horse before the court house, with a view, it was thought, of intimidating the jury; while a general clamor was raised out of doors for his conviction."[70]

Clow, apparently without counsel, vigorously defended himself against the charges. Sheriff Clayton took the stand to testify that Moore was probably "accidentally killed by one of his own men," and he provided surprisingly modern forensic-style evidence to support that view. After members of the posse testified to the same exculpatory effect, the state secured a conviction with another subgenre of modern prosecutorial practice by calling a jailhouse snitch. John Bullen, one of Clow's ex-cellmates, swore that Clow had said "if he did kill Moore it was by accident." In a bitterly politicized environment, in which the underpaid Continental army was wrathfully disbanding near West Point, even though its British counterpart had not yet left its garrison quarters in New York City, this was more than enough to get a cardsharp hanged.[71]

However, with the war over, American political gears shifted, and debates broke out over whether and how to curb the radical impulses that drove the political process in the previous decade. Conservative forces joined under the banner of the Federalists to seek a national constitution to shift power back into the hands of elites. Delaware distinguished itself as the "First State" by its quickness in ratifying that document. Loyalists, who had fled by the thousands after 1783, finding refuge in Atlantic Canada, the British Isles, and the West Indies, now sought to return. Delawareans in the 1780s elected a series of governors in no hurry to carry out the 1783 sentence against China Clow. But some citizens remembered his raids and were unwilling to forego justice. Finally, in 1788, allegedly at his own request, after he had despaired of release, Clow met his fate at the end of a rope. He was described in one account as walking to the gallows, singing what for all we know may have been a Methodist camp hymn.[72]

Most of the bile, but little of the mystique, of this episode died with Clow. Memories dispersed with participants, like ripples from the surface of a pond. One account had witnesses to the public hanging sinking into "unavailing remorse" at the deed's finality. Another had Caesar Rodney declaring that he wished he was still governor so he could pardon Clow. A story was propagated about Sheriff Clayton sleeping in the jail cell with his prisoner for months to spare him the wrath of his angry neighbors. A countervailing image circulated, in which a militiaman, who had tried to kidnap Clow on his way to trial for private justice, was hounded by Clow's vindictive family and friends into the barren wilderness of southwestern Pennsylvania. The relentless Freeborn Garrettson, pursuing souls with the fervor of a British customs inspector tracking down smuggled molasses, charged into the "neighborhood of Chaney Clow" at the time of his arrest in 1782. He pronounced the prospect before him once again a "prosperous work."[73]

Individuals hoping to recover costs for their role in the initial pursuit of the bandit were still badgering the Delaware Assembly as late as 1785. Five years after that, Colonel Pope requested an adjustment in his compensation for the case on the grounds that he had received it in "depreciated Currency." Clow's widow quietly buried his remains in an unknown place, and much of his family dispersed to the Ohio and Kentucky frontiers, which ironically had been opened up by the very Independence he had opposed. Marylanders more quickly put the episode behind them, but James Tilghman was still trying in 1792 to acquit himself from the charge of having taken part in the insurrection. He secured at least paper redemption in the form of certificates from a militia commander stating that his arrest of Tilghman in 1778 had been intended only to protect him and to restore order to the militia. Tilghman gratefully published the news, saying that he hoped that "the Ghost of Clow, which . . . has been so often conjured up against me, is now laid forever."[74]

Conclusion

That was not to be, and this chapter cannot claim to have stilled the ghost. A determined social historian, haunting church attics or courthouse cellars in Delmarva, might yet extract some useful facts about the actor behind the spectral shade. Enough is known, however, to offer a few generalizations. The peninsula was a peculiarly apt host for insurgencies because of its physical isolation in the larger sense of things and its countervailing accessibility from large bodies of navigable waters through tributary creeks. The remoteness of centers of political authority—with their institutional penchant to record complex realities on the ground—makes it hard to grasp the contours of this insurgency, or to fathom an obscure figure such as China Clow. Governors, legislative bodies, militia officers, and neighbors cannot have been mistaken in assuming that there *was* such a man, or that he was centrally involved in antirevolutionary disorders. But it is not clear that the insurgency was *his* in any appropriately possessive sense, or whether it merely helped Whig leaders to assume that they were battling an identifiable personality. There is no record on the British side, even among persons who were urging intervention in Delmarva, that anyone with such a colorful name was the man to call on for action. This episode may illustrate the American compulsion—from Opechancanough's attacks on the seventeenth-century Virginia palisade to Osama Bin Laden's adventures in our own day—to be able to put a name and a face to a mysterious evil.

The ways that military authorities on both sides addressed the episode are interesting. Although there were no formal military *lines*, of the sort that Harry M. Ward has examined, on either side of the peninsular arena, in a more metaphorical sense, both sides recognized that the events in Delmarva begged a response, even if that was to take no action. Both generally chose a minimalist intervention, and—as was the case for much of the war—this development favored the revolutionaries. William Howe declined to send an expedition to Dover to capture "topmost rebels," but he let his marine forces harass the marshes and creeks on both sides of the peninsula. Washington sent Henry Lee on a supply mission to Dover, but when confronted with the strategic problem of what to *do* about the peninsula, he chose to protect carefully delineated critical resources and hoped for the best with respect to the rest. Those were Wilmington, which anchored his line of encampment to the Delaware River, and Head of Elk, which anchored his southern supply lines.

As for securing friendly civilians in Delmarva from their malevolent neighbors, there is no record that Washington even considered that question. His subordinate, William Smallwood, loaned a resourceful Continental officer, Colonel Pope, and left it to the states involved to find the necessary manpower. Interestingly, they did so and even subordinated their jealousies long enough for Pope to oversee a combined operation. That operation pragmatically confined itself to pushing China Clow's gang off of its comfortable roost. When this was done, Pope returned to Wilmington, the state authorities briefly lamented their failure to bring in their man, and everyone else moved on. This sequence of events partially mirrored Washington's prudent management of the intersection between strategy and politics near Philadelphia during the same winter and spring. He offered rhetorical empathy and even some tactical support to local Whig authorities trying to contain revolutionary violence that the movement of his own army had in some ways provoked. But he refused to be drawn into an open-ended guerilla contest based in the countryside, and his British counterparts tacitly agreed. The situation on the ground and its resulting challenges in Delmarva, in fact, more closely resembled those phenomena as they would manifest themselves in the southern backcountry between 1779 and 1781 than they did the more geometrically, even linear, shape of battle north of Maryland from 1775 until late 1778. Perhaps lessons in military restraint and political pragmatism learned there and in Pennsylvania helped turn the war in the South slowly in the direction of an American victory.[75]

Notes

The author would like to thank Christopher Hodson and Laura Keenan-Spero, who read an earlier version of this chapter and provided useful comments. Jacqueline Thibaut-Ewbanks and I discussed China Clow many times years ago and wondered who he actually might have been.

1. This is not to suggest that there is no significant historiography of Loyalism, but efforts to recover the context of divided opinion about the Revolution have forever moved against the winds of American cultural optimism. Some of the benchmark efforts through the generations include Lorenzo Sabine, *The American Loyalists: Or Biographical Sketches of Adherents to the British Crown in the War of the Revolution* (Boston, MA: Little, Brown, 1847); Claude Halstead Van Tyne, *The Loyalists in the American Revolution* (New York: Macmillan, 1902); Wallace Brown, *The King's Friends* (Providence, RI: Brown University Press, 1965); Wallace Brown, *The Good Americans: Loyalists in the American Revolution* (New York: Morrow, 1969); Robert McCluer Calhoon, *The Loyalists in Revolutionary America, 1760–1781* (New York: Harcourt Brace Jovanovich, 1973). For early exceptions to this point, see Eileen Ka-May Cheng, "American Historical Writing and the Loyalists, 1788–1856: Dissent, Consensus, and American Nationalism," *Journal of the Early Republic* 23 (2003): 491–519.

2. Harry M. Ward, *Between the Lines: Banditti of the American Revolution* (Westport, CT: Praeger, 2002).

3. Clow's given name may have been "Cheney." For an account of the "marginal" character of the Delmarva region into the nineteenth century, see Gabrielle M. Lanier, *The Delaware Valley in the Early Republic: Architecture, Landscape, and Regional Identity* (Baltimore, MD: Johns Hopkins University Press, 2005), ch. 3.

4. Ward, *Between the Lines*. John Shy, "Armed Loyalism: The Case of the Lower Hudson Valley," and "The Military Conflict Considered as a Revolutionary War," in his *A People Numerous and Armed: Reflections on the Military Struggle for*

American Independence (New York: Oxford University Press, 1976), 183–92, 195–224, are both very useful for thinking about this phenomenon.

5. "Delmarva" combines elements of the three states that shared the peninsula: Delaware, Maryland, and Virginia. A dated, but still useful, overview of this subject is Charles J. Truitt, *Breadbasket of the Revolution: Delmarva in the War for Independence* (Salisbury, MD: Historical Books, 1975).

6. J. Frederick Fausz, "Merging and Emerging Worlds: Anglo-Indian Interest Groups and the Development of the Seventeenth-Century Chesapeake," in *Colonial Chesapeake Society*, ed. Lois Green Carr, Philip D. Morgan, and Jean B. Russo, 47–98, esp. 65–68 (Chapel Hill, NC: University of North Carolina Press, 1988).

7. The literature on this subject is voluminous, but a reliable perspective may be had in the following works, all by C. A. Weslager: *Dutch Explorers, Traders, and Settlers in the Delaware Valley, 1609–1644* (Philadelphia, PA: University of Pennsylvania Press, 1961); *The English on the Delaware, 1610–1682* (New Brunswick, NJ: Rutgers University Press, 1967); and *New Sweden on the Delaware, 1638–1655* (Lanham, MD: Middle Atlantic Press, 1988).

8. Francis Jennings, "Glory, Death, and Transfiguration: The Susquehannock Indians in the Seventeenth Century," *Proceedings of the American Philosophical Society* 112 (1968): 15–53.

9. Edwin Danson, *Drawing the Line: How Mason and Dixon Surveyed the Most Famous Border in America* (New York: John Wiley, 2001); Nicholas B. Wainwright, "The Missing Evidence: Penn v. Baltimore," *Pennsylvania Magazine of History and Biography* (*PMHB*) 80 (1956): 227–35, and "Tale of a Runaway Cape: The Penn-Baltimore Agreement of 1732," *PMHB* 87 (1963): 251–93.

10. Paul G. E. Clemens, *The Atlantic Economy and Colonial Maryland's Eastern Shore: from Tobacco to Grain* (Ithaca, NY: Cornell University Press, 1980), esp. ch. 6.

11. Ibid., 176–79; Thomas M. Doerflinger, *A Vigorous Spirit of Enterprise: Merchants and Economic Development in Revolutionary Philadelphia* (Chapel Hill, NC: University of North Carolina Press, 1986), esp. 106–107, and map 2, p. 93.

12. Useful introductions to this subject are Patience Essah, *Slavery and Emancipation in Delaware, 1638–1865* (Charlottesville, VA: University Press of Virginia, 1996), ch. 2, esp. 44–49, and William H. Williams, *Slavery and Freedom in Delaware, 1639–1865* (Wilmington, DE: SR Books, 1996), esp. 40–46.

13. For a general treatment of the Awakening, see Frank Lambert, *"Pedlar in Divinity": George Whitefield and the Transatlantic Revivals, 1737–1770* (Princeton, NJ: Princeton University Press, 1994). For the impact of this episode on the career of one individual who played a secondary role in the pre-Revolutionary crisis and its outcome, see Mark H. Jones, "Herman Husband," in *American National Biography*, 24 vols., ed. John A. Garraty and Mark C. Carnes, 11: 574–75 (New York: Oxford University Press, 1999).

14. See William H. Williams, "The Attraction of Methodism: The Delmarva Peninsula as a Case Study, 1769–1820," in *Perspectives on American Methodism: Interpretive Essays*, ed. Russell E. Richey, Kenneth E. Rowe, and Jean Miller Schmidt, 31–45 (Nashville, Tenn., 1993); Dee E. Andrews, *The Methodists and Revolutionary America, 1760–1800: The Shaping of an Evangelical Culture* (Princeton, NJ: Princeton University Press, 2000), esp. 50–62.

15. John A. Munroe, *Federalist Delaware, 1775–1815* ((New Brunswick, NJ: Rutgers University Press, 1954), part 1; Ronald Hoffman, *A Spirit of Dissension: Economics, Politics, and the Revolution in Maryland* (Baltimore, MD: Johns Hopkins University Press, 1973); Robert J. Brugger, *Maryland, a Middle Temperament, 1634–1980* (Baltimore, MD: Johns Hopkins University Press, 1988), 159–60.

16. Wayne Bodle, *The Valley Forge Winter: Civilians and Soldiers in War* (University Park, PA: Pennsylvania State University Press, 2002), ch. 2; Steven R. Taafe, *The Philadelphia Campaign, 1777–1778* (Lawrence, KS: University Press of Kansas, 2003).

17. Trish Surles and Dottie Philippe, *Clough's Chance: Remembering Bygone Generations of the Clough/Clow Family* (Baltimore, MD: Gateway Press, 1994), 1–2; Clemens, *The Atlantic Economy*, 147–50; "Return of the Recruits Rais'd by Capt'n Benj'n Noxon," 1758, *Pennsylvania Archives*, 5th ser., 1: 186–89.

18. Surles and Philippe, *Clough's Chance*, 16; "History of Cheney Clow," *Delaware Register and Farmer's Magazine* (1838), 223; Reverend Joseph Brown Turner, "Cheney Clow's Rebellion," *Papers of the Historical Society of Delaware* 57 (1912): 3–16.

19. See F. W. Anderson, "Why Did Colonial New Englanders Make Bad Soldiers? Contractual Principles and Military Conduct during the Seven Years' War," *WMQ*, 3rd ser., 38 (1981): 394–417, and his *Crucible of War: The Seven Years' War and the Fate of Empire in British North America* (New York: Alfred A. Knopf, 2000); Matthew Ward, *Breaking the Backcountry: The Seven Years' War in Virginia and Pennsylvania, 1754–1765* (Pittsburgh, PA: University of Pittsburgh Press, 2003).

20. S. K. Stevens et al., eds., *The Papers of Henry Bouquet*, vol. 2 (Harrisburg, PA: The Pennsylvania Historical Museum Commission, 1951), 508, 566–67, 596–97, 673–74, and passim. Although the Delaware troops did see some action and took a few casualties, they were probably mostly used for road building and temporary garrison activities than for direct combat—of which there was a minimum here.

21. For a local study of eighteenth-century wealth and mobility in rural Pennsylvania just north of Delmarva, see Duane E. Ball, "The Dynamics of Population and Wealth in Eighteenth-Century Chester County, Pennsylvania," *Journal of Interdisciplinary History* 6 (1976): 21–44. The interpretive literature on this subject is immense, and the debates are complicated. See Alfred F. Young, ed., *The American Revolution: Explorations in the History of American Radicalism* (DeKalb, IL: Northern Illinois University Press, 1976); Young, *Beyond the American Revolution: Explorations in the History of American Radicalism* (DeKalb, IL: Northern Illinois University Press, 1993); Gary B. Nash, *The Unknown American Revolution: The Unruly Birth of Democracy and the Struggle to Create America* (New York: Penguin Books, 2005); Gordon Wood, *The Radicalism of the American Revolution* (New York: Alfred A. Knopf, 1993).

22. On the prevalence of tenancy in late colonial Maryland, see Gregory A. Stiverson, *Poverty in a Land of Plenty: Tenancy in Eighteenth-Century Maryland* (Baltimore, MD: Johns Hopkins University Press, 1977), 5 (map), 152–53. For intersections between poverty, landlessness, and the Revolution, see Edward C. Papenfuse and Gregory A. Stiverson, "General Smallwood's Recruits: The Peacetime Career of the Revolutionary Private," in *WMQ*, 3rd ser., 30 (1973): 117–32.

23. Clemens, *The Atlantic Economy*, esp. 198–205.

24. Danson, *Drawing the Line*, 103–109; Surles and Philippe, *Clough's Chance*, 1–5. It is possible that the Mason and Dixon survey *allowed* China Clow to become a landowner. When Delaware received land as part of the settlement with Maryland, much of it was vacant as part of Calvert proprietary holdings, and a late colonial land rush allowed some claimants to benefit. See Munroe, *Federalist Delaware*, 26; Henry C. Conrad, *History of the State of Delaware from the Earliest Settlements to the Year 1907*, 3 vols. (Wilmington, DE: The Author, 1908), 2: 644–50.

25. Criminal Indictment, RG 3805, May 1774, Maryland Hall of Records, reproduced in facsimile in Surles and Philippe, *Clough's Chance*, between pp. 16–17. For a perceptive treatment of the social and legal environment of Little Creek Hundred in these years, see Laura T. Keenan, "Reconstructing Rachel: A Case of Infanticide in the Eighteenth-Century Mid-Atlantic and the Vagaries of Historical Research," *PMHB* 130 (2006): 361–85.

26. See Aubrey C. Land, *Colonial Maryland: A History* (Millwood, NY: KTO Press, 1981), 309–23.

27. John A. Munroe, *History of Delaware*, 4th ed., (Newark, DE: University of Delaware Press, 2001), 61–73.

28. Sailing up the bay, a British officer wrote that inhabitants on the Eastern Shore of Maryland behaved as though they might "return to obedience," but that those on the Western Shore seemed "very averse to a reconciliation." Colonel Charles Stuart to Lord Bute, August 21, 1777, in Violet Stuart Wortley, ed., *A Prime Minister and His Son: From the Correspondence of the 3rd Earl of Bute and of Lt.-General the Hon. Sir Charles Stuart, K. B.* (New York: E. P. Dutton, 1925), 114–15.

29. John F. Reed, *Campaign to Valley Forge: July 1, 1777 to December 19, 1777* (Philadelphia, PA: University of Pennsylvania Press, 1965), 99–103.

30. Munroe, *History of Delaware*, 72–75; Reed, *Campaign to Valley Forge*, 2–4, 206.

31. Munroe, *History of Delaware*, 74–75.

32. Caesar Rodney to Thomas McKean, March 9, 1778, in George Herbert Ryden, *Letters to and from Caesar Rodney, 1756–1784* (Philadelphia, PA: University of Pennsylvania Press, 1933), 253–54.

33. Colonel George Dashiell (Somerset County, Maryland) to Governor [Thomas Johnson?], March 12 and March 18, 1778, the latter enclosing depositions from Captain John Williams, William Winders, and Reverend Thomas Hopkinson, all in Maryland State Archives/Hall of Records, 1/6/5/27. See also Luther Martin to Governor [Johnson?], ibid.

34. Charles Pope to Caesar Rodney, March 17, 1778, in Ryden, *Letters to and from Rodney*, 256.

35. Minutes of the Delaware Council, March 20, 1778, *Proceedings of the Historical Society of Delaware* (Wilmington, DE: Historical Society of Delaware, 1887), 200–201; Rodney to McKean, March 9, 1778, *Letters to and from Rodney*, 253.

36. Bodle, *The Valley Forge Winter*, ch. 5, esp. 167–72, 175–78; Jacqueline Thibaut, *This Fatal Crisis: Logistics, Supply, and the Continental Army at Valley Forge, 1777–1778* (Valley Forge, PA: United States Department of the Interior, 1980), 162–91.

37. Bodle, *The Valley Forge Winter*, 169, 175–76, for the selection of Lee, and 133–34 for his earlier demonstrated sensitivity to civilian opinion and well-being.

38. Ibid., 210.

39. Henry Lee to Washington, February 21 and 22, 1778, in Edward G. Lengyel, ed., *Papers of George Washington*, Revolutionary War Series, 13 [December 1777–February 1778] (Charlottesville, VA: University Press of Virginia, 2003), 632–33, 642–43.

40. Lt. Col. William Henry to Col. William Bordley, April 13 and 14, 1778, MSA/HR, 1/6/5/27.

41. Lt. Col. Henry to Col. Bordley, April 15, 1778; Bordley to Gov. Thomas Johnson, April 16, 1778, ibid. Where Clow had been since his trial for cardsharping in 1774 is unknown.

42. Maryland Council to W. Hemsley, April 17, 1778; Maryland Council to Col. Bordley, April 17, 1778, in William Hand Browne, ed., *Archives of Maryland: Journals and Correspondence of the Council of Maryland, April 1, 1778–October 26, 1779* (Baltimore, MD: Maryland Historical Society, 1901), 40.

43. Samuel Patterson to General Smallwood, April 15, 1778, *Calendar of Maryland State Papers*, number 4, part 1, The Red Books (Annapolis, MD: Hall of Records Commission, 1950), 94.

44. Charles Pope to Smallwood, April 14, 1778, ibid.

45. Charles Pope to President Caesar Rodney, April 14, 1778, in Ryden, *Letters to and from Rodney*, 259–60.

46. General William Smallwood to President Henry Laurens, April 17, 1778, *Calendar of Maryland State Papers*, number 4, part 2, The Red Books, 94–95.

47. For examples of this circular correspondence, see Samuel Chase to ? (April 1778); J. Henry Jr. to Gov. Thomas Johnson, April 20, 1778; Charles Carroll to Gov. Thomas Johnson, April 21, 1778, in Browne, *Archives of Maryland*, 44–45 45–46, 49–50. Congress was not immediately reassured. Thomas McKean told Caesar Rodney that his colleagues had created "a Committee specially appointed early last winter to take the direction of Delaware, as it was understood that the Government was at an End." As late as May 31, that body "expect[ed] a report from these Gentlemen daily," although the imminent British abandonment of Philadelphia seemed to be a hopeful sign. McKean to Rodney, May 31, 1778, in Paul H. Smith, ed., *Letters of Delegates to Congress, 1774–1789*, vol. 9 (Washington, DC: Library of Congress, 1982), 791–92.

48. Donaldson Yeates, statement to an unnamed recipient, August 6, 1792, Lloyd Papers, 1658–1910, Ms. 2001, Maryland Historical Society (MHS).

49. Ibid; Donaldson Yeates to Col. Edward Lloyd, Esq., September 11, 1792, and September 14, 1792; statement of Arthur Bryan to an unnamed recipient, [n.d., but 1792], Lloyd Papers, 1658–1910, Ms. 2001, MHS.

50. Caesar Rodney to Henry Laurens, April 24, 1778, in Ryden, *Letters to and from Rodney*, 263–64.

51. Col. William Bordley to Gov. Thomas Johnson, April 20, 1778, *Calendar of Maryland State Papers*, number 4, part 2, The Red Books, 247.

52. Thomas McKean to President Caesar Rodney, April 28, 1778, in Ryden, *Letters to and from Rodney*, 264–65.

53. Charles Pope to Caesar Rodney, May 3, 1778, ibid., 265–66. Pope complained bitterly to the governor that the gallows was "a debt due one third of your people."

54. Ernst Kipping and Samuel Stelle Smith, eds., *At General Howe's Side, 1776–1778: The Diary of William Howe's Aide-de-Camp, Captain Friedrich Muenchhausen* (Monmouth Beach, NJ: Philip Freneau Press, 1974), 51 [April 21, 24, 1778]. It is not clear how literally to take Muenchhausen's description of the intended captives. He may have confused state representatives and Continental congressmen.

55. Caesar Rodney to Thomas McKean, May 8, 1778, in Ryden, *Letters to and from Rodney*, 267–68. Rodney closed the letter with news that ten residents from Port Penn, on the Delaware, had been carried onto enemy ships the previous night. Indeed, he admitted, "I fear I must Decampt" if the security situation did not improve.

56. William Hemsley to Gov. Thomas Johnson, May 23, 1778 [enclosing petition], in *Calendar of Maryland State Papers*, The Red Books, 251, and Minutes of the Council of Maryland, May 23, 1778, in Browne, *Archives of Maryland*, 107–108.

57. Edward Tilghman Jr. to Gov. Thomas Johnson, June 25, 1778, in *Calendar of Maryland State Papers*, number 4, part 2, The Red Books, 256. Tilghman, then, had several plantations.

58. Harold B. Hancock, *Delaware Loyalists* (Boston, MA: Gregg Press, 1972), 34–35; Munroe, *Federalist Delaware*, 52–57; Andrews, *The Methodists and Revolutionary America*, 55–62; James W. May, "Francis Asbury and Thomas White: A Refugee Preacher and His Tory Patron," *Methodist History* 14 (1976): 141–64.

59. Robert Drew Simpson, ed., *American Methodist Pioneer: The Life and Journals of the Rev. Freeborn Garrettson, 1752–1827* (Rutland, VT: Academy Books, 1984), 74. (entry for September 12, 1778).

60. Sheriff William Wright to Gov. Thomas Johnson, September 29, 1778, *Calendar of Maryland State Papers*, number 4, part 2, The Red Books, 1778.

61. Caesar Rodney to Thomas McKean, June 11, 1778, in Ryden, *Letters to and from Rodney*, 271. Modern scholars agree that the peninsula became more orderly by late 1778. See Hoffman, *A Spirit of Dissension*, 236–37; Hancock, *Delaware Loyalists*, 38–39.

62. Hancock, *Delaware Loyalists*, 32.

63. Rodney to McKean, June 11, 1778, in Ryden, *Letters to and from Rodney*, 271.

64. For an evocation of this "dull period" in the war in the north, see Bodle, *The Valley Forge Winter*, 250–55, esp. n. 18; John Shy, ed., *Winding Down: The Revolutionary War Letters of Lieutenant Benjamin Gilbert of Massachusetts, 1780–1783* (Ann Arbor, MI: University of Michigan Press, 1989), esp. the introduction, 9–17.

65. "Indictments For Treason: Cheney Clow" [1778], *Delaware Archives*, 5 vols. (Wilmington, DE: Public Archives Commission, 1911–1919) 3: 1296–99.

66. "History of Cheney Clow," 222–23.

67. Ibid.

68. Ibid., 223–24; "Conviction of Cheney Clow" (in reality, the record of the grand jury proceeding with text of the indictment), May 5, 1783, *Delaware Archives*, 3, 1296–99.

69. Reverend Joseph Brown Turner, "Cheney Clow's Rebellion," *Papers of the Historical Society of Delaware* 57 (1912): 3–16. Turner discounted much of the story of Clow's "rebellion" as a romantic "myth" but agreed that a person of that name "was no creation of countryside gossip."

70. "History of Cheney Clow," 224–25.

71. Ibid. Clayton's testimony suggested that Moore had been shot in the back while facing Clow's "fort." For circumstances surrounding the embittered disbandment of the Continental army in 1783, see Charles Royster, *A Revolutionary People at War: The Continental Army and American Culture* (Chapel Hill, NC: University of North Carolina Press, 1979), esp. 331–41; Richard H. Kohn, "The Inside History of the Newburgh Conspiracy: America and the Coup d'Etat," *WMQ*, 3rd ser., 27 (1970): 187–220.

72. "History of Cheney Clow," 225–26; Turner, "Cheney Clow's Rebellion," 11–14; Surles, *Clough's Chance*, 24–26. The general but never uncontested conservative drift of Delaware's politics between 1783 and 1791 is described in Munroe, *Federalist Delaware*, 94–109, 195–203.

73. "History of Cheney Clow," 226; Turner, "Cheney Clow's Rebellion," 9–10; *Life and Journals of Freeborn Garrettson*, 206; Claudia L. Bushman, Harold B. Hancock, and Elizabeth Moyne Homsey, eds., *Proceedings of the House of Assembly of the Delaware State, 1781–1792, and of the Constitutional Convention of 1792* (Newark, DE: University of Delaware Press, 1988), 242–43, 675–76. Rodney's purported remorse would have been a very interesting phenomenon, as he had died in 1784.

74. Ibid. See also James Tilghman Jr., "To the Public," 5th September 1792, Lloyd Papers, 1658–1910, Ms. 2001, MHS.

75. For resemblances between Washington's symbolically assertive but tactically cautious approach to undermining British ascendancy in Pennsylvania between the fall of 1777 and the summer of 1778, and in Delmarva, see Bodle, *The Valley Forge Winter*, esp. 254–57.

CHAPTER 2

"Loyalty Is Now Bleeding in New Jersey"

Motivations and Mentalities of the Disaffected

David J. Fowler

Early in the morning of April 12, 1782, six months after Cornwallis's surrender at Yorktown, Richard Lippincott, a captain in the Associated Loyalists, went aboard the guard ship *Britannia* stationed off of Sandy Hook to take custody of Joshua Huddy, a prisoner he had previously confined there. Huddy was a rebel captain who had been captured on March 24 in a Loyalist raid on Toms River, New Jersey (see Map of New Jersey, 1775, Figure 2.1). He also was a zealous member of the Monmouth County Association for Retaliation, a Patriot vigilante organization. Eighteen months earlier, Huddy had been wounded and captured during another raid but had managed a daring escape; he would not be so fortunate this time. Before Captain Lippincott left the vessel, he also requested a length of rope. The party of two dozen men then sailed to the mainland opposite "the Hook." After they reached the shore, the prisoner made out his will; he was placed atop a barrel under a makeshift gallows, and Lippincott "shook hands with Huddy, by . . . Huddy's request." A black Loyalist then executed the prisoner, who was left hanging for several hours. A label pinned to the victim's chest justified the summary execution and gave vent to Loyalist frustration and rage:

> We the Reffugees having with Greif Long beheld the Cruel Murders of our Brethren and finding Nothing but Such Measures Daily Carrying into Execution.
>
> We therefore Determine not to Suffer without taking Vengance for numerous Cruelties and thus begin and have made use of Captn Huddy as the first Object to present to your Veiws, and Further <u>Determine</u> to Hang Man for Man as Long as a Reffugee is Left Existing.

Up Goes Huddy
for
Phillip White

White was an Associated Loyalist who had recently died under questionable circumstances while in Patriot custody.[1]

The Huddy-Lippincott affair was the culmination of a lengthy, "savage kind of desultory war."[2] The focus here will not be on Loyalists such as William Franklin or his ilk but instead on the common sort of "Friends to Government," as the Loyalists called themselves, who often experienced

Figure 2.1 Map of New Jersey, 1775

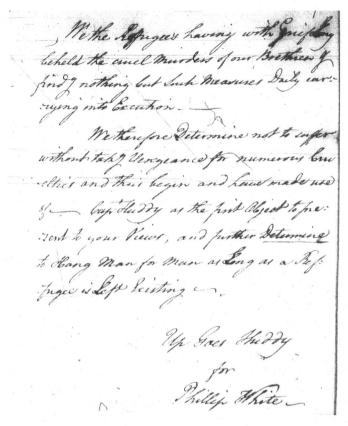

Figure 2.2 "Up Goes Huddy"

the conflict on a visceral level. Some were "middling" farmers who were unknown outside of their own townships. Others were poor husbandmen, artisans, laborers, seamen, and woodsmen who formed the backbone of a rural society in which an enervating civil war raged for eight years. Although actuated by a variety of motives, hundreds of them followed a tortuous path that led them to become enthusiastic proponents of the *lex talionis* (law of retaliation) and the "principle of self-preservation."

The shocking circumstances of Huddy's execution caused a sensation, launched two obscure officers onto an international (and a historical) stage, and highlighted an internecine civil conflict in New Jersey. Monmouth County Whigs, who were among the most ardent in the state, demanded vengeance for Huddy's murder. George Washington declared the killing "the most wanton, unprecedented, and inhuman murder that ever disgraced the arms of a civilized people" and insisted that British Commander in Chief Sir Henry Clinton surrender Lippincott. Clinton refused and countered by relaying a list of fifteen "acts of cruelty and barbarity" committed against New Jersey Loyalists; he did, however, authorize an inquiry into the matter.[3] Exasperated, Washington had a British prisoner of similar rank, Charles Asgill, chosen by lot for the "fixed purpose of exemplary retaliation." After much discussion, the British court-martialed Lippincott.[4] The trial, which lasted May 3 to June 22, 1782, provided the defendant with a forum for an impassioned Loyalist apologia, which gave voice to emotions that hundreds of common, inarticulate Loyalists had long harbored.

Lippincott pleaded not guilty to the charge of murder. In his opening statement, he professed himself "an unalterable friend to his Government": "My loyalty has not been of the passive kind, for I have often hazarded *my life.*" His defense centered on the fact that instead of being treated as prisoners of war when captured, his loyal friends and neighbors had become victims of "retaliative justice" and had been "arraigned for *Treason* before *Treasonable Tribunals*" and tried "by *Rebels* as *Rebels.*" The defendant argued that he harbored no personal animosity toward the victim but had executed him in retaliation for the killing of Phillip White and to prevent "a Repetition of the like barbarities." He alluded to precedents in which "retaliation has been practiced with some Degree of Success" and justified Loyalists' behavior by "the principle of self preservation."[5] Importantly, his defense hinged on the allegation that he had received "verbal orders" from William Franklin, president of the Board of Associated Loyalists and erstwhile royal governor of New Jersey, authorizing the execution. Speaking for his oppressed brethren, Lippincott lamented, "Loyalty has been bleeding at every Vein, and is now bleeding in New Jersey."[6] Although the court found that Huddy had been executed "without proper Authority," it ruled that Lippincott had acted without malice and in obedience to orders and consequently acquitted him of murder.[7]

"Little Freeholds, Cultivated by the Owners"

In 1775, a writer characterized New Jersey as consisting of "little freeholds, cultivated by the owners."[8] During the late colonial period, East Jersey and West Jersey were dependent on the respective "gateway ports" of New York City and Philadelphia for markets and commercial services. "The Jerseys" were profitable marketplaces for imported goods channeled through the two entrepôts, as well as being important secondary grain-producing areas for cargoes exported from them.[9] Laws passed between 1760 and 1775—concerning debt, road repairs, building dams, and dogs killing sheep—give ample evidence of the "localist tendencies of public life." The province was culturally and ethnically diverse, which for pragmatic reasons tended to foster a "psychology of accommodation." It is thus ironic that this small, rural, conservative colony was destined to experience "some of the bitterest civil war in all the provinces."[10]

During the 1760s and 1770s New Jersey authorities generally reacted with "reluctance and irresoluteness" in protesting British policies. As in other colonies, independence provoked a crisis of conscience for many people. Disaffected Joseph Cogil of Gloucester County, for example, declared that "he was as Good a Whig as Ever Sat on a pot till Independicy Was Declared." An unknown but significant number of pacifists, neutrals, and the apathetic comprised "the sensible core of wary people who hoped to avoid war's violence altogether." In the last article of the new state constitution passed on July 2, 1776, an escape clause evidenced the equivocation of New Jersey's Patriots: "If a Reconciliation between *Great-Britain* and these Colonies should take Place, . . . this Charter shall be null and void, otherwise to remain firm and inviolable."[11] While Whigs dithered, New Jersey's Loyalists were fomenting counterinsurrections.

Determining the total number of Loyalists in New Jersey is difficult. The most detailed estimate by Paul H. Smith suggests that about 36 percent to 37 percent of the population (or nearly 52,000 persons) was disaffected. If accurate, the figure is close to John Adams's statement that "about a third of the people . . . were against the revolution." Even if this estimate is too high, New Jersey still had significantly more Royalists than the 16 percent that Smith postulated as the aggregate Loyalist population for all of the colonies. It also is telling that hundreds of common Jerseymen filled the ranks of the New Jersey Volunteers, the largest of all Provincial (i.e., Loyalist) regiments.[12] The situation was highly fluid: "Loyalism meant different things to different persons in different situations."[13] Factors of time and place thus complicate any analysis of New Jersey's Loyalist population.

As in other colonies, the motivations of New Jersey's Loyalists, whether "high born," "middling," or of the "common sort," were varied. It often is "practically impossible to place many people at any certain point on the political spectrum."[14] Many were conservative and satisfied with a status quo in which they enjoyed the highest standard of living in the world, "better than the same people in Britain."[15] Some feared the "loss of British community" and the benefits of membership in the "empire of goods." An influential few were linked to the royal patronage system. Others were devout Anglicans who revered "Church and King." Many pacifist Quakers evinced a "conscientious Nonconformity to the times." According to one New Jersey Whig, Tories in general displayed a "foolish, doting passion for Great Britain and the old Constitution."[16] Members of ethnic and religious

minorities perceived the Crown as a buffer against the tyranny of the majority, which was a potentially important issue in the heterogeneous colony.[17]
Although some local responses to rebellion in New Jersey were doubtless
the outgrowth of simmering personal or "community feuds," most cases are
"unascertainable based on surviving evidence."[18]

For some, "repressive revolutionary programs" tipped the scales in favor
of the royal cause. James Moody, a farmer in the northwestern county of
Sussex, learned firsthand that "to be the victim of politicized communal
outrage . . . was a terrifying experience": he was confronted by his Whig
neighbors with the choice "Join or die!" Although he strove to remain
neutral, a mob flourished tomahawks around Moody's head; the last straw
came when they shot at him, whereupon he commenced his career as
New Jersey's foremost Tory partisan.[19] For conservatives and moderates who
desired reform and reconciliation within the existing British constitutional
framework, independence was anathema. As one conservative complained,
"Those who are not for us are against us is the cry."[20] Dramatic family splits
notwithstanding, family, kinship, and other networks exerted a compelling
force in determining allegiance.[21] The Revolution was not class warfare. Loyalists, like their Patriot counterparts, came from all ranks of society. Indeed,
the typical white male in New Jersey, Whig or Loyalist, was a native-born
farmer of middling status.[22]

A writer in 1765 noted that there was in New Jersey "almost every
religious persuasion under heaven . . . they were like so many jarring elements
pent up together." The statement was prophetic of how events unfolded during the Revolutionary War. Religion was an important thread of causation
in determining allegiance in New Jersey, but unlike neighboring colonies
such as New York, the lack of detailed community studies impedes making
blanket generalizations. One study of six townships in East Jersey, however,
found evidence of the rise of Presbyterian hegemony at the expense of the
Quakers.[23] But the large number of latitudinarian "generic Protestants" in
the colony, who were either "outside the membership of any church" or
not particular about which services they attended, complicates the issue.[24]
In sum, for a variety of reasons—religious and economic rivalries, personal
animosities, differences of temperament, hostility to coercion, and prewar
local conditions—the "psychology of accommodation" broke down between
1775 and 1783, and civil war ensued.

The state itself was a mosaic of allegiances. Although Loyalists who
petitioned the British government for compensation in the postwar period
were "not statistically representative" of all New Jersey Loyalists, they do in
some instances, along with other sources, provide a rough yardstick of disaffection. Overall, New Jersey had the fourth largest number of claimants (239).
By far the plurality of claimants (63) came from Middlesex County, where

Perth Amboy, one of New Jersey's two colonial capitals, was located; it was also the headquarters of the East Jersey proprietors.[25] In contrast, there were no Loyalist claimants at all from remote and sparsely populated Cape May, where one Whig committeeman boasted that he personally visited nearly everyone in the county in order to gather signatures for the Continental Association. Such exercises could be merely "forced hypocrisy": Gilbert Giberson of Monmouth County, for instance, claimed that in 1775 he signed the Continental Association "in consequence of many Threats."[26]

A high proportion of the disaffected inhabited the arc of East Jersey counties—Bergen, Essex, Middlesex, and Monmouth—that constituted the military frontier opposite British-held New York; the majority of the state's population also was clustered here. One prominent Patriot evidenced this pattern when he wrote to his friend: "I wonder that you venture to live in Monmouth as I have always thought that county was as bad as Bergen."[27] The large number of Quakers in West Jersey counties such as Burlington and Gloucester helps explain the lukewarm reaction there to Revolutionary agitation. Other counties such as quasifrontier Sussex, where James Moody resided, are more difficult to explain. Even though Monmouth County, on the Atlantic seaboard, had strong Whig communities, such as Freehold, it also had troublesome pockets of disaffection, such as Shrewsbury.[28] Monmouth consequently bred some of the most radical Patriots, as well as some of the most violent opponents of the new political order.

Loyalist Counterinsurrections, June 1776–January 1777

The arrival of the British fleet and army off of Sandy Hook in late June 1776 heartened covert Loyalists throughout New Jersey. Indeed, the decision to occupy New York was based in part on the notion that the Middle Colonies were friendly to the royal cause, a premise that ultimately proved the undoing of British strategy in late 1776.[29] Loyalists armed themselves, signed articles of association, and attempted to regain control of local militias that the fledgling state had purged and co-opted. An armed band from Shrewsbury joined the British, and it was rumored that large groups were organizing in the nearby cedar swamps intending to link up with the redcoats. Others provided supplies and intelligence. Loyalist agitators and recruiters were evidently active. Promises were being made that recruits would have "the Land taken from the Whigs"; this caused one recruit to think that "it was a fine thing to be a tory, to be so secure." Some recruiters were more heavy-handed. When Isaac Potter of Dover township in southern Monmouth proved hesitant, Lieutenant Colonel John Morris promised to "strip him of everything he had" and throw him in the guard house if he did not enroll. Another recruiter "threatened if any man did reveal the secret [plot] . . . he (pulling out a pistol) would blow that charge through him instantly."[30]

After the decisive American defeat at the Battle of Long Island in late August 1776, Jersey Loyalists became even more emboldened. A Tory recruiter boasted that he "should see the Time when he dare walk the Road when the damn Rebels dare not shew their Faces." At the very time the authors of the Declaration of Independence were charging that George III had "excited domestic insurrections amongst us," Loyalist insurgencies broke out in Bergen, Essex, Gloucester, and Hunterdon counties. In volatile Monmouth County, Patriot forces attempted to disarm and round up the disaffected no less than six times between June 1776 and January 1777.[31]

The best documented of all the New Jersey Loyalist uprisings was the one centered in Upper Freehold township, Monmouth County, in the latter half of 1776. It was a locale about which one Continental officer complained, "I have to deal with a sett of the most discontented disaffected wretches that ever existed." This situation was not surprising. During the Stamp Act crisis (1765–1766), relatively few Upper Freehold inhabitants had "shew'd themselves Friends to Liberty."[32] An analysis of the local insurrectionists indicates that people usually went to war as part of family and associational networks. A cell of prosperous, locally prominent Quaker farmers named Woodward led the uprising. Chief among the insurgents was Anthony Woodward Jr. ("Little Anthony" or "Little Nat"); his relatives Anthony ("Black Nat"), Jesse, Thomas, Thomas L., Samuel, and John; and their neighbors Richard Robins and Moses Ivins. Although the leaders of the Loyalist uprising were of the middling prosperous sort, they probably were virtually unknown outside of their own community. Younger family members and local marginal men, who were landless, transient wage laborers, formed the rank and file.[33]

The Loyalist "Club Men" first assembled in Upper Freehold in the late spring of 1776 at a militia muster held at the mill of pro-British Quaker merchant Richard Waln.[34] Little Anthony exhorted the crowd, claiming that the rebel merchants "oppressed them by Raising [prices] upon their Goods more than England would do," and that those who refused to sign the Continental Association were disenfranchised. A common element of Tory propaganda was the charge that the Continental Association was a scheme whereby Whig merchants could unload their merchandise at inflated prices.[35]

A majority of those assembled appointed Richard Robins and Moses Ivins as the new militia captains, and Robins urged that those who were "against the Measures of Rebellion" should follow him. Gilbert Giberson, another Upper Freehold Loyalist, claimed that he accepted a militia captaincy in order "to keep a troublesome man from being appointed."[36] Around the same time in the recalcitrant Shrewsbury township, Joshua Huddy's future nemesis, Richard Lippincott, became a lieutenant in a militia company. By the summer of 1776, membership in the militia, whether Whig or Loyalist, had become "a political act," and the contest between both groups for control of this instrument of indoctrination and coercion had become crucial.[37]

By the early summer of 1776, the New Jersey Provincial Congress noted the Upper Freehold Loyalists' efforts at organization and summoned Richard Robins, Moses Ivins, and Thomas L. Woodward, who were consequently required to bond themselves for their good behavior. Given their subsequent actions, they were apparently putting on a "penitential trim." Little Anthony, for his part, fled behind British lines, and the rebels consequently inventoried his estate in preparation for auctioning it.[38] But Loyalists were not long on the defensive. After the Battle of Long Island in late August, Little Anthony and other Loyalists returned from behind the lines bearing vague promises of reward. By mid-December, American forces had abandoned New Jersey, and the Woodward insurgents embarked upon their most active period. Jesse Woodward boasted that "now the Staff is in our . . . Hands." Their activities centered around disarming Whigs, intimidating them into accepting British protections, and commandeering horses, wagons, and provisions for the use of the British.[39]

Exulting in their success, the Upper Freehold insurgents "railed violently against the Congress, damming them, that they had now run away, that they had commenced the War in order to make Estates and aggrandize themselves, that they made Congress money, which they were changing at a great Under-value for Gold and Silver in order to run away with." There also was the outrageous rumor that "Franklin and Adams were prisoners in New York, with whom there was found three Millions of half Joannes." Quaker Richard Robins cursed one Presbyterian Whig, "saying that he was the cause of all this Bloodshed."[40]

The utterances of the Woodward insurgents from May 1776 to December 1776 provide an invaluable insight into the grassroots Loyalist mind. The younger, marginal, more impressionable men were no doubt being influenced and swayed by their elders, who themselves reflected Tory propaganda. Legitimate complaints about harassment, disenfranchisement, fines, and compulsory oath taking were intermingled with more questionable ones such as a plot by Whig merchants to inflate prices and outrageous rumors regarding rebel leaders. It also was a Loyalist commonplace subscribed to by both elites and the lower sort that the rebellion was a Presbyterian conspiracy. As the conflict intensified, Quakers and Anglicans came to view the Revolution as a religious confrontation, a charge that exposed an underlying fault line in colonial society. As late as 1781, Joseph Cogil of Gloucester County would complain that "the Presbyterians were

Striving to Get the Rule into their own hands And that he Never Wold be Subject to a Presbyterian Government."[41] In the Hackensack Valley, other religious tensions influenced allegiances. A prewar schism within the Dutch Reformed church apparently motivated the Coetus faction, which favored Americanizing the church, to support the Revolution, while the orthodox Conferentie opposed independence.[42]

The American victories at Trenton and Princeton dramatically burst the bubble of Loyalist ascendancy in New Jersey. On December 19, merchant Richard Waln had been willingly selling flour to the British; eleven days later, he was supplying the Americans "per Bayonet Order."[43] Hoping for the return of the redcoats, several Woodward insurgents fled to hideouts in the nearby forests and swamps of Monmouth and Burlington counties, where "tory-hunters" pursued them. James Moody compared such experiences to being stalked "as a partridge in the mountains." An ill-conceived plot in early 1777 by several Woodward rank and filers to ambush a Whig manhunter backfired when one of the would-be ambushers was killed. This was the only blood shed during the insurgency. The elusive Little Anthony apparently escaped to the British, but others failed to do so.[44]

Meanwhile, the Chesterfield Monthly Meeting of Friends in Burlington County, with which the Upper Freehold Preparative Meeting was affiliated, disciplined several Quaker insurrectionists for participating in martial activities.[45] The seeming paradox of Friends violating the pacifist tenets of their sect suggests the power of other compelling forces at work: "primal honor," which sought vengeance against family or community enemies; preexisting local disputes that affected allegiance; the influence of relatives and friends; charismatic leaders; and, in some cases, temperaments that were ill suited to play a passive role in the face of a perceived threat.[46] As unfounded as some of their fears now seem, their anxieties impelled them to action.

By early 1777, Patriot forces had rounded up most of the active Upper Freehold insurgents. They endured miserable confinement until January 1778, when the Monmouth County court of oyer and terminer dealt with their insurrectionary activities committed in late 1776. Multiple indictments were handed down for riot, assault, trespass, and false imprisonment; punishments included heavy fines and incarceration for specified periods.[47] Ringleaders such as Richard Robins and Jesse Woodward were chastised and allowed to remain in their communities, where local Whigs coerced them with social ostracism, harassment, fines, and forfeiture of property. Others continued to serve the British in more conventional ways by joining Loyalist regiments. Some, such as Little Anthony Woodward, continued to act as partisans.[48]

What had happened in New Jersey between June 1776 and January 1777 was a typical form of Loyalist counterinsurrection. It began as a relatively bloodless affair but became more violent over time. Despite Whig propaganda, the ringleaders were definitely not men "of the most abandoned characters and desperate fortunes."[49] Indeed, their high local social status and possible connections to moderate authorities doubtless played a part in their treatment. At this early stage of the conflict, moreover, adversaries seemed reluctant to inflict draconian punishments. In a few short months, these Loyalist insurgent leaders ran the gamut from being pillars of their local community, to being the politically oppressed, to being the politically ascendant, to being the hunted in their own locale. As was true throughout the war, the hope of succor from the British proved an illusion. Loyalist insurgencies of this period proved to be only the first phase of civil violence in New Jersey, however.

Egregious Villains: Loyalist Irregulars and Banditti

In order to deal decisively with insurgencies and other forms of disaffection, the state legislature created the Council of Safety on March 15, 1777.[50] The lawmakers compensated for a constitutionally weak executive by investing the council with unprecedented powers. Governor William Livingston chaired each of the council's more than 400 meetings. Gathering in ten different locations during its eighteen-month tenure, the body became a de facto directorate. The peripatetic tribunal arrested and interrogated suspects, summoned and examined witnesses, administered oaths of allegiance, set bail and security, banished the families of Loyalist refugees, and remanded the recalcitrant to jail until county criminal courts convened. Although the council observed legal formalities, it was zealous in the prosecution of its duties: at one meeting, in July 1777, it summoned 126 men to take oaths and arrested 48 suspects; at another meeting later that year, it arraigned 94 people.[51] For Patriots of every degree of commitment, the council's visitations represented a tangible manifestation of state authority on the local level. For the grassroots disaffected, the rumor of the council's appearance, or the threat of being hauled before it, could be terrifying.

When the assembly allowed the Council of Safety to expire in October 1778, the governor's Privy Council carried on its functions, using both legislation (especially property confiscation and test laws) and the county courts.[52] The proceedings of Patriot criminal courts sometimes revealed a class bias, if not outright judicial murder. In June 1778, for instance, John Wood and Thomas Emmons ("alias Burke"), a private in the Loyalist New Jersey Volunteers, were captured and indicted in Monmouth County for "felony and robbery from the person." Upon their being found guilty, the court invoked an ominous formula: "that they have no lands, goods, chattels or tenements." In short, they were propertyless and perhaps illiterate and therefore ineligible for benefit of clergy, which by the eighteenth century had evolved into a plea-bargaining device for the literate and propertied. When they were executed on July 17, Wood and Emmons were probably among the earliest of the unlucky thirteen reputedly put to death during the war at "the noted hanging place" near Freehold. Like all such eighteenth-century public rituals, their hanging provided gruesome entertainment that attracted large crowds; a Continental army surgeon who had traveled to see the spectacle regretted that the condemned were "turned off a few minutes before we arrived."[53] Such executions allegedly served as a deterrent, but that is questionable, for the deaths of both men were subsequently included in the British list of "acts of cruelty and barbarity" that infuriated Loyalists. Wood and Emmons were executed not because they were marginal members of society, because of the nature of their crimes, or because of their allegiance but because of all three factors combined.

Some unfortunate Loyalists of the common sort were unquestionably used by the Whigs as object lessons. William Hammet, a nineteen-year-old Anglican who had reportedly "suffered much by the rebel plunderers," captured two Patriot officers in New Jersey in March 1778 and conveyed them to the provost in British-occupied Philadelphia. Hammet himself was eventually apprehended and late in 1778 was one of eighteen men tried and convicted for treason by the Gloucester County court of oyer and terminer. Although the governor's Privy Council pardoned the seventeen others—a common occurrence—Hammet was sentenced to be hanged on January 29, 1779. The council was apparently unwilling to overlook his capture of the two Whig officers and the fact that he had borne arms for the king after being pardoned for the same offense two years earlier. Swedish Lutheran minister Nicholas Collin visited the condemned youth in his final hours and provided spiritual solace to both him and his distraught mother. On the day of execution, Reverend Collin accompanied Hammet "past a great crowd of spectators" to the gallows, where "he was hung and died quickly."[54] The reasons William Hammet placed himself in double jeopardy are unknown. Perhaps he was sincerely dedicated to church and sovereign, was seeking vengeance, was influenced by others, or was moved by some combination of factors. But it is clear that the Whig political order intended to make an example of him as a deterrent to others.

The only trial of a Tory partisan leader was that of Joseph Mulliner of Little Egg Harbor in Burlington County. Mulliner, an Associated Loyalist and whaleboat privateer captain, was an obscure figure who at the hands of later antiquarians inexplicably underwent a process of "Robinhooding."[55] Captured in Monmouth County in 1781, he was tried in late July by the Burlington County court of oyer and terminer for high treason. Mulliner pleaded not guilty but was found guilty, even though, according to the British, "he Produced his Commission as Captain of said Privateer at his Tryal." There is no indication in the surviving court minutes that his defense was based on that evidence, which suggests that it was disallowed, suppressed in the record, or subsequently trumped up by the Associated Loyalists. But a few months after his execution, Governor Livingston noted that Mulliner had "committed many depredations at Sea." As in the cases of John Wood and Thomas Emmons, the court invoked the fatal formula that "he has not any Goods, or Chattels, Lands or Tenements." He was consequently hanged in Burlington on August 8.[56] While Mulliner's case may (or may not) represent an instance of judicial murder, it definitely highlights an issue that toward the end of the war inflamed Loyalists. As Captain Richard Lippincott declared at his court-martial: "If I took a Rebel Prisoner, he was subject to be exchanged, according to the Laws of War and of Nations[.] If I should happen to have fallen into the hands of Rebels, my life was subject to be taken, as a Rebel to a Rebel state."[57]

Some Loyalists never appeared before a legitimate Patriot tribunal or court. One such person was Stephen Edwards of Shrewsbury, whom Loyalists regarded as "the first of our brethren, who fell a Martyr to republican fury in Monmouth County." In October 1777, Edwards was "taken out of his Bed at his own house," found to be in possession of compromising papers, given a drumhead court-martial presided over by General David Forman and Captain Joshua Huddy, and then hanged "on a large Oak near the Court House at Monmouth." Huddy later admitted that he "ty'd the knot and greased the Rope that it might slip easily," and that Forman "assisted in pulling the Rope, hand over hand."[58] Forman was a brigadier general of militia, a Continental army colonel, a Whig radical, and an influential county political boss whose zeal against Monmouth Tories earned him the sobriquet "Black David . . . the most persecuting Rebel in the Country."[59]

Other Loyalists were punished without even the benefit of the kangaroo court that convicted Edwards. The phase of militant opposition to the rebels that followed the counterinsurrections of 1776 proved the most deadly for Loyalists. Moreover, from that year onward, gangs of Loyalist "banditti," led by Wiert Banta, Claudius Smith, and John Mason, utilized the Highlands of the New York–New Jersey border as a base from which to conduct irregular operations against rebels and neutrals. In the pine barrens of the central and southeastern parts of the state, several similar gangs also operated within Whig lines. Although nominally Loyalist, the sometimes indiscriminate marauding expeditions of these gangs call their motives into question.[60]

Monmouth County was particularly hard hit by partisan violence. Among the most notorious Loyalist offenders was Jacob Fagan ("alias Jameson"), a former petty criminal in his early twenties who had deserted from the rebel army and joined the Second Battalion of the New Jersey

Volunteers commanded by Lieutenant Colonel John Morris. Although evidently "detached" for the purposes of recruiting, his activities also included plundering isolated homesteads and highway robbery. After a Whig mole infiltrated Fagan's gang, the outlaw Loyalist was ambushed and killed in September 1778. Patriots then "dug him up, carried the Corps to Freehold, and hung it on a Gibbet," a "degradation ceremony" traditionally accorded executed slaves, pirates, and perpetrators of other heinous crimes.[61] In January 1779, three of Fagan's gang members—Stephen Emmons ("alias Burke"), who had deserted from a state regiment and whose kinsman Thomas had been executed in Monmouth County the year before, Stephen West, and Ezekiel Williams—were likewise ambushed by Whig militia while attempting to return to New York. Despite their cry for quarter, they were killed, and two of them also were reportedly "hanged in chains."[62] All four victims belonged to the Loyalist New Jersey Volunteers at the time of their deaths, and their fates demonstrated the folly of authorizing or allowing enlisted men to conduct irregular operations behind American lines.

Patriots described Loyalist irregulars in loaded and dehumanizing terms, including "banditti," "land pirates," "infamous robbers," "freebooters," "miscreants," "fiends," "monsters in wickedness," "wood robbers," and "egregious villains," terms that doubtless made it psychologically easier to extirpate them. But the questionable nature of Fagan, Emmons, West, and Williams's activities, as well as their use of aliases, makes their motives suspect. Patriots tended to regard all Loyalists irregulars as they did Lewis Fenton of Freehold, a notorious wartime criminal who apparently had neither a formal nor an informal affiliation with the British.[63] There is, admittedly, a large gray area concerning the motivations and behavior of Loyalist irregulars. Sometimes they were conducting legitimate partisan operations, such as horse stealing or disrupting rebel commerce. At other times they were merely plundering and committing criminal acts. For example, when Patriots interrogated a member of one "Marauding Gang" who was captured in June 1780, he said "he is not a Soldier, Neither was he to receive any pay ... their Sole Business was to take Numbers of the Inhabitants from their Houses and to Plunder & that the plunder was to be divided amongst them."[64] But since Loyalist irregulars were of the inarticulate common sort, and since the sources regarding their operations are largely Patriot sources, we will never know in many cases what their real aims were.

"An Eye for an Eye" versus "A Predatory Kind of War"

A factor determining the amount and type of violence that Loyalist insurgents inflicted on counties in the neutral ground of northeastern New Jersey was the "raw power" that emanated from British garrison towns. The fortified post at Paulus Hook on the New Jersey bank of the Hudson opposite New York City, for example, influenced both allegiance and trade patterns in southern Bergen County. During the British occupation of Philadelphia (1777–1778), a similar lodgment was established at Billingsport on the Delaware. Had it remained, the king's forces could have succeeded in cutting the state in half. Pro-British marauding expeditions often were launched from Staten Island, where the New Jersey Volunteers and the Queen's Rangers were cantoned. Centered at the Sandy Hook lighthouse, "Refugee-Town" was a lodestone that attracted irregulars, deserters, refugees, spies, double agents, horse thieves, and illicit traders. In August 1778, one American officer frantically reported that there were 2,500 men on "the Hook." More typically, a report in July 1780 noted that there were up to sixty black and white refugees camped on the peninsula "in the Cedars." Among the most notable leaders of these marauding gangs was "Colonel Tye" (formerly Titus), the runaway slave of a Monmouth County farmer. With good reason, Patriots characterized Refugee-Town as "where the horse thieves resort."[65] Gangs operating from outposts such as Staten Island and Sandy Hook were, in effect, "insurgent extensions of British power" that frequently exerted a destabilizing influence on the Whig-controlled New Jersey hinterland.[66]

Among the most notable leaders of marauding expeditions launched into "the neutral ground" was Colonel Tye, the erstwhile slave Titus, who had absconded from his Monmouth County master in November 1775. He was one of hundreds of New Jersey blacks who responded to British proclamations offering freedom in return for service to the Royalist cause. Another who answered the clarion call in 1778 was the "stout wench" Hagar, formerly owned by David Forman. Refugee blacks were "familiar with every corner of the country" and thus were very effective in targeting Whigs and their property. During the summer of 1780, Tye led several raids into Monmouth County; the last was in early September, when he captured Captain Joshua Huddy, who escaped. As a result of a wound received in this action, however, Tye died. For blacks such as Tye, Hagar, and no doubt the anonymous black Loyalist who executed Huddy, flight and service to the British offered a form of "legal revenge" against an oppressive slave system.[67]

Patriots in frontier counties such as Monmouth were in a vise grip between forces operating out of British-held New York and "intestine enemies," such as Joseph Mulliner, William Giberson Jr., and John Bacon, who operated from "skulking places" in the state's southeastern pinelands. Just how dangerous Monmouth was is demonstrated by the fact that between 1776 and 1782, no less than fifty-two prominent Whigs, including civil and military officials, were killed, plundered, kidnapped (some more than once), paroled, or had their homes burned.[68] By April 1780, one county militia colonel felt that the situation had deteriorated worse than in late 1776, "when they layed Down arms." So many Whigs in Shrewsbury and Middletown townships had been captured or paroled that there were too few to muster for frequent alarms. The sparsely populated and heavily forested southern townships of Dover and Stafford were "in continual Possession of the enemy," who roved about in "camps" of as many as sixty men that frequently outnumbered local Whig militia forces.[69] An accident of geography explains much of Monmouth's predicament. In addition to its proximity to New York, Monmouth's coastline was "a very extensive one and the Number of Men in no Degree equal to the Task" of defending it.[70]

Four hundred thirty-six Monmouth County Whigs responded to this destabilizing situation in mid-1780 by creating the Association for Retaliation, a vigilante organization that acted independently of the duly elected county officials. Appropriately, Colonel David Forman, who now combined his military commission with his civil role as common pleas justice, chaired the organization. Its avowed purpose was, as Dr. Nathaniel Scudder, another county leader, argued, "An Eye for an Eye and a Tooth for a Tooth." He admitted that the organization was extralegal but rationalized its existence on "the principle of self-preservation" and on the belief that the "Laxness, Timidity, and Indecision" of Whig magistrates made the law "a screen for Tories."[71]

Loyalists countered late the same year by establishing the Associated Loyalists, whose board of directors was presided over by New Jersey's last royal governor, William Franklin. Two of the objectives set forth in the board's "Declaration" of December 28 help explain much of what occurred in New Jersey in the conflict's waning years. One was that in pursuing "a predatory kind of war," the associators would engage in "Annoying the Sea Coasts of the revolted Provinces and distressing their Trade"; the other pledged that as long as the rebels continued the distinction of prisoners of war from prisoners of state, the directors would "Make the enemy feel the just vengeance due to such Enormities."[72] Both the Monmouth Retaliators and the Loyalist Associators in effect institutionalized the law of retaliation and thereby demonstrated that the Revolution "brought together extremists of every sort."[73]

"The Pernicious Clandestine Commerce," 1780–1783

The final phase of Loyalist insurgency in New Jersey during the early 1780s was the most effective in disrupting the rebel war effort. This phase was driven by trade in contraband which, one militia officer claimed, was "so much Esteemed that their Lives are Embarked for it."[74] In one form or another, contraband trade had been a thorn in the side of the Patriots ever since the arrival of the British off New Jersey in July 1776. During the British occupation of Philadelphia (1777–1778), a similar symbiotic relationship developed between that city and southwestern New Jersey. On Easter Sunday 1778, Reverend Nicholas Collin of Swedesboro, Gloucester County, was startled by a "terrific cry" near his church of a captured trader who was being flogged so severely that he subsequently died. By the early 1780s, the "London" or "New York" trade that emanated, especially, from southern Monmouth and eastern Burlington and Gloucester counties, had become an intractable problem. Nearly all of the partisan activity in New Jersey during the early 1780s, much of which occurred after the British surrender at Yorktown, was either directly or indirectly linked to the furtherance of contraband trade.[75]

As scores of indictments for "going into enemy lines" indicate, the numerous laws enacted to suppress the illicit commerce were ineffective. Part of the problem was that the legislation was either not sufficiently draconian or not enforced. Captured traders were eligible for bail and, if convicted, were only fined, "which the villains can afford to pay out of their iniquitous profits and still make a lucrative business of it."[76] Washington doubted whether the entire Continental army could suppress the trade and suggested that the only way to control it was to impose the death penalty: "We are . . . the only Nation who suffer their people to carry on a commerce with their enemy in time of War."[77]

In an address to the legislature in May 1782, Governor Livingston pointed out that the trade enabled the enemy "to Support the war against us by promoting the sale of their manufactures, by draining of our Specie, & by depriving us of many articles necessary for the Support of our army or greatly enhancing the price." The trade was driven by lawbreakers who supplied the British much-needed livestock, provisions, cordwood, and lumber and who were in turn paid in specie and in luxury and manufactured items. In response to a query by a foreigner in 1782 regarding New Jersey's commerce, Livingston replied tongue in cheek: "Latterly the chief trade of the State has been carried on from little Egg harbour, being by much the most convenient for the lumber business."[78] An inventory of goods seized from traders in 1782 demonstrated the popularity of teapots, tea sets, and tea. Thus although the ubiquitous beverage had served to politicize people in the 1770s, by the early 1780s citizens were "seduced by British gew-gaws" away from their allegiance. As David Forman observed: "These Temptations are too mutch for Weak Whiggs to with stand—Tories want no Temptations."[79]

The "pernicious clandestine commerce" drew people of all allegiances into its vortex. In fragile local economies disrupted by long years of civil turmoil, survival strategies, as well as greed, help explain behavior on all sides.[80] For Loyalists, contraband trade was a means of earning income, recompensing losses, and subverting the Patriot war effort. In 1782, an unfounded rumor that the refugees were fortifying Osborn's Island in lower Barnegat Bay caused Patriot authorities some concern, but they concluded that the Tories were "a set of out Casts," many of whom had previously been paroled, who were "Constantly plying up & Down the Bay and Supporting the Illicit Trade" in armed boats. Their objective was chiefly "to Protect their Trading Boats of which they have a Number."[81] It was, in short, their livelihood.

Perhaps the most outlaw community in New Jersey during the early 1780s was Little Egg Harbor township in eastern Burlington County, where the tavern at Clamtown (Tuckerton) was the traders' chief rendezvous. Indeed, in 1790, the legislature frankly admitted that between 1780 and 1782 the township was "subject to the ravages of the Enemy, and not fully protected by this State or the United States."[82] For various reasons, Little Egg Harbor became the hotbed of the "pernicious traffic." The population was sparse, estimated in 1784 at approximately 600 persons (or about five inhabitants per square mile). It also was a preponderantly Quaker township in a predominately Quaker county. This assured the traders of complaisance if not compliance, because conscientious pacifists would not use force to suppress the trade. One of the traders' hideouts was, in fact, situated within a half mile of the Friends' meetinghouse.[83] It also was opposite a major inlet that provided access to the sea-lanes approaching New York, and the traders' shallow-draft vessels could use the back bays and intricate network of waterways to their advantage. The Little Egg Harbor militia had been moribund for several years. In May 1781, refugees and locals forcibly drove the Monmouth Whig militia back to the border of their county; that November, when a Whig outsider was suspected of reviewing the local militia, he was "beat exceedingly." These incidents demonstrate that the traders and their abettors would brook no interference with their business. Little Egg Harbor also was an important link in a network that channeled fugitive Loyalists and escaped British prisoners to New York.[84]

A rare insight into the traders' "roving partisan community" was provided in December 1782 in the aftermath of a skirmish at Cedar Creek Bridge in southern Monmouth between the Burlington County Whig militia and John Bacon's "Infernal Gang." Bacon, a shingle maker who had resided in Manahawkin before the war, did not emerge as a Tory partisan leader until 1780. His extensive repertoire of offenses included going within enemy lines, killing a rebel officer at sea for attempting to interdict the illicit trade, waging a "publick and cruel war" against the state, plundering rebel homesteads, horse stealing, engaging in firefights with the Whig militia, robbing the Burlington County collector, and perpetrating the Long Beach "massacre."[85] After the skirmish, Thomas Bird, who was Bacon's "Cheif Runner" (i.e., fencer) was captured; he eventually confessed that he and others had "Agreed to Assist Bacons Gang at a minits warning." Another prisoner, William Holmes, revealed "a Gang of theaves and traders." Joe "Crummil" (Cromwell), a local black who had used his wagon to transport the wounded outlaws, had been sworn to secrecy by them. The Patriots also discovered that there were others in the area who "frequently Bought Bacons Stolen Goods [and] Supplide him with provitions, both men and women." Women were, in fact, less likely to be searched and thus were effective at crossing the lines and fencing goods. Bacon's roving band, therefore, included not only a cadre of armed Loyalists but also an extensive network of receivers, abettors, and customers. Fittingly, the ambush and killing on April 3, 1783, of Bacon, whose economically motivated depredations had disrupted isolated Patriot homesteads and communities for three years, rang down the curtain on an exhausting chronicle of civil violence in New Jersey. He was New Jersey's, and perhaps the Revolutionary War's, last reported casualty.[86]

Aftermath

In July 1783, Johann David Schoepf, a surgeon serving with the German auxiliaries, decided to tour the new United States. Before sailing from New York to Elizabethtown, however, his vessel's captain was threatened with "a lading of blows . . . by a man of the King's party who fancied the skipper had injured him," which caused Schoepf to fear "experiencing on the other shore something of the law of reprisals" from the "still irritated" Americans.[87] Although the German doctor's fears were unfounded, many others were not as fortunate. For many who had experienced the prolonged ordeal of brutality, retribution, and violence, old animosities and memories died hard. Even sixty years after the war, many veterans recalled going on "scouts" to ferret out irregulars and London traders from their "lurking places" in the pines. When in the 1840s Benson Lossing was compiling material for his *Pictorial Field-Book of the Revolution*, he encountered eighty-four-year-old Polly Van Norden, who during the war lived near Freehold. Lossing found that she still "became excited with feelings of the bitterest hatred against the Tories while telling me of their deeds—a hatred, the keenness of which a lapse of seventy years had scarcely blunted."[88]

In the immediate postwar period, zealous Whigs assailed the state legislature with apoplectic petitions that called active Loyalists "atrocious Monsters of Wickedness," compared them to "turks and Canibals," and urged that "No Indulgence" be granted them to return.[89] Some, such as Anthony Jr. and Jesse Woodward and several of their relatives, as well as Richard Robins and Gilbert Giberson, migrated to Canada. Largely because they brought money back into the state during a cycle of economic downturn, by the late 1780s punitive legislation was relaxed and the arch-traitors were permitted to return. The reaction to them in their former communities could be violent, however. When Gilbert Giberson returned to Upper Freehold, his family was harassed, so he relocated to Pennsylvania. In contrast, his nephew, Tory partisan William Giberson Jr., may have successfully reintegrated into society in southwestern New Jersey. Little Anthony Woodward, who apparently had a sizeable family network still present in Upper Freehold, eventually managed to reestablish himself in the community.[90]

Many Loyalists never left the state. In 1782, the legislature did away with the secret ballot in elections for fear that proponents of "Anti-Republican Principles" would work within the system to subvert the government. Hotly contested elections between 1782 and 1784 in Burlington County "indicate ongoing wartime tensions," as well as an attempt by formerly disenfranchised Quakers to "reestablish themselves as public leaders in a new political context created by a war that they had officially opposed.[91] Early in 1784, a dissident faction in the county attempted to use the courts to punish a captain who was seeking to collect militia fines and distrain goods from delinquents. By August, a donnybrook erupted in Chesterfield township between the militia and a "Tory party" over the matter of fines; the contending parties fought with "Stones, Brick bats, Axes, Hoes, Waggon Tires, hinges, stalk knives, Hot water, etc." The women played their part too, "scalding several so that their clothes were obliged to be cut off"; one woman was seen "with a Club in one hand and a Urinary in the other, at other times beating upon a brass Kettle which she had for a drum." Even though the incident lasted for half an hour, no one was killed, but it caused one Patriot leader to ponder, "where it will end God only knows, as the Tories and London traders are bent upon ruling the country, and the Whigs are determined to oppose it." One month later, a "mutiny" happened in the same county over the framing of an election ticket, which gave rise to fears that a Tory faction was attempting "to introduce Characters so notoriously disaffected to the present happy Constitution . . . that they must have some latent design in view, which if carried into execution will be productive of the worst of Consequences to those who have heretofore distinguished themselves as Whigs." In 1784, the disaffected in Burlington County actually succeeded in electing delegates to the state legislature.[92] Well into the postwar period, political opponents leveled the mudslinging charge of "Tory."

Patriots accused Tories of being "of a timid Cast, & of weak Nerves." Thomas Paine alleged, "Every Tory is a coward . . . fear is the foundation of Toryism." Yet as the wartime careers of James Moody, Little Anthony Woodward, William Giberson Jr., John Bacon, Richard Lippincott, and many others indicate, "timidity was not always, or perhaps not even usually, the rule."[93] Nor was it the case with Loyalist women such as Mrs. Howard, who threatened to "let the enemy have her close line" for the purpose of hanging three Whigs at New Brunswick. Nor with the wife of Richard Robins, who in January 1777 brazenly confronted rebels that were impressing supplies from their farm. Nor with the sister of the Tory partisan William Giberson Jr., who in 1782 reputedly facilitated his comic-opera escape from Burlington jail by changing clothes with him.[94] But there were "many gradations below the active, dedicated, consistent Tory." James Moody differentiated between those who were "loyal only through resentment and interest, not from conviction and principle"; in the course of his picaresque career, he found that "Loyalists . . . from principle" never failed him. Dr. Benjamin Rush categorized such people as "rank" Tories; William Livingston thought "a real Tory is by any human Means absolutely inconvertible."[95] But such comments validate, however grudgingly, that dedicated Tories, like dedicated Whigs, at least had the integrity of their convictions.

In 1779, the *Annual Register* (London) observed, "Civil wars are unhappily distinguished from all others, by a degree of rancour in their prosecution, which does not exist in the hostilities of distinct nations, and absolute strangers." To those who desperately tried to remain neutral, it seemed as though "both parties fought not like real men with sword and gun, but like robbers and incendiaries."[96] New Jersey Loyalists were initially motivated by factors similar to those that motivated the disaffected in other colonies, including self-interest, personality, religious affiliation, experience, and prewar disputes. Contemporaries and later observers agree that private grudges played a role in determining allegiance. But as the war escalated, grievances such as property confiscation, prosecutions in Whig criminal courts, and especially capital punishment caused Loyalists to invoke the "ethic of self-redress."[97] Patriots such as Nathaniel Scudder and Loyalists such as Richard Lippincott both invoked the Mosaic law and the principle of self-preservation. In 1782, Sir Guy Carleton, who became British commander in chief in the midst of the Huddy uproar, recognized the vicious circle: "It would be as Difficult as it seems useless to trace from what first Injuries those Acts of Retaliation, which have lately passed, are Derived."[98] There was, indeed, blame enough to go around. From the comparatively moderate activities of the Woodward insurgents, to the more questionable motives of Fagan and his ilk, to the economically driven operations of Bacon's gang, a crescendo of retributive violence led seemingly irreversibly to Huddy and Lippincott's final handshake.

Notes

1. The foregoing narrative is summarized from the transcript of the trial in L. Kinvin Wroth, ed., "Vengeance: The Court-Martial of Captain Richard Lippincott,"

in *Sources of American Independence: Selected Manuscripts from the Collections of the William L. Clements Library*, ed. Howard H. Peckham, 2 vols., 2: 535–612 (Chicago, IL: University of Chicago Press, 1978), hereafter cited as Wroth, "Court-Martial of Lippincott." There are numerous references to the Huddy incident: see Katherine Mayo, *General Washington's Dilemma* (New York: Harcourt, Brace, 1938); Frederick B. Wiener, *Civilians under Military Justice: The British Practice since 1689 Especially in North America* (Chicago, IL: University of Chicago Press, 1967), 113–22; Larry Bowman, "The Court-Martial of Captain Richard Lippincott," *New Jersey History* 89 (1971): 23–36 (hereafter cited as *NJH*); Arthur D. Pierce, *Smugglers' Woods: Jaunts and Journeys in Colonial and Revolutionary New Jersey* (New Brunswick, NJ: Rutgers University Press, 1960), 252–78; and William S. Stryker, *The Capture of the Block House at Toms River, New Jersey* (Trenton, NJ: Naar, Day, and Naar, 1883). A useful compilation of primary documents on the incident is the catalog accompanying an exhibit at the Monmouth County Archives, "The Joshua Huddy Era: Documents of the American Revolution" (Manalapan, NJ: Monmouth County Archives, 2004). On the Associated Loyalists, see Edward H. Tebbenhoff, "The Associated Loyalists: An Aspect of Militant Loyalism," *New-York Historical Society Quarterly* 63 (1979): 115–44 (hereafter cited as *NYHSQ*); and Edward J. DeMott, "The Board of Associated Loyalists at New York," MA thesis, St. John's University, Queens, New York, 1971. On the Association for Retaliation, see Michael S. Adelberg, " 'A Combination to Trample All Law Underfoot': The Association for Retaliation and the American Revolution in Monmouth County," *NJH* 115 (1997): 3–36. On Huddy's daring escape, see Nathaniel Scudder to Joseph Scudder, September 11, 1780, MG 4, New Jersey Historical Society, Newark; and *Pennsylvania Packet*, October 3, 1780. Amazingly, both the label pinned to Huddy's chest and the will he signed have survived; see, respectively, George Washington Papers (microfilm edition) (Library of Congress, 1964), reel 84, and MG 4, New Jersey Historical Society.

    2. The phrase is from George Washington to David Forman, December 3, 1782, in John C. Fitzpatrick, ed., *The Writings of George Washington*, 39 vols. (Washington, DC: Government Printing Office, 1931–1944), 25: 388–90.

    3. Washington to Sir Henry Clinton, April 21, 1782, in Fitzpatrick, *The Writings of Washington*, 24: 146–47. William Franklin to Clinton, April 25, 1782 (enclosure regarding "acts of cruelty and barbarity"), a copy of which Clinton forwarded to Washington on May 1, British Headquarters Papers, no. 4475, and Papers of the Continental Congress, reel 171, item 152, v. 10, p. 543.

    4. Worthington C. Ford et al., eds., *Journals of the Continental Congress, 1774–1789*, 34 vols. (Washington, DC: Government Printing Office, 1904–1937), 22: 217. For an extended discussion of the context of the Huddy incident, see Wroth, "Court-Martial of Lippincott," 499–534.

    5. Wroth, "Court-Martial of Lippincott," 558, 559, 560, 561, emphases in original.

    6. Lippincott used the phrase "verbal orders" several times in his defense; ibid., 589, 590, 591.

    7. Ibid., 559, 601.

    8. Anon., *American Husbandry, Containing an Account of the Soil, Climate, Production and Agriculture of the British Colonies in North America and the West*

Indies . . . by an American, edited by Harry J. Carman (Port Washington, NY: Kennikat Press, 1964), 110.

9. Richard Buel, *In Irons: Britain's Naval Supremacy and the American Revolutionary Economy* (New Haven, CT: Yale University Press, 1998), 15, 20–21, 107, 109. For an overview of New Jersey's colonial economy and social structure, see David J. Fowler, " 'These Were Troublesome Times Indeed': Social and Economic Conditions in Revolutionary New Jersey," in *New Jersey in the American Revolution*, ed. Barbara J. Mitnick, 15–20 (New Brunswick, NJ: Rutgers University Press, 2005).

10. For laws passed during the period 1760–1775, see Bernard Bush, comp., *Laws of the Royal Colony of New Jersey*, vols. 4–5 (Trenton, NJ: New Jersey State Library, 1982, 1986); the quote is from Gordon S. Wood, *The Radicalism of the American Revolution* (New York: Alfred A. Knopf, 1992), 245. On the cultural and ethnic diversity of New Jersey, see Peter O. Wacker, *Land and People: A Cultural Geography of Preindustrial New Jersey; Origins and Settlement Patterns* (New Brunswick, NJ: Rutgers University Press, 1975). On the "psychology of accommodation" in the Middle Colonies, see Jack P. Greene, *Pursuits of Happiness: The Social Development of Early Modern British Colonies and the Formation of American Culture* (Chapel Hill, NC: University of North Carolina Press, 1988), 140–41, and James A. Henretta, *The Evolution of American Society: An Interdisciplinary Analysis* (Lexington, MA: D. C. Heath, 1973), 112, 115–16, 124, 166. The quote is from Wallace Brown, *The King's Friends: The Composition and Motives of American Loyalist Claimants* (Providence, RI: Brown University Press, 1965), 116. According to Dennis P. Ryan, "No state was so deeply affected by the internal and external convulsions of those years," "Landholding, Opportunity, and Mobility in Revolutionary New Jersey," *William and Mary Quarterly*, 3rd ser., 36 (1979): 578 (hereafter cited as *WMQ*). In 1784, a British officer who had campaigned in New Jersey also observed that the state "suffered extremely by the war, much more in proportion than any other." See J. F. D. Smyth, *A Tour in the United States of America* (1784; reprinted New York: New York Times, 1968), 40.

11. The most comprehensive study of events in New Jersey leading up to independence is Larry R. Gerlach, *Prologue to Independence: New Jersey in the Coming of the American Revolution* (New Brunswick, NJ: Rutgers University Press, 1976). The quote is from John E. O'Connor, *William Paterson, Lawyer and Statesman* (New Brunswick, NJ: Rutgers University Press, 1979), 89. Cogil (Cowgill) quote is from Wm. Tatem affidavit, no. 0314, Stewart Collection, Savitz Library, Rowan University, Glassboro, New Jersey. On the "sensible core of wary people," see Liam Riordan, *Many Identities, One Nation: The Revolution and Its Legacy in the Mid-Atlantic* (Philadelphia, PA: University of Pennsylvania Press, 2007), 44. The "Proviso" in New Jersey's constitution is published in John D. Cushing, comp., *First Laws of the State of New Jersey* (Wilmington, DE: M. Glazier, 1981), x, emphasis in original.

12. Paul H. Smith, "New Jersey Loyalists and the British 'Provincial Corps' in the War for Independence," *NJH* 87 (1969): 76. Dennis P. Ryan has questioned Smith's estimate; see "Six Towns: Continuity and Change in Revolutionary New Jersey, 1770–1792." PhD diss., New York University, 1974, 177, n. 23; his study is based on evidence regarding only six townships, however. Adams's oft-cited estimate is in Thomas McKean to Adams, January 1814, in *The Works of John Adams*, ed.

Charles Francis Adams, 10: 87 (1856; reprinted Freeport, NY: Books for Libraries Press, 1969). The aggregate figure for Loyalists is from Paul H. Smith, "The American Loyalists: Notes on Their Organization and Numerical Strength," *WMQ*, 3rd ser., 25 (1968): 269.

13. Ibid., 261.

14. O'Connor, *William Paterson*, 102. General statements concerning the backgrounds and motivations of New Jersey Loyalists are in Dennis P. Ryan, *New Jersey's Loyalists*, no. 20, in *New Jersey's Revolutionary Experience* series (Trenton, NJ: New Jersey Historical Commission, 1975), 7–13, 23–25; Leonard Lundin, *Cockpit of the Revolution: The War for Independence in New Jersey* (Princeton, NJ: Princeton University Press, 1940), 70–108; Brown, *The King's Friends*, 111–26; and Robert M. Calhoon, *The Loyalists in Revolutionary America, 1760–1781* (New York: Harcourt, Brace, Jovanovich, 1973), 360–69.

15. Anon., *American Husbandry*, 110. For a summarization of sources concerning the colonial American standard of living, see Fowler, " 'These Were Troublesome Times Indeed,' " in *New Jersey in the American Revolution*, 201, n. 26.

16. Richard Waln to Joseph Galloway, March 29, 1789, Richard Waln Letterbook, Historical Society of Pennsylvania, Philadelphia. On the ramifications of colonial membership in the British "empire of goods," see T. H. Breen, "An Empire of Goods: The Anglicization of Colonial America, 1690–1776," in *Colonial America: Essays in Politics and Social Development*, 4th ed., ed. Stanley N. Katz et al., 378–84 (New York: McGraw Hill, 1993). William Paterson, "Address at a Conference," [1777], William Paterson Papers, Special Collections, Rutgers University Libraries, New Brunswick, New Jersey. The quote regarding Quakers is from "Journal of Samuel Rowland Fisher, 1779–81," *Pennsylvania Magazine of History and Biography* 41 (1917): 149 (hereafter cited as *PMHB*).

17. William H. Nelson, *The American Tory* (Boston, MA: Northeastern University Press, 1992), 88, 91.

18. On the "community feud," see Richard Maxwell Brown, *Strain of Violence* (New York: Oxford University Press, 1975), 251; on the Revolution as "a series of local civil wars," see Michael S. Adelberg, " 'I Am as Innocent as an Unborn Child: The Loyalism of Edward and George Taylor," *NJH* 123 (2005): 5, 29. The quote is from Ryan, "Six Towns," 177.

19. Paul H. Smith, *Loyalists and Redcoats: A Study in British Revolutionary Policy* (New York: W. W. Norton, 1972), 66. Robert M. Calhoon, "Introduction" in *Loyalists and Community in North America*, ed. Calhoon, et al., 3 (Westport, CT: Greenwood Press, 1994). *Lieutenant James Moody's Narrative of His Exertions and Sufferings in the Cause of Government, since the Year 1776*, 2nd ed. (1783; reprinted New York: Ayer Publishing, 1976), 5–6; on Moody, see also Susan Burgess Shenstone, *So Obstinately Loyal: James Moody, 1744–1809* (Montreal: McGill-Queen's University Press, 2000).

20. Gerlach, *Prologue to Independence*, 239–40, 252, 276–77, 282–83, 354, 452, n. 47; and Daniel Coxe to Cortlandt Skinner, July 4, 1775, quoted in ibid., 276. For examples of New Jersey's Whig-Loyalists—those who were leaders in the colonial protest movement against British policies but who recoiled from independence and armed rebellion—see Adelberg, "I Am as Innocent as an Unborn Child," 3–37.

21. On the importance of kinship in influencing allegiance, see Ryan, "Six Towns," 75, 143, 144, 155, 162, 173. Gerlach points out that "many communities were genealogically one extended family," *Prologue to Independence*, 14; similarly, Wood notes that due to intermarrying, some "enlarged families" encompassed entire villages or townships, *Radicalism of the American Revolution*, 44, 48.

22. Brown, *The King's Friends*, 111, 117–19, 121, 265–67.

23. Robert Rogers, *A Concise Account of North America* (1765; reprinted New York: SR Publishers, 1966), 78. On the importance of religion in six East Jersey communities (Newark, Morristown, Woodbridge, Piscataway, Middletown, and Shrewsbury), see Ryan, "Six Towns," 154, 155, 162, 163, 168, 185, 187, 189, 219, 237, 294, 309. On the influence of the Presbyterians in the protest movement in New Jersey, see also Gerlach, *Prologue to Independence*, 200, 258, 323–25, 354. For an overview of the influence of Presbyterianism, see Joseph S. Tiedemann, "Presbyterianism and the American Revolution in the Middle Colonies," *Church History* 75 (2005): 306–44.

24. John Fea notes that many New Jersey Protestants "moved freely among churches, ministers, and meetinghouses, rarely committing to one denomination." See "Rural Religion: Protestant Community and the Moral Improvement of the South Jersey Countryside, 1676–1800" (PhD diss., State University of New York at Stony Brook, 1999), 20, 310, 317. Wallace N. Jamison questions the active religious affiliation of many people, *Religion in New Jersey: A Brief History* (Princeton, NJ: Van Nostrand, 1964), 70; Jean R. Soderlund likewise argues that "probably a large proportion of colonists had no active religious affiliation," *Quakers and Slavery: A Divided Spirit* (Princeton, NJ: Princeton University Press, 1985), 209.

25. Eugene R. Fingerhut, "Uses and Abuses of American Loyalists' Claims: A Critique of Quantitative Analyses," *WMQ*, 3rd ser., 25 (1968): 248, 258; Brown, *The King's Friends*, 111, 117, 289, 315.

26. Brown, *The King's Friends*, 118. "Letter of Thomas Leaming Jr. to Hon. William Paterson, 1789," in *PMHB* 38 (1914): 116. Gilbert Giberson Loyalist Claim, Audit Office (AO) 12/15, Public Record Office (PRO), Great Britain. On "involuntary allegiance" and "compulsory oath-taking," see Michael Kammen, "The American Revolution as a *Crise de Conscience*: The Case of New York," in *Society, Freedom and Conscience: The Coming of the Revolution in Virginia, Massachusetts, and New York*, ed. Richard M. Jellison, 125–89; the quote is on p. 157 (New York: Norton, 1976).

27. On the distribution of population, see Fowler, "'These Were Troublesome Times Indeed,'" in *New Jersey in the American Revolution*, 196, n. 2. John Fell to Robert Morris (of New Jersey), July 10, 1779, quoted in Adrian C. Leiby, *The Revolutionary War in the Hackensack Valley: The Jersey Dutch and the Neutral Ground* (New Brunswick, NJ: Rutgers University Press, 1980), 213.

28. On the Freehold and Shrewsbury townships, see David J. Fowler, "Egregious Villains, Wood Rangers, and London Traders: The Pine Robber Phenomenon in Revolutionary New Jersey," PhD diss., Rutgers University, 1987, 30–33.

29. Shortly before the Battle of Trenton, General William Howe admitted that his chain of cantonments across New Jersey was "rather too extensive," but he justified the disposition of posts because he was "induced to occupy Burlington,

to cover the county of Monmouth, in which there were many loyal inhabitants; and trusting to the almost general submission of the country to the southward," Howe to Lord Germain, December 20, 1776, in K. G. Davies, ed., *Documents of the American Revolution, 1770–1783*, 21 vols. (Shannon, Ireland: Irish University Press, 1972–81), 12: 267.

30. Wm. Livingston to John Hancock, December 7, 1776, and Deposition of Isaac Potter, April 7, 1777, in *Livingston Papers*, 1: 192, 299–300; Evidence of Thomas Clark against John Mason "respecting the plot," Apr. 8, 1777, Council of Safety Records, New Jersey State Archives, Trenton; and Fowler, "Egregious Villains," 34, 42, 46, 48.

31. Deposition of Wm. Sands, April 23, 1777, in Carl E. Prince, et al., eds. *The Papers of Willioam Livingston*, 5 vols. (New Brunswick, NJ: New Jersey Historical Commission, 1979–1988) (hereafter cited as *Livingston Papers*), 1: 312–14; Gerlach, *Prologue to Independence*, 353. On the counterinsurrections in Monmouth, see Fowler, "Egregious Villains," 27–114.

32. Francis Wade to a Committee of Congress, March 4, 1777, Papers of the Continental Congress, reel 104, p. 383. On the Woodward insurrection, see Fowler, "Egregious Villains," 54–114.

33. On the backgrounds of the Woodward insurgents, see Fowler, "Egregious Villains," 60–66. On transient rural laborers, see Peter O. Wacker and Paul G. E. Clemens, *Land Use in Early New Jersey: A Historical Geography* (New Brunswick, NJ: New Jersey Historical Society, 1992), 10–12, 24, 29.

34. Examination and Confession of Thomas Fowler, 1777, Council of Safety Records, New Jersey State Archives. Six years after the war's end, Waln was still hoping for a restoration of British rule, Waln to Joseph Galloway, and Waln to Joseph Warder, both March 29, 1789, Richard Waln Letterbook, Historical Society of Pennsylvania.

35. On the Continental Association as a scheme by Whig merchants, see Harold Hyman, *To Try Men's Souls: Loyalty Tests in American History* (Berkeley, CA: University of California Press, 1959), 69.

36. Examination and Confession of Thomas Fowler, 1777, Council of Safety Records, New Jersey State Archives. John Robins affidavit in Richard Robins Loyalist Claim, and Gilbert Giberson Loyalist Claim, both AO 12/15, PRO.

37. Gerlach, *Prologue to Independence*, 258–60, 270. On Lippincott, see Revolutionary War Numbered Mss., no.1139, New Jersey State Archives.

38. Peter Force, *American Archives*, 4th ser., 6: 1647, 1661, and 5th ser., 1: 726; *Minutes of the Provincial Congress and the Council of Safety of the State of New Jersey, 1775–1776* (Trenton, NJ: Naar, Day, and Naar, 1879), 509–10, 539. The phrase is from Wm. Paterson, "Address at a Conference," [1777], Wm. Paterson Papers, Special Collections, Rutgers University Libraries.

39. On the depredations of the Woodward insurgents in late December 1776, see Fowler, "Egregious Villains," 68–73.

40. Examination of Abraham Hendricks, April 10, 1777, Depositions of Wm. Imlay, April 12, 1777, and Deposition of Thomas Forman, April 23, 1777, in *Livingston Papers*, 1: 301, 304–05, 310–11; Fowler, "Egregious Villains," 69, 71–72, 73.

41. Cogil quoted in Wm. Tatem affidavit, no. 0314, Stewart Collection, Savitz Library, Rowan University, Glassboro, New Jersey. For other examples, see Wallace

Brown, *The Good Americans: The Loyalists in the American Revolution* (New York: Morrow, 1969), 132, 223, 253, and Wood, *Radicalism of the American Revolution*, 112.

42. Leiby, *The Revolutionary War in the Hackensack Valley*, 19–20, 112–14, 228–31; Randall Balmer, *A Perfect Babel of Confusion: Dutch Religion and English Culture in the Middle Colonies* (New York: Oxford University Press, 1989), ix, 149–50, 152.

43. Richard Waln Accounts: Grain Purchase, 1773–1786, Waln Family Papers, Historical Society of Pennsylvania.

44. Fowler, "Egregious Villains," 79–87; Moody, *Narrative*, 22.

45. Fowler, "Egregious Villains," 90.

46. On primal honor, see Bertram Wyatt-Brown, *Southern Honor: Ethics and Behavior in the Old South* (New York: Oxford University Press, 1982), xi, xiii, xv, xvii, 3, 14, 17, 25, 26, 33, 34. On the "ethic of individual violent self-defense and self-redress," see Brown, *Strain of Violence*, viii, 238. On the influence of kinship, friends and associates, and charismatic leadership, see Jack Marietta, *The Reformation of American Quakerism* (Philadelphia, PA: University of Pennsylvania Press, 1984), 234–36; Ryan, "Six Towns," 75, 143, 144, 155, 162, 173.

47. Minutes of the Monmouth County Court of Oyer and Terminer, January 20–February 7, 1778, and Supreme Court case files 37836 and 39543, all at New Jersey State Archives; Jesse Woodward Loyalist Claim, AO 13/21, PRO.

48. On the later careers of the Woodward insurgents, see Fowler, "Egregious Villains," 94–101.

49. Force, *American Archives*, 5th ser., 1: 1534–35. Wallace Brown points out that in no state were Loyalist counterinsurrections successful; see *Good Americans*, 41.

50. Cushing, *First Laws*, 14.

51. David A. Bernstein, "New Jersey in the American Revolution: The Establishment of a Government amid Civil and Military Disorder, 1770–1781," PhD diss., Rutgers University, 1969, 280–99; Agnes Hunt, *The Provincial Committees of Safety of the American Revolution* (New York: Haskell House, 1968), 76–83. An unannotated and unindexed transcription of the council's minutes is *Minutes of the Council of Safety of the State of New Jersey* (Jersey City, NJ: J. H. Lyon, 1872); supporting depositions, affidavits, confessions, and other documents related to the council's proceedings are in Council of Safety Records, 1776–1781, New Jersey State Archives.

52. On the Privy Council, see David A. Bernstein, ed., *Minutes of the Governor's Privy Council, 1777–1789* (Trenton, NJ: New Jersey State Library, 1974). Extant records of Revolutionary era-criminal courts—specifically, courts of quarter sessions and courts of oyer and terminer, as well as Supreme Court case files—for the counties of Monmouth, Burlington, and Gloucester are at the New Jersey State Archives. On property confiscation, see Bernstein, "New Jersey in the American Revolution," 359–65; Michael P. Riccards, "Patriots and Plunderers: Confiscation of Loyalist Lands in New Jersey, 1776–1786," *NJH* 86 (1968): 14–28; Ruth M. Keesey, "New Jersey Legislation Concerning Loyalists," *Proceedings of the New Jersey Historical Society* 79 (1961): 87–94 (hereafter cited as *PNJHS*).

53. Wroth, "Court-Martial of Lippincott," 567; *New Jersey Archives*, 2nd ser. (Newspaper Extracts), 2: 31 (hereafter cited as *NJA*); Minutes of the Monmouth County Court of Oyer and Terminer, June, 1778, New Jersey State Archives;

Dr. Samuel Adams (Massachusetts surgeon) diary, entry for July 17, 1778, New York Public Library; Fowler, "Egregious Villains," 166–68. In later years, "the noted hanging place" on Daniel Barkalow's property served as a reference point in deeds, Samuel Forman deed to David Forman, March 1790, James Neilson Papers, Special Collections, Rutgers University Libraries. On benefit of clergy, see *Black's Law Dictionary*, 8th ed. (St. Paul, MN: West Group, 2002), s.v., "benefit of clergy."

54. Hammet pleaded guilty to the charge of treason; see Minutes of the Gloucester County Court of Oyer and Terminer, November–December 1778, New Jersey State Archives. On Hammet, see also *NJA*, 2nd ser. (Newspaper Extracts), 2: 126, 583, 588; David A. Bernstein, ed., *Minutes of the Governor's Privy Council, 1777–1789* (Trenton, NJ: New Jersey State Library, 1974), 109; "List of Disaffected Persons Sent Me from Gloucester County," Israel Shreve Papers (Ac. 825), Special Collections, Rutgers University Libraries; and Wm. Livingston to county sheriffs, January 22, 1779, Livingston Papers (microfilm edition), reel 9, Massachusetts Historical Society, Boston, MA. Details regarding Hammet and a poignant vignette of his last hours appear in Amandus Johnson, ed., *Journal and Biography of Nicholas Collin, 1746–1831* (Philadelphia, PA: New Jersey Society of Pennsylvania, 1936 (hereafter cited as Collin, *Journal*), 249, 250–51. Ironically, Collin does not name the condemned prisoner, but his identity is evident from the foregoing sources. Collin mentions that Hammet was a "member of the English [i.e., Anglican] Church, of good character and great courage," ibid., 250.

55. Fowler, "Egregious Villains," 213–37. Wm. Franklin to Henry Clinton, April 25, 1782 (enclosure), British Headquarters Papers (microfilm), no. 4475, a copy of which was relayed as an enclosure from Clinton to Washington, Papers of the Continental Congress, reel 171, item 152, v. 10. On the process of "Robinhooding" outlaws, see Kent L. Steckmesser, "Robin Hood and the American Outlaw: A Note on History and Folklore," *Journal of American Folklore* 79 (1966): 354.

56. Minutes of the Burlington County Court of Oyer and Terminer, July 25–August 1, 1781, New Jersey State Archives; *NJA*, 2nd series (Newspaper Extracts), 5: 265; Wm. Livingston to Thomas Sim Lee, October 29, 1781, in *Livingston Papers*, 4: 323.

57. On "judicial murder" of Tories, see Brown, *Strain of Violence*, 75, Wroth, "Court-Martial of Lippincott," 560, 561.

58. Wroth, "Court-Martial of Lippincott," 566, 579, 611; David Forman to George Washington, October 15, 1777, George Washington Papers (microfilm edition), reel 44. A Royalist newspaper reported that Edwards was executed for attempting to bring "a few cheeses" to New York, *New York Gazette*, October 27, 1777, *NJA*, 2nd ser. (Newspaper Extracts), 1: 479; another Royalist account of Edwards's capture and death appeared in the *Pennsylvania Ledger*, November 26, 1777.

59. Wroth, "Court-Martial of Lippincott," 567–68, 611. On April 9, 1782, three days before he executed Joshua Huddy, Richard Lippincott proposed an expedition into Monmouth in order to "Seize on . . . General Forman," ibid., 562. On Forman, see *American National Biography* (New York: Oxford University Press, 1999), v. 8, s.v. "Forman, David."

60. On the Highlands gangs, see Leiby, *Revolutionary War in the Hackensack Valley*, 186–99; on the Pine Robber gangs, see Fowler, "Egregious Villains." A general

study of Revolutionary outlaws, which includes chapters on New Jersey, is Harry M. Ward, *Between the Lines: Banditti of the American Revolution* (Westport, CT: Praeger, 2002), 51–116.

61. Fowler, "Egregious Villains," 144–56. Between 1774 and 1776, Fagan was indicted in both Monmouth and Burlington counties for pilfering clothing; see *NJA*, 2nd ser. (Newspaper Extracts), 1: 104; Monmouth County Court of Quarter Sessions, and Court of Oyer and Terminer (loose papers), Indictments, October 1774, Monmouth County Archives; and re Burlington county, Supreme Court case files 20690* and 20691*, New Jersey State Archives. On September 1, 1777, Fagan was listed as a deserter from the Second New Jersey Regiment, Military Service Record cards, New Jersey State Archives. The proclamation offering a reward for Fagan's capture is in *Livingston Papers*, 2: 454–55. A lurid description of Fagan's gibbeting is in John W. Barber and Henry Howe, *Historical Collections of the State of New Jersey* (1868; reprinted Spartanburg, SC: Reprint Company, 1966), 352–53. Sir Henry Clinton included Fagan's disinterment and gibbeting when in the aftermath of the Huddy incident he complained about "acts of cruelty and barbarity" against Loyalists, Clinton to Washington (enclosure), May 1, 1782, Papers of the Continental Congress, reel 171, item 152, v. 10.

62. Wroth, "Court-Martial of Lippincott," 568; Fowler, "Egregious Villains," 156–59; *NJA*, 2nd ser. (Newspaper Extracts), 3: 53–54.

63. Fowler, "Egregious Villains," 161–66; *NJA*, 2nd ser. (Newspaper Extracts), 3: 641, 649–50. After Fenton was killed in an ambush by dragoons of Major Henry Lee's Legion, his body was reputedly thrown out of a wagon in front of the courthouse in Freehold; see Barber and Howe, *Historical Collections*, 352. His name was not included in the list of "acts of cruelty and barbarity" against Loyalists, Clinton to Washington (enclosure), May 1, 1782, Papers of the Continental Congress, reel 171, item 152, v. 10.

64. David Forman to Washington, June 23, 1780, Washington Papers (microfilm edition), reel 67. In 1781 it was reported that "the trade of Horse stealing flourishes amazingly," Silas Condict to Wm. Livingston, July 20, 1781, in *Livingston Papers*, 4: 242–43.

65. On the influence of "raw power" on allegiance, see John Shy, "Hearts and Minds in the American Revolution: The Case of 'Long Bill' Scott and Peterborough, New Hampshire," in *A People Numerous and Armed: Reflections on the Military Struggle for American Independence* (New York: Oxford University Press, 1976), 178; "Conclusion," in *The Other New York: The American Revolution beyond New York City, 1763–1787*, ed., Joseph S. Tiedemann and Eugene R. Fingerhut, 224 (Albany: State University of New York Press, 2005). On Paulus Hook, see Ruth M. Keesey, "Loyalism in Bergen County, New Jersey," *WMQ*, 3rd ser., 18 (1961): 560, 569–70. On the interrelationships between Staten Island and East Jersey, see Philip Papas, "Richmond County, Staten Island," in *The Other New York*, 84, 86, 88–89, 90, 91, 92, 94; on Provincial regiments stationed there, see ibid., 93. On Billingsport, see Lundin, *Cockpit of the Revolution*, 343, 372, 375. On Sandy Hook, see Michael S. Adelberg, " 'So Dangerous a Quarter': The Sandy Hook Lighthouse during the American Revolution," *The Keeper's Log* (1995): 10–15; Asher Holmes to Wm. Livingston, August 4, 1778, Livingston Papers (microfilm edition), reel 7; David

Forman to Washington, July 9, 1780, Washington Papers (microfilm edition), reel 67; and *NJA*, 2nd ser. (Newspaper Extracts), 5: 344. On Colonel Tye, see Graham R. Hodges, *Slavery and Freedom in the Rural North: African Americans in Monmouth County, New Jersey, 1665–1865* (Madison, WI: Madison House, 1997), 92–93, 97–104; Hodges, "Black Revolt in New York City and the Neutral Zone: 1775–83," in *New York in the Age of the Constitution, 1775–1800*, ed. Paul A. Gilje and William Pencak, 24, 34–38 (Cranbury, NJ: Associated University Press, 1992). On the influence of the garrison town of New York on the adjoining no-man's-land, see Cynthia Dubin Edelberg, "Jonathan Odell and Philip Freneau: Poetry and Politics in the Garrison Town of New York City" in *Loyalists and Community*, 105–106.

66. Lindley S. Butler, "David Fanning's Militia: A Roving Partisan Community," in *Loyalists and Community*, 147, 155.

67. On Colonel Tye and black resistance during the Revolution, see Hodges, *Slavery and Freedom in the Rural North*, 91–112; Hodges, "Black Revolt in New York City and the Neutral Zone: 1775–83," in *New York in the Age of the Constitution, 1775–1800*, 20–47. The quotes are from the latter, pp. 23, 24. On Hagar, see Hodges, ed., *The Black Loyalist Directory: African Americans in Exile after the American Revolution* (New York: Garland Publishing, 1996), 40.

68. Adelberg, " 'A Combination to Trample All Law Underfoot,' " *NJH* 115 (1997): 29–30, n. 5.

69. Samuel Forman to Wm. Livingston, April 7, 1780, Livingston Papers (microfilm edition), reel 11.

70. Asher Holmes to Wm. Livingston, March 10, 1780, Livingston Papers (microfilm edition), reel 11.

71. On the Association for Retaliation, see Adelberg, "A Combination to Trample All Law Underfoot," 3–36; Fowler, "Egregious Villains," 194–97. The exact date of the founding of the Retaliators is uncertain, but it is mentioned in Nathaniel Scudder to Joseph Scudder, July 5, 1780, MG 4, New Jersey Historical Society, and N. Scudder to Henry Laurens, July 17, 1780, Dreer Collection, Historical Society of Pennsylvania. The original list of 436 associators is apparently not extant, but a transcription is in Barber and Howe, *Historical Collections*, 371–74; the majority of the signers appear to be members of county militia regiments.

72. The phrase is from Board of Associated Loyalists to Henry Clinton, December 1, 1780, in Davies, ed, *Documents of the American Revolution*, 18: 242; see also Lord Geo. Germain to Clinton, April 21, 1780, ibid., 79–80. The Board of Directors' "Declaration" of December 28 was published in the *Royal Gazette*, December 30, 1780; the *Articles of the Associated Loyalists under the Honourable Board of Directors* was printed as a broadside [c. 1780], Early American Imprints, no. 43764. See also Tebbenhoff, "The Associated Loyalists," *NYHSQ* 63 (1979): 115–44.

73. Fowler, "Egregious Villains," 184, 194. The quote is from O'Connor, *William Paterson*, 89.

74. Samuel Forman to Wm. Livingston, May 20, 1781, Livingston Papers (microfilm edition), reel 14.

75. Collin, *Journal*, 246. On contraband trade in New Jersey, see Fowler, "Egregious Villains," 184–212, 238–89.

76. On the numerous laws passed concerning contraband trade, see Cushing, *First Laws*, 60, 75, 117, 146, 155, 195, 214, 241, 287, 314, and Appendix, 8, 11, 13, 16, 29, 22. On the scores of indictments concerning traders, see Minutes of the Burlington County Court of Oyer and Terminer, July 1782; Minutes of the Gloucester County Court of Oyer and Terminer, February 1781; Minutes of the Monmouth County Court of Oyer and Terminer, January, May, November, 1781, and May 1782, all of which are at the New Jersey State Archives. The quote is from Livingston to Washington, January 26, 1782 (letterbook copy), Livingston Papers, Massachusetts Historical Society, reel 7; the phrase was deleted from the recipient's copy of the letter published in *Livingston Papers*, 4: 372–74.

77. Washington to Wm. Livingston, January 12, 1782; Washington to the Secretary at War, November 6, 1782, and Washington to Livingston, November 13, 1782, in Fitzpatrick, *Writings of Washington*, 23: 444–45, 25: 332, 337.

78. Livingston to M. Marbois, July 26, 1782; Livingston to the Assembly, May 17, 1782, in *Livingston Papers*, 4: 446, 415.

79. "Account of Sales of Sundry Goods, Wares, & Merchendize Taken . . . and Sold at Monmouth agreeable to Law," June 8, 1782, Court of Common Pleas (loose papers), Monmouth County Archives; *NJA*, 2nd ser. (Newspaper Extracts), 5: 462; David Forman to [the Governor and Council?], [c.1780–1781], Livingston Papers (microfilm edition), reel 11.

80. The phrase is from Washington to the Secretary at War, November 6, 1782, in Fitzpatrick, *Writings of Washington*, 25: 322. On the influence of "imperatives of survival" on people's behavior, see Sung Bok Kim, "The Limits of Politicization in the American Revolution: The Experience of Westchester County, New York," *Journal of American History* 80 (1993): 883; the situation in Westchester County bore many similarities to that in northeastern New Jersey. In 1782 a scandal arose concerning the involvement in contraband trade of several prominent Whigs in New Jersey and Pennsylvania; their motives are more difficult to ascribe to "imperatives of survival." See Fowler, "Egregious Villains," 206–207.

81. Andrew Brown to Wm. Livingston, January 10, 1782; John Cook to Livingston, January 1782; Abiel Akin to Livingston, January 10, 1782, in Richard J. Koke, ed., "War, Profit, and Privateers along the New Jersey Coast: Letters of 1782 Relating to an Obscure Warfront of the American Revolution," *NYHSQ* 41 (1957): 311–13.

82. "An Act for the Relief of the Township of Little Egg-Harbour, in the County of Burlington," *Acts of the General Assembly of the State of New Jersey*, November 12, 1790.

83. John Black county tax collector's account book, 1784, New Jersey Historical Society. Richard Peters to Wm. Livingston, November 9, 1781, in *Livingston Papers*, 4: 327. For the disaffection of Quakers and Anglicans in western Burlington County, see Liam Riordan, *Many Identities, One Nation: The Revolution and Its Legacy in the Mid-Atlantic* (Philadelphia, PA: University of Pennsylvania Press, 2007), 43–46.

84. Samuel Forman to Wm. Livingston, May 20, 1781, *Livingston Papers* (microfilm edition), reel 14; and S. Forman to Livingston, November 7, 1781, in *Livingston Papers*, 4: 326–27. On the difficulty in meeting militia quotas in Burlington

County, see Joseph Budd to Wm. Livingston, August 18, 1780, in *Livingston Papers* 4: 43–44. Fowler, "Egregious Villains," 135, 205, 257–58.

85. Butler, "Fanning's Militia," in Calhoon, *Loyalists and Community*, 147, 155. On Bacon's background and wartime career, see Fowler, "Egregious Villains," 238–89. Three summonses for debt in the period 1775–1776 mention him as a "Shingle Maker," Monmouth County Court of Common Pleas (loose papers), Monmouth County Archives. Eyewitness accounts of the skirmish at Cedar Creek Bridge appear in the pension applications of Benjamin Shreve, John Saltar, Abner Page, Eneas Lippincott, and William Potts, Revolutionary War Pension Application Files, U.S. National Archives.

86. Israel Shreve to Wm. Livingston, December 28, 1782, and William Shreve to Livingston, January 6, 1783, *Livingston Papers* (microfilm edition), reels 18 and 19, respectively; *New Jersey Gazette*, January 8, 1783. On Bacon's death, see George F. Fort, "An Account of the Capture and Death of the Refugee John Bacon," *PNJHS*, 1st ser., 1 (1845): 151–52. Bacon is recorded as the Revolutionary War's last casualty in Howard H. Peckham, ed., *The Toll of Independence: Engagements and Battle Casualties of the American Revolution* (Chicago, IL: University of Chicago Press, 1974), 99.

87. Johann David Schoepf, *Travels in the Confederation, 1783–1784*, translated and edited by Alfred J. Morrison, 2 vols. (Philadelphia, PA: W. J. Campbell, 1911; reprinted New York: B. Franklin, 1968), 1: 11–12.

88. See, for example, pension applications of Jesse Mount, John Saltar, William Lloyd, John Brown, William Everingham, Samuel Lippincott, Thomas Smith, Benjamin L. Smith, Samuel Sooy, James Leeds, William Potts, Joseph Mount, David Baird, Cornelius McCollum, Abner Page, and Benjamin Shreve, Revolutionary War Pension Application Files, National Archives; Lossing, *Pictorial Field-Book of the Revolution*, 2 vols. (New York: Harper, 1851), 1: 332–33; Fowler, "Egregious Villains," 271–72, 285–88, 292–93, 329–31. Riordan points out that although local skirmishes "had no strategic impact on the course of the war, they shaped local life in lasting ways." See *Many Identities, One Nation*, 48.

89. For examples of anti-Loyalist petitions, see RD 78, 79, 132, 133, 134, 135, 147, New Jersey State Archives.

90. On the migration of the Woodward insurgents and the Gibersons to Canada, see Fowler, "Egregious Villains," 99–101, 135–36; Gilbert Giberson Loyalist Claim, AO 12/15, PRO. On William Giberson Jr.'s possible return to New Jersey, see Fowler, "Egregious Villains," 136–37. By the late 1780s, Anthony Woodward Jr. reappears on the Upper Freehold township tax lists, Tax Ratables, New Jersey State Archives.

91. The law was repealed, however, in 1783; see Richard P. McCormick, *Experiment in Independence: New Jersey in the Critical Period* (New Brunswick, NJ: Rutgers University Press, 1950), 36; Riordan, *Many Identities, One Nation*, 85, 96.

92. On these events, see Israel Shreve to Wm. Livingston, February 14, 1784, and Wm. Shreve to Livingston, February 15, 1784, *Livingston Papers* (microfilm edition), reel 20; Marmaduke Curtis to Israel Shreve, August 10, 1784, quoted in E. M. Woodward, *History of Burlington County* (Philadelphia, PA: Everts and Peck, 1883; reprinted Burlington, NJ: Burlington County Historical Society, 1980), 31; John

Cox to Israel Shreve, September 18, 1784, Israel Shreve Papers, Special Collections, Rutgers University Libraries; McCormick, *Experiment in Independence*, 38.

93. The phrase is from Wm. Paterson, "Address at a Conference," [1777], Wm. Paterson Papers, Special Collections, Rutgers University Libraries. Paine is quoted in Brown, *Good Americans*, 64; both Thomas McKean of Pennsylvania and Lord Cornwallis regarded Loyalists as "timid," ibid.

94. On Mrs. Howard, see Affidavit of Matthew Horson [Harrison?], New Jersey Council of Safety Records, New Jersey State Archives. On the incident involving Robins's wife, see *New Jersey Gazette*, July 16, 1783. There is no contemporary corroboration for the anecdote concerning Giberson's unnamed sister, but it is certain that he was wounded and captured in 1782, taken to Burlington Jail, and somehow effected an escape—one of many escapes from rebel jails; see Fowler, "Egregious Villains," 132–35.

95. Brown, *Good Americans*, 227; Moody, *Narrative*, 35–36; "Historical Notes of Dr. Benjamin Rush, 1777," *PMHB* 27 (1903): 143; Livingston to the Assembly, May 29, 1778, in *Livingston Papers*, 2: 349.

96. Quoted in Brown, *Good Americans*, 102; Collin, *Journal*, 249.

97. Brown, *Strain of Violence*, viii, 238.

98. Carleton to Wm. Livingston, May 7, 1782, in *Livingston Papers*, 4: 405.

PART 2

Groups

CHAPTER 3

Black Loyalists and African American Allegiance in the Mid-Hudson Valley

Michael E. Groth

The freedom struggle waged by Ebenezer Hulsted's slave Rachel was as heroic and dramatic as those fought by any other during the War for Independence. The thirty-five-year-old woman fled her Patriot owner in Great Nine Partners, Dutchess County, in the Mid-Hudson Valley, during the early summer of 1781, despite the threat of capture and the significant danger she assumed as a lone black woman on the run. In doing so, she joined thousands of slaves across British North America who fled to British lines seeking freedom during the war. Rachel, however, was not content simply to escape from bondage. One week after her flight, she allegedly returned to her master's home with an accomplice and burned Hulsted's house to the ground. In the newspaper advertisement that her traumatized owner took out for the fugitive after the incident, Hulsted described Rachel as a "tall and lusty woman"—physically imposing and sexually intimidating—who was devious and calculating, "as cunning and subtle a creature as any of the kind." An outraged Hulsted exhorted "all well-wishers to their country to apprehend and secure her, so that she may be brought to justice."[1]

Rachel was only one of many ordinary and largely unknown Americans whose decisions and actions helped determine the course of the American Revolution. Historians have long debated the extent, depth, and duration of social upheaval during the Revolutionary era, but it is clear that the convulsive experience of war had profound social consequences. What had begun ostensibly as a political struggle between the mainland British colonies and the Mother Country in the 1760s over taxation and the right to self-government had dramatic and unanticipated social consequences as the political crisis exploded into war in 1775. In New York, republicanism and a new egalitarian spirit directly challenged traditional patterns of deference and irrevocably undermined a hierarchical social order, in which a privileged elite that included many slaveholders wielded disproportionate political, social, and economic power. The politicization of ordinary Americans from the middle and lowers ranks of society radicalized the struggle. As Alfred Young has suggested, the Revolution was a series of multiple "revolutions," freedom struggles waged by common people largely excluded from power during the Colonial era. The Revolution in British North America was made in part by artisans, small farmers, shopkeepers, tenants, laborers, seamen, servants, women, Native Americans—and slaves.[2]

The Revolution was a watershed in the African American experience. Emotional appeals to "life," "liberty," and "freedom" had profound, immediate, and personal meanings to those held in bondage in the Mid-Hudson Valley. Drawing upon a long history of resistance to slavery, African Americans such as Rachel seized opportunities available to them during the War for Independence in what was the largest slave uprising in American history prior to the Civil War. Their actions—and, just as significantly, what political and military leaders on both sides of the conflict feared African Americans would or could do—directly influenced political decisions and military strategies. The Revolution, however, ultimately had contradictory implications for slavery and race in the newborn republic. On the one hand, Christian evangelicalism born of the Great Awakening and radical republican ideology converged to fuel the first organized movement against slavery in North America. The Revolution weakened slavery in the Upper South and struck the death knell of the institution in the North, where it came to be perceived as a moral evil, an economic anachronism, and a threat to free republican institutions. Paradoxically, however, Revolutionary ideology also enshrined fundamental rights of property. In one sense, slaveholding Patriots went to war in 1775 and declared independence in 1776 to defend their rights to own slaves. Freedom and slavery had been inextricably linked to the American Colonial experience. The existence of a permanently degraded racial underclass had served to elevate the status of all free white people. In other words, Euro-Americans were free precisely *because* they were not black slaves. The prospect of emancipation during the Revolutionary era, then, simultaneously constituted a fundamental challenge to eighteenth-

Figure 3.1. Detail, Van Bergen Overmantel, ca. 1733, Hudson Valley

century notions of property and freedom and threatened the existing social and political order. Resistance to emancipation in the North was nowhere more pronounced than in New York, where African Americans comprised a comparatively larger proportion of the total population than in neighboring states, and where slaves played more significant economic roles. Abolition was among the most controversial issues confronting New Yorkers during the Revolutionary period, sharply dividing even ardent Patriots. Delegates at the state's first constitutional convention in 1777 deemed any debate over slavery "highly inexpedient," given the immediate crisis, and quickly deferred the volatile question to the future.[3]

What happened in New York's Dutchess and Ulster counties exemplified these developments. Slaves such as Ebenezer Hulsted's Rachel undoubtedly weighed such contradictions and assessed the hypocrisy of Whig slaveholders when considering British appeals to join the Loyalist cause during the War for Independence. Seizing opportunities created by the war, some African Americans in the Mid-Hudson Valley fled their owners in the hope of procuring freedom in His Majesty's service. Determining one's own allegiance, however, could be a complicated and an agonizing experience for blacks in the valley. Loyalty was not necessarily obvious for many Hudson Valley residents, and the war brought about a "crisis of conscience" for blacks as well as whites in the region. The loyalties of a great majority of African Americans in the Hudson Valley were torn. The vast majority of the region's slaves did not act as boldly and decisively as did Rachel but instead chose to tread more cautiously and act more prudently. Whatever their decisions, however, as the crisis unfolded, many slaves in the central Hudson Valley grew increasingly bold and defiant in their daily dealings with whites. In so doing, they directly challenged the authority of their owners and undermined the institution of slavery in the region.

Slavery and Slave Resistance in the Mid-Hudson Valley

Slavery was entrenched firmly on both sides of the Mid-Hudson Valley by the third quarter of the eighteenth century. The region grew dramatically during the 1700s as the Colonial economy expanded rapidly. Rich soils and a temperate climate, especially on the eastern side of the river in Dutchess County, and access to distant markets via the Hudson River beckoned land-hungry immigrants from New York City, Long Island, and New England. An expanding economy, however, only exacerbated a chronic shortage of labor. Impediments to European immigration and the cost of indentured servants forced producers in the Mid-Hudson Valley to turn to Africans and African Americans, who provided a comparatively cheaper and more convenient labor source. Opportunities for slave ownership increased with the expansion of the transatlantic and domestic slave trades during the eighteenth century, and the black population of the colony grew dramatically. The number of Africans and African Americans in New York doubled between 1723 and 1756 and tripled during the six decades between 1731 and 1790, jumping from 7,231 to 25,983 persons, making the province the largest slave society north of the Chesapeake. The rate of increase was particularly dramatic in the central Hudson Valley. On the eve of the Revolution, more than 3,200 blacks resided and worked in Dutchess and Ulster counties, comprising almost 10 percent of the regional population.[4]

The African American freedom struggle during the Revolutionary era was only one episode in a broader saga of slave resistance and rebellion in early New York, British North America, and the wider Atlantic world. Resistance to bondage was most often indirect. African Americans throughout the colonies adopted a variety of tactics in the struggle for power that slave and master waged on a daily basis. Slaves defied their masters' authority by slowing the pace of work, feigning illness, sabotaging tools, vandalizing property, talking insolently to their owners, "stealing" from the master's storehouse or barn, assembling or fraternizing with others in defiance of law, and engaging in other illicit activities.[5]

Resistance, however, also could be direct and violent. Slave rebelliousness in eighteenth-century New York intensified as the black population expanded and slavery grew increasingly brutal and oppressive. The 1702 "Act for Regulateing [sic] of Slaves" acknowledged apprehensively that the number of slaves in the province "doth daily increase, and that they have been found oftentimes guilty of Confederating together in running away, or other ill practices."[6] Conflict between master and slave exploded in New York City during the spring of 1712, when approximately two dozen insurgents set fire to a building and murdered several whites who rushed to extinguish the blaze. Hysterical recriminations followed. Panicked authorities brutally executed twenty-one alleged conspirators, and lawmakers rushed to strengthen the state's slave code.[7] The detection of another alleged conspiracy in the city in 1741 reverberated throughout the entire colony. In the frantic response to the supposed insurgency, authorities arrested 175 conspirators, savagely executed 30 blacks by hanging or burning, and deported 70 more to the West Indies.[8]

Despite the convulsive consequences of the 1712 and 1741 conspiracies, however, there were in fact few organized slave insurrections in colonial New York. Violent resistance more commonly took the form of individual acts. Arson, assault, murder, and rape committed by slaves struck terror in the hearts of residents of the Mid-Hudson Valley. During the winter of 1714–1715, for example, a slave named Tom attempted to murder his master Johannes

Dykeman, a tenant on Livingston Manor.[9] Such violence usually resulted in swift and brutal punishment. Authorities executed a Kingston slave named Tom for the attempted rape and murder of a white woman. Jack, convicted of torching a barn full of wheat in Kingston in 1732, and a Red Hook slave found guilty of the same offense were each burned alive for their crimes.[10] Although isolated acts of violence did not in and of themselves threaten the slave system, they generated fears and anxieties that profoundly shaped how slaveowners perceived and acted toward their slaves.

Slave resistance and fears of slave rebellion in the Mid-Hudson Valley intensified as the Revolutionary crisis unfolded. Some slaves, such as Ezra Rutty's slave Minsor, accused of assaulting Fenner Palmer of Pawling in early 1774, grew increasingly bold and insolent as war approached.[11] Fears of insurrection led authorities to respond decisively, even ruthlessly, to individual acts of defiance. One twenty-six-year-old slave terrified the residents of Poughkeepsie shortly before the Revolution when he torched his master's barn and outbuildings. Detected by smoke that emanated from combustible materials in his pocket, the twenty-year-old man confessed to the crime, and the judges at his trial (in a cruel irony) sentenced him to death by burning. His horrific execution was a public spectacle that must have been indelibly imprinted upon the collective memories of those who witnessed it. The crowd surrounding the pyre was allegedly so dense that it "excluded the air, so that the flames kindled but slowly, and the dreadful screams" of the victim could be heard for a distance of three miles.[12]

Slave insurrectionists came extremely close to executing one well-orchestrated plot in Ulster County in February 1775. The conspiracy was discovered only hours before the event, when Johannes Schoonmaker, a Kingston area farmer, overheard a conversation between two leaders of the conspiracy named Joe and York. Schoonmaker rushed to spread the alarm. Authorities quickly arrested twenty alleged conspirators and confiscated a sizeable cache of powder and shot. The subsequent investigation uncovered a chilling conspiracy. According to the insurgents' plan, rebels from as many as four towns surrounding Kingston were to organize themselves into three groups. While one group torched several Kingston buildings, the second contingent was to assume the grisly task of murdering the occupants as they fled their burning homes. The third group, meanwhile, was to beat drums to muffle the cries and screams of the victims. After the initial assault, the insurgents planned to join forces with as many as 500 to 600 Indians.[13] Newspapers carried accounts of the conspiracy throughout the colonies, and the episode had a chilling effect in the Mid-Hudson Valley. The terrifying plot in Ulster undoubtedly weighed heavily on the minds of the freeholders in the Rombout Precinct of Dutchess County, when they assembled in Fishkill in the spring of 1775. To prevent any such conflagration on the river's east bank, the freeholders organized a committee for defense, whose principal concerns included the "affairs of the Negroes." Immediately across the river in Newburgh, the town council imposed a sundown curfew on all slaves and ordered up to thirty-five lashes for any individual found in violation of the ordinance. Revolutionary lawmakers also responded to the perceived threat, permitting any individual in time of invasion to shoot without fear of legal reprisal any slave found more than one mile from his master's abode.[14]

The Mid-Hudson Valley in Revolution

The course of events and the military struggle that unfolded in New York intensified fears of subversion and insurrection. The Hudson Valley occupied a pivotal strategic position during the War for Independence. The Hudson River was a major avenue of transportation and commerce that linked the major port of New York to the interior and Canada. British control of the valley would have severed New England from the other states, conceivably strangling the rebellion itself. The military defense of the Hudson became especially critical after New York City fell to British forces during the late summer and early autumn of 1776. The central Hudson Valley also provided a wealth of resources vital to the American war effort. Dutchess and Ulster counties not only boasted a large number of potential recruits for American armies, but the farms, mills, shops, shipyards, and forges in the region provided a large quantity of foodstuffs and other materials essential to the military struggle. Communities on both banks of the river became armed camps crowded with soldiers, camp followers, and refugees. Fishkill was a major encampment, supply depot, hospital, prison, and burial ground. New York's provisional government and various revolutionary committees sat in Fishkill, Kingston, and Poughkeepsie at different times during the war.[15]

Residents of the Mid-Hudson Valley, however, were divided as the Revolution unfolded. The crisis exacerbated internal tensions and conflicts that had been simmering for years before the war, particularly on the east bank of the river, where tenants, yeoman farmers, small manufacturers, merchants, professionals, and other ambitious men from the middling ranks increasingly challenged the political and economic hegemony of the region's landlords.[16] The struggle for power tore individual loyalties. As many as one third of almost 2,800 Dutchess County residents refused to sign the Continental Association, pledging allegiance to the country and to the Continental and Provincial Congresses during the summer of 1775.[17] Although it is likely that a majority of those refusing to sign were desperately attempting to maintain a neutral stance in the struggle, some actively joined the Loyalist cause. Tories organized small partisan bands and recruited residents for His Majesty's service. In Dutchess's Charlotte Precinct, a trio of heavily armed Tories allegedly terrorized the inhabitants and threatened to abduct and turn over Whig leaders to British authorities. Egbert Benson, the chairman of the Dutchess County Committee, repeatedly warned New York's Provincial Congress that the number of "disaffected" residents in the county was so great that only "spirited measures" would eliminate the Loyalist threat.[18]

Violence and partisan activity intensified in the wake of the decision for independence and the subsequent capture of New York City by British forces in the late summer of 1776. The proximity of His Majesty's forces and rumors of British advances up the Hudson River emboldened Loyalists on both sides of the river. Ulster County Committee Chairman Robert Boyd Jr. had boasted in the early summer of the "unanimity of sentiment" and "regularity in practice" in the county, but decisive British victories and the prospect of invasion threatened the Whig consensus on the west bank. By the late summer and fall, conflict had broken out on the frontier, and "many dangerous persons" had begun to organize in Ulster County (and the neighboring Orange County) to enlist recruits for His Majesty's cause.[19] The most serious threats to the rebellion, however, continued to come from the east side of the river. Only weeks after the state had ordered the organization of troops to quell "disaffection" in Dutchess, a group of between 150 and 200 Tories launched an uprising in Nine Partners in early July, which was put down only by local units and a sizeable contingent of Connecticut troops.[20] In early autumn, Whigs in the Southeast Precinct, the southernmost part of Dutchess County, which was perilously close to British forces, appealed for military assistance to suppress Loyalism and restore law and order. Conflict erupted on the county's northern border as well. Reporting the violence and destruction in Claverack and on Livingston Manor to the Committee of Safety, Colonel Livingston concluded that the northern regions of the county were "infested with disaffected persons." Rebellion broke out on Livingston Manor in May 1777, followed by an uprising of upward of 400 Tories at Washington Hollow a couple of months later.[21] To meet the threat, the Committee and subsequent Commission for Detecting and Defeating Conspiracies engaged in a zealous campaign to root out disaffection in the region. Meeting alternately in Fishkill, Poughkeepsie, Rhinebeck, and Kingston between September 1776 and 1778, authorities arrested hundreds of suspected traitors for assault, conspiracy, desertion, espionage, murder, providing aid and comfort to the enemy, sedition, theft, and other criminal or seditious activities. The Loyalist threat in the region gradually receded after General Burgoyne's defeat at Saratoga in October 1777, and British military strategists redirected their attention southward, but angry popular demonstrations against shortages and rising prices and other expressions of "disaffection" in the central valley continued until the end of the war, at times degenerating into banditry and indiscriminate violence.[22]

Black Loyalists

An untold number of African Americans in the Mid-Hudson Valley seized opportunities created by the wartime crisis. Many exploited the breakdown of law and order to flee from their owners. Short of violence, flight represented the most direct defiance of a master's authority. The sixty fugitive slaves from the region appearing in local newspapers between 1777 and 1783 likely represent only a fraction of those who absconded during the conflict.[23] Escape from bondage, not Loyalism, was likely the goal of most fugitives from the Mid-Hudson Valley during the war; eleven of the fifteen runaways, whose destinations were surmised by their owners, were alleged to have made a permanent break for freedom.[24]

Although cautious not to endorse full emancipation for all slaves, British strategists appealed to Africans and African Americans both to deprive American rebels of their slaves' labor and to meet their own pressing manpower needs. As early as November 1775, Virginia's Royal Governor Lord Dunmore took the momentous and highly provocative step of promising freedom to slaves of rebel masters who fled their owners and rallied to the king's standard. The governor's incendiary appeal had an electrifying and a far-reaching impact. Thousands of slaves from across the thirteen colonies fled to the British, who put them to work in a variety of military and nonmilitary capacities. General William Howe offered refuge to slaves of rebel masters after British forces seized New York City in 1776. Three years later, British Commander in Chief Sir Henry Clinton officially endorsed what had become a well-established practice when he formally offered sanctuary and employment to any slave belonging to a rebel master reaching British lines.[25]

Between the late summer of 1776 and the conclusion of the war, British-occupied New York City served as a magnet for fugitives from the Mid-Hudson Valley. Several Mid-Hudson Valley slaveowners, including Ananias Cooper, Cornelius Haight, Zaccheus Newcomb, Comfort Sands, Stephen Hogeboom, Herman Pest, Ebenezer Hulsted, and Lewis Barton, all suspected that their fugitives were heading toward the enemy.[26] Porous military lines in the lower Hudson Valley facilitated and encouraged escape, especially for those slaves in closest proximity to the city.[27] Marmeet, a slave belonging to "Miss Verplank," for example, joined an unknown number of other slaves in the vicinity of southern Dutchess and northern Westchester counties in a plot to flee to freedom during the summer of 1780. Whether one of the conspirators became an informant or whether Whig authorities learned of the plot through other means, the local constabulary upset the group's plans and apprehended Marmeet. Marmeet, however, refused to see the plan thwarted and his hopes dashed. While being escorted to the county jail, he set upon his captors and wrestled from them forty shillings "hard money" and, not insignificantly, "a very handsome carbine." Marmeet then fled and, under cover of darkness, he hastened to the Verplank household, where he waited silently. Once the dwelling's occupants were asleep, he surreptitiously entered his quarters and gathered all his clothing. The fugitive then made his way to the river and southward to New York City. Perhaps despairing of actually apprehending the fugitive, the advertiser who took out the notice in the *New York Journal and General Advertiser* expressed only a desire to recover the carbine.[28] The prospect of freedom in New York City was powerful enough to entice slaves from more distant locations in the valley. Tom, a thirty-year-old slave, fled his master in Rhinebeck in northern Dutchess County and cautiously made his way southward toward the enemy in May 1780. The fugitive, who carried a fraudulent pass, was purportedly spotted ten days after his escape several miles to the south.[29]

Hudson Valley fugitives who successfully reached occupied New York not only found refuge behind British lines but discovered economic and social opportunities unavailable to them in the countryside. African Americans readily found wartime employment, some earning wages for the first time in their lives. Black Loyalists served His Majesty as artisans, couriers, guides, interpreters, laborers, musicians, partisans, pilots, pioneers, privateers, servants, soldiers, spies, and teamsters. Men and women from the rural Mid-Hudson Valley must have found the social opportunities available in the city particularly exciting. Mixing with other fugitives, refugees, residents, and soldiers, African Americans engaged in a vibrant cultural life on the city's streets and alleys, and in taverns, gambling halls, theaters, and dance halls.[30]

Not all Mid-Hudson Valley fugitives who rallied to the British cause fled as far away as New York City. Some remained in the region and found refuge among local Loyalists. Pomp, a "Guinea born" slave belonging to the Whig Comfort Sands, was allegedly protected in the Hanover Precinct of Ulster County by some "disaffected people," who had assisted him in his escape.[31] In some instances, runaways enlisted in Tory paramilitary organizations. Black Loyalists served with partisan bands such as "Rodger's Rangers" and otherwise served His Majesty's cause by engaging in sundry seditious activities in the region. Jonathan, a mulatto slave in the hire of James Doughty, allegedly enticed a group of young men to flee conscription by escaping to Long Island. Another African American operating in the vicinity of southern Dutchess and northern Westchester counties assisted Loyalists attempting to flee to New York City by hiding them in the woods and by serving as their pilot on the Croten River.[32] The British, for their part, exploited and encouraged seditious activity by actively employing black agents and operatives in the region. During the summer campaigns of 1777, as General Burgoyne's army in northern New York marched southward, a mulatto woman allegedly brought intelligence from British authorities in New York City to local Tory organizations. After passing on the critical information, the woman purportedly continued northward in the hope of reaching Burgoyne's army.[33]

If many African Americans in the Mid-Hudson Valley were sympathetic to the Loyalist cause, then their willingness to act on those sympathies was another matter. Fugitives assumed tremendous risks. Although British-occupied New York served as a powerful beacon for slaves in the greater region, the geographic distance remained daunting. Moreover, while the dislocation of war presented opportunities to escape, disorder and violence in war-torn New York also made flight that much more dangerous. Apprehension could mean brutal punishment and reenslavement. Whigs considered captured slaves of Tory masters spoils of war liable to be impressed into service. Seized when heading to the enemy in early 1777, James Weeks and Pompey were put to labor at "the works" in New Windsor.[34] Another black Loyalist, who served with a partisan organization in the Pawling vicinity, was less fortunate. After the band ransacked the home of an elderly man in Quaker Hill, a posse pursued and eventually caught up with the raiders. Finding the black partisan wearing the shoes and carrying a handkerchief belonging to the elderly victim, the captors proceeded to hang the man "as a sort of scapegoat for the rest of the party."[35]

Not only did those in bondage have to weigh carefully the formidable risks of flight, but African Americans also had to consider their prospects in occupied New York City. Although many found wartime employment in His Majesty's service, successful runaways joined thousands of refugees and soldiers in the overcrowded metropolis that suffered from serious wartime shortages of food, fuel, and housing. The poorest residents clustered in the filthiest and least healthy neighborhoods. Labor for the British army, moreover, could be grueling, and military authorities regularly impressed laborers. And although British leaders promised freedom to slaves of rebel masters, African Americans had cause to doubt British motivations and even to question the British commitment to black freedom. The institution of slavery persisted in occupied New York City, and buyers and sellers participated in a brisk wartime slave trade. No black Loyalist was completely secure from kidnapping and reenslavement.[36]

Black Patriots

If African Americans had some cause to doubt the motivations and designs of their British and Loyalist allies, then British authorities entertained similar suspicions about the loyalties of African Americans. Tories in the Mid-Hudson Valley knew that they could not take for granted the allegiance of African Americans. Conspiring with fellow Loyalists in April 1777, "Captain Jacocks" warned that "Blacks in the Kitchen" could betray them and admonished the conspirators to keep slaves ignorant of the group's plans.[37] Norma, a slave of the Van Voorhis family in Fishkill, and Dinah, a slave in the Anthony household in Poughkeepsie, were just two such women. Each stood faithfully at her owner's side when a British expedition sailed up the Hudson River in October 1777; Dinah even allegedly spared her master's Poughkeepsie home from the ravages of an enemy raiding party by "softening" British hearts with her freshly baked bread.[38]

Defense of homes and families, loyalty to their owners, hope in the egalitarian rhetoric and republican principles of the Whig Revolution, or simple circumstance impelled African Americans such as Norma and Dinah to side not with the Crown but with the cause of independence. Some black men in the region took up arms in defense of the American cause. Fierce resistance on the part of slaveholders to black military service originally had led Congress and individual states to prohibit the enlistment of black troops, but pressing manpower needs ultimately forced New England and the Mid-Atlantic states to accept African American soldiers.[39] A handful of African Americans served in different Dutchess County and Ulster County militia companies, and a group of slaves in the vicinity of Marlborough in Ulster County even organized their own company, drilling under the command of a slave named Harry.[40] Philip Field, a Dutchess County native who served in Captain Pelton's Second New York Regiment, made the ultimate sacrifice for the cause of independence, dying at Valley Forge in 1778.[41]

A policy of exclusion, however, did not necessarily discourage the aspirations of black Patriots.[42] New York allowed the substitution of slaves for those drafted into the state militia in 1776. Five years later, it provided for the emancipation of any slave who enlisted and served either for three years or until honorably discharged and granted a land bounty to the slave's master or mistress.[43] Although most of the approximately 5,000 African Americans who took up arms to fight for the rebel cause during the war came from New England and the Chesapeake area, several black New Yorkers were active participants in the military struggle. Philip Field, a Dutchess County native who served in Captain Pelton's Second New York Regiment, made the ultimate sacrifice for the cause of independence, dying at Valley Forge in 1778.[44]

Although a sizeable proportion of fugitives from the central Hudson Valley ran away to occupied New York City or sought refuge among local Loyalists, others rejected British appeals and fled instead to American forces. Young men, such as fifteen-year-old John Johnson, who fled his owner and assumed a new name and identity as a free man, did so in order to enlist in military service.[45] The prospect of wartime employment also attracted some fugitives. As did the British, American armies employed African American laborers in a variety of military and nonmilitary capacities.[46] Other runaways, however, simply sought to disappear among the large numbers of soldiers, laborers, camp followers, and refugees who flooded local communities. Charles Clinton, for example, surmised that his mulatto slave Bob would "put on regimental clothing" to disguise himself as a soldier, having been "frequently in camp when the army were dispersing."[47] Yet others, such as one poorly clad African American boy, who wandered into the Fishkill encampment of the Second Maryland Regiment, might have had no other place to go.[48] Military encampments were destinations for women as well as men. Joshua Shearwood's thirty-year-old female slave—an allegedly "talkative and polite" woman—was supposedly "lurking about Col. Butler's Regiment" in Fishkill during the summer of 1782.[49] As long as soldiers were willing to provide refuge or at least tolerate their presence, women like Shearwood's slave managed to support themselves as servants, cooks, nurses, and washerwomen for the army.

The Dilemma of Allegiance

The matter of choosing sides ultimately proved an agonizing experience for most slaves in the Mid-Hudson Valley. Practical considerations weighed heavily. The proximity of British forces in New York City, the sizeable presence of American troops throughout the region, social unrest, political instability, and partisan violence in the countryside rendered the position of African Americans in the region especially tenuous. Running away, moreover, was a particularly dangerous undertaking; prudence, attachment to family or home, fear of the unknown, and simple psychological or physical incapacity prevented the vast majority of slaves in the Mid-Hudson Valley from absconding. Given the formidable risks associated with flight, younger men clearly predominated among fugitives during the war years. Only four of the sixty runaways appearing in the wartime newspapers were females. Almost nine of ten fugitives during the war years, whose ages were known, were between sixteen and thirty-five years of age; three fifths of all runaways were under age twenty-six.[50] Given ambivalent loyalties and the uncertainty of the struggle's outcome in embattled New York, most African Americans, like a sizeable number of their free white neighbors, adopted a "wait and see attitude," hoping to maintain a cautious neutrality as long as possible.[51] When circumstance or conscience dictated a commitment to one side in the conflict, African Americans not atypically arrived at different conclusions. For example, two men in the Rhinebeck Precinct of Dutchess County, each named Jack, found themselves on opposite sides of the struggle. One, presumably a fugitive slave, joined Teunis Peer and other Loyalists in a guerilla campaign against local Whigs in northern Dutchess County that included violence and sabotage. During the summer of 1777, Jack and Peer made repeated attempts to coax the second Jack, a slave in the Freligh family, to escape from his "Damn'd Rebel" master. Freligh's slave, however, treaded cautiously. He originally resisted their entreaties, but he also apparently kept his silence and failed to inform his master of their efforts to recruit him—at least for a while. When Peer attempted to induce Freligh's slave to set fire to a barn in the neighborhood belonging to Captain Isaac Sheldon—immediately after his master's own barn had burned to the ground under suspicious circumstances—Jack came to the conclusion that it was "his duty" to inform his master and the captain. Freligh's slave, however, went beyond serving as a mere informant. He proceeded to join Peer's partisan band "while in concealment" to gather incriminating evidence, which the Commission for Detecting Conspiracies ultimately used to convict Peer and his accomplices of seditious activity.[52]

African Americans in the Mid-Hudson Valley made decisions and pursued courses of action that best served their personal interests or improved their own positions. Some runaways acted out of motivations that had little to do with either Toryism or Whiggery. Although flight could represent an attempt to escape bondage, it also could be a tactic that slaves employed in dealing with their owners. Some fugitives took advantage of the circumstances simply to take some time off or to visit loved ones. Runaways fled to previous places of residence, if only to a neighboring town. John Elsworth, for example, suspected that his twenty-three-year-old slave, Jack, was likely in the neighborhood of his former master in "Wiccoppy" in eastern Dutchess County. Henry G. Livingston's fugitive mulatto boy, Caesar, was likely to be found during the winter of 1782 in Nine Partners or Rhinebeck, having lived previously in both places. And Bill, a nineteen-year-old mulatto belonging to Fletcher Matthews in Orange County, fled not southward to the British in New York City but northward to Esopus. Yet another fugitive named Ben allegedly attempted to leave the region altogether. Fleeing neither to British nor American forces, Ben escaped from his owner in the Charlotte Precinct of Dutchess County and headed for his previous home in Virginia.[53]

Even when escaping to British or American encampments, runaways could act out of personal or self-interested motives, including the desire to be reunited with loved ones. Sam, a slave from Stono Ferry, six miles north of Albany, allegedly headed to Fishkill to see his wife and nine-year-old daughter. In another powerful testament to the strength of family bonds, one thirty-four-year-old fugitive from Maryland named Sarah (who also used the alias Rachel) was "big with child" when she fled Baltimore with her six-year-old son to join her husband, who served in the First Maryland Regiment.[54]

Personal freedom, of course, was the most powerful inducement to flee one's owner. Freedom, however, was found not only with the British or in American military service. For Job Mulford's slave, Levi, it lay northward and westward; in the fall of 1779, Levi allegedly crossed the Hudson River from Staatsburg in a bold attempt "to get beyond our frontiers."[55] Loyalty to one side in the struggle was ultimately a means to an end for most black participants. Allegiance could be fickle; those who actively supported one side at one point in the conflict did not hesitate to shift or even betray allegiances when necessary. For example, one man named Caesar evidently had no intention of returning to his owner when he "hired into" Captain Wright's Company in Colonel Cortlandt's regiment during the summer of 1778. Stephen Haight placed an advertisement in the *New York Packet* in June 1779 seeking information on the whereabouts of the twenty-eight-year-old slave. According to Haight, Caesar had been discharged at Valley Forge on account of ill health but had failed to return to his master in Albany County.[56]

Whatever course of action they chose, and whatever their allegiances, many African Americans directly challenged the slave system in the Mid-Hudson Valley during the War for Independence. Even if only a small proportion of slaves in the Mid-Hudson Valley absconded from their owners, fugitives had an inordinate impact on how whites perceived all slaves in the region. Few slaveowners were likely as traumatized by their slave's actions as Ebenezer Hulsted, whose escaped slave Rachel had torched the Hulsted home, but masters of runaway slaves typically characterized their fugitives as calculating, devious, sinister, and dangerous. Hezekiah Collins, for example, regarded twenty-five-year-old Nero as a "smooth-tongued fellow," and Charles Cullen of the Southeast Precinct described his forty-year-old fugitive slave as "artful and plausible."[57] Another slaveowner, Cornelius Haight, was obviously unsettled by the flight of his slave, Prim, in 1780. The twenty-three-year-old woman had evidently planned her escape well in advance, secreting all of her clothing to an unknown location before her flight. In the advertisements he took out in both the *New York Journal and General Advertiser* and *New York Packet*, Haight predicted that Prim would hasten to the hiding place to alter her appearance and warned readers to be "particularly careful to secure her, so that she does not give them the slip, as she is very sly and artful . . . and if they trust her [she] will certainly deceive them."[58] Although runaways most directly challenged their owners, the Revolution ultimately empowered all slaves in the region. Even those who did not abscond or enlist in the British or American cause grew self-confident, assertive, and even insolent in their dealings with their owners. Petitioning the Provisional Congress in February 1777 for their release from detention for refusing to swear allegiance to the American cause, Dirck Gardenier and Matthew Goes complained that "having no person at Home to Superintend their Domestic Affairs but Females," their slaves "Absolutely Refuse all Obedience, Taking Advantage from your Petitioners absence."[59]

The Aftermath of Revolution

Despite the bold actions of runaways and the growing defiance of slaves toward their owners, ultimately only a handful of African Americans in the Mid-Hudson Valley procured their freedom by war's end. Among them were at least some of those who successfully found refuge behind British lines. Francis Griffin, a slave who once belonged to Jacob Duryea of Dutchess County, was one who narrowly escaped reenslavement. Early in the war, Duryea had entrusted to Griffin the care of the family's New York City home, when Duryea and his family fled northward in 1776. As the months and years passed, Griffin evidently found life in British-occupied New York to his liking, marrying a free black woman. As the war approached its close, Francis and his master reestablished contact to negotiate the terms of their postwar relationship. Duryea proposed what he must have considered generous terms; he not only proposed to hire Griffin's wife as a free laborer but also extended to the couple the option of remaining in New York City. Having tasted freedom in occupied New York, however, Griffin balked at Duryea's offer. Incensed at the rebuff, Duryea hired two men, proceeded to New York City, and located the defiant slave. With the assistance of his two accomplices, Duryea seized Francis, bound him, and attempted to return up the river on a sloop. A witness to the abduction, however, had spread the alarm. The city inspector pursued and overtook the kidnappers and then freed the captive with the help of several Hessian soldiers. At Duryea's subsequent trial, a British magistrate affirmed Francis's freedom and ordered Duryea to pay a fine to contribute to the relief of the city's indigent black population.[60]

Francis was only one of more than 3,000 African Americans from throughout the colonies in New York City at war's end. Resisting the insistent demands of American slaveholders and General George Washington that the departing British forces return their slave property, Sir Guy Carleton, commander in chief of His Majesty's forces in North America in 1783, refused to turn over black Loyalists who had managed to reach British lines before November 1782. Among them were several refugees from the central Hudson Valley. Lists of black Loyalists boarding British vessels compiled by inspectors and commissioners in 1783 include at least a dozen men from the region, ranging in age from twenty to forty-eight. From Fishkill came twenty-two-year-old Casar Nicholls, formerly the slave of "Dr. Van Wyck," and forty-year-old Bristol Storm, who had fled from his master Garnet Storm in 1780. York, a "stout fellow," age twenty-three, had escaped from Leonard Van Klock in Poughkeepsie five years previously; thirty-one-year-old Joseph Bartlet had fled another Poughkeepsie slaveowner, Gilbert Livingston, in 1779. Forty-three-year old John Simonsbury and twenty-year-old Abraham Thomas had escaped their respective owners in Fredericksburg in southern Dutchess County; Thomas, a "stout lad" identified by inspectors as the former slave of Lemuel Willet, claimed to have been born free in Westchester County. Twenty-seven-year-old John Cooper had successfully made his way from as far away as Livingston Manor. From Esopus in Ulster County came thirty-nine-year-old Robert James and forty-eight-year-old John Been.

Other black refugees from the west bank included William Sampson, who had escaped from his master in New Windsor in 1777, and forty-year-old Nero Denton, who had fled his owner in Goshen in 1776. A twenty-seven-year-old mulatto, Robert Freeman, who had served time with a powder maker near Goshen in Walkill, claimed to have been born free. Among the women who crowded New York City in 1783 were thirty-year-old Massey Antin, who had formerly served Joseph Tomkins in Dutchess County, and fifty-year-old Catharine Livingston, who had fled eight years earlier from none other than Robert Livingston of Livingston Manor.[61] Having escaped bondage, however, black Loyalists boarding English vessels at war's end faced very uncertain futures in other parts of the British empire. While some exiles struggled against poverty and discrimination in efforts to establish lives as free people in Canada, Britain, or West Africa, others ultimately became indentured servants or even slaves in the British Caribbean.[62]

Although the Revolutionary experience proved a transformative event for black New Yorkers, the institution of slavery in New York not only survived the war but also proved remarkably resilient. Opposition to emancipation in post-Revolutionary New York was fierce, and sixteen years would pass before slaveholders acceded to what was an exceptionally conservative scheme of gradual abolition. Nevertheless, African American resistance to slavery during the War for Independence had laid decisive groundwork for the antislavery struggle during the years that followed. Capitalizing on the

Hudson Valley's pivotal geographic position and exploiting the breakdown of law and order in the region, African Americans waged their own freedom struggle against a violent and an oppressive system of small-scale slavery that was both part of and separate from either the American struggle for independence or the British effort to crush the rebellion.

A sizeable number of African Americans in the region answered British appeals and defied their rebel masters to become Loyalists, either by fleeing to New York City or by joining partisan organizations in the countryside. The matter of allegiance, however, proved a difficult one for slaves in the valley. Some fugitives fled to join Americans forces. Others exploited the breakdown of authority to take time off from their work routines and to visit loved ones. Comparatively few slaves in the region in fact resorted to violence or even ran away. And while some became Patriots and perhaps a larger number became Loyalists, many more went to great lengths to remain neutral. Whatever their loyalties and whatever courses of action they pursued, African Americans were central actors in the Revolutionary drama in the Mid-Hudson Valley who mounted a serious challenge to slavery in the region and challenged the existing social and political order.

Notes

1. *New York Packet*, June 7, 1781.

2. See Alfred F. Young, ed., *Beyond the American Revolution: Explorations in the History of American Radicalism* (DeKalb, IL: Northern Illinois University Press, 1993), 3–24, 317–64. The social implications of the Revolution and the roles ordinary Americans played in the conflict are explored in Ray Raphael, *A People's History of the American Revolution: How Common People Shaped the Fight for Independence* (New York: Perennial, 2002).

3. Edward Countryman, *A People in Revolution: The American Revolution and Political Society in New York, 1760–1790* (Baltimore, MD: Johns Hopkins University Press, 1981), 244, 248–49; *Journals of the Provincial Congress, Provincial Convention, Committee of Safety and Council of Safety of the State of New York, 1775–1777*, vol. 1 (Albany: T. Weed, 1842), 887, 889. The African American experience during the Revolution is explored in Herbert Aptheker, *The Negro in the American Revolution* (New York: International Publishers, 1940); Philip S. Foner, *Blacks in the American Revolution* (Westport, CT: Greendwood Press, 1975); Sylvia R. Frey, *Water from the Rock: Black Resistance in a Revolutionary Age* (Princeton, NJ: Princeton University Press, 1991); Sidney Kaplan and Emma Nogrady Kaplan, *The Black Presence in the Era of the American Revolution*, rev. ed. (Amherst, MA: University of Massachusetts Press, 1989); Daniel C. Littlefield, *Revolutionary Citizens: African Americans, 1776–1804* (New York: Oxford University Press, 1997); William C. Nell, *The Colored Patriots of the American Revolution* (Boston, MA: R. F. Wallcot, 1855); Benjamin Quarles, *The Negro in the American Revolution* (Chapel Hill, NC: University of North Carolina

Press, 1961); Willie Lee Rose, "The Impact of the American Revolution on the Black Population," in *Slavery and Freedom*, expanded ed., ed. William Freehling, 3–17 (New York: Oxford University Press, 1982); and Donald R. Wright, *African Americans in the Colonial Era: From African Origins through the American Revolution* (Arlington Heights, MA: Harlan Davidson, 1990). The scholarship on slavery, emancipation, and race during the Revolutionary era and the Early Republic is extensive. For New York, see Graham Hodges, *Root and Branch: African Americans in New York and East Jersey, 1613–1863* (Chapel Hill, NC: University of North Carolina Press, 1999); Shane White, *Somewhat More Independent: The End of Slavery in New York City, 1770–1810* (Athens, GA: University of Georgia Press, 1991); Arthur Zilversmit, *The First Emancipation: The Abolition of Slavery in the North* (Chicago, IL: University of Chicago Press, 1967). The classic text that analyzes the paradox of slavery and freedom in the American experience is Edmund Morgan, *American Slavery, American Freedom: The Ordeal of Colonial Virginia* (New York: Norton, 1975).

4. Evarts B. Greene and Virginia D. Harrington, *American Population before the Federal Census of 1790* (New York: Columbia University Press, 1932), 96–104; 1,360 slaves in Dutchess County comprised 6 percent of the county's population in 1771. The proportion was notably higher in Ulster County, where almost 2,000 slaves comprised 14 percent of Ulster's population. Thomas Davis explores the demography of New York's eighteenth-century slave population in "New York's Black Line: A Note on the Growing Slave Population," *Afro-Americans in New York Life and History* 2 (1978), 41–59. See also Edgar McManus, *A History of Negro Slavery in New York* (Syracuse, NY: Syracuse University Press, 1966), 24–25, 42–46.

5. Herbert Aptheker, *American Negro Slave Revolts*, 5th ed. (1943; New York: International Press, 1983), 140–49.

6. *The Colonial Laws of New York from the Year 1664 to the Revolution*, vol. 1 (Albany, NY: J. B. Lyon, 1894), 520.

7. Aptheker, *Slave Revolts*, 169–73; Hodges, *Root and Branch*, 63–68; Kenneth Scott, "The Slave Insurrection in New York in 1712," *New York Historical Society Quarterly* 45 (1961): 43–74.

8. Authorities also executed two white men and two white women. The 1741 plot is the subject of Thomas J. Davis, *A Rumor of Revolt: The "Great Negro Plot" in Colonial New York* (New York: Free Press, 1985). See also Aptheker, *Slave Revolts*, 192–96; Hodges, *Root and Branch*, 88–98.

9. Roberta Singer, "The Livingstons as Slave Owners: The 'Peculiar Institution' on Livingston Manor and Clermont," in *The Livingston Legacy: Three Centuries of American History*, ed. Richard T. Wiles, 81–82 (Annandale-on-Hudson, NY: Bard College Office of Publications, 1987).

10. Henry Noble MacCracken, *Old Dutchess Forever!: The Story of an American County* (New York: Hastings House, 1956), 125; A. J. Williams-Myers, "The African Presence in the Mid-Hudson Valley Before 1800: A Preliminary Historiographical Sketch," *Afro-Americans in New York Life and History* 8 (1984): 33. Graham Hodges analyzes slave resistance in the greater New York City region during the eighteenth century in *Root and Branch*, 69–138.

11. "Ancient Documents Collection," Dutchess County Archives, Poughkeepsie, New York, January 1774.

12. According to one account of the incident, such brutal executions "were by no means rare." See William J. Allinson, *Memoir of Quamino Buccau, A Pious Methodist* (Philadelphia, PA: Henry Longstreth, 1851), 4–5. The episode also is cited in MacCracken, *Old Dutchess Forever!*, 125; Philip H. Smith, *General History of Dutchess County, from 1609 to 1876, Inclusive* (Pawling, NY: The Author, 1877), 104; and Zilversmit, *First Emancipation*, 21–22.

13. "Negro Plot in Ulster County, 1775," Kingston Senate House, Kingston, New York; A. J. Williams-Myers, *Long Hammering: Essays on the Forging of an African-American Presence in the Hudson River Valley to the Early Twentieth Century* (Trenton, NJ: African World Press, 1994), 58–59; Peter H. Wood, " 'The Dream Deferred': Black Freedom Struggles on the Eve of White Independence," in *In Resistance: Studies in African, Caribbean, and Afro-American History*, ed. Gary Okihiro, 173 (Amherst, MA: University of Massachusetts Press, 1986); Wood, " 'Liberty Is Sweet': African-American Freedom Struggles in the Years before White Independence," in *Beyond the American Revolution*, 163. In addition to the two essays by Peter Wood, see also Aptheker, *Negro in the American Revolution*, 22–27, and Raphael, *A People's History of the American Revolution*, 309–20, for the growing restlessness of slaves throughout the colonies on the eve of war.

14. Jonathan C. Clark, "A Government to Form: The Story of Dutchess County and the Political Upheaval in Revolutionary New York," in *From English Colony to Sovereign State: Essays on the American Revolution in Dutchess County, New York*, ed. Richard B. Morris, Jonathan C. Clark, and Charlotte Cunningham Finkel, 73 (Millbrook, NY: Dutchess County American Revolution Bicentennial Commission, 1983); Williams-Myers, "The African Presence in the Hudson River Valley," 84; Williams-Myers, *Long Hammering*, 47; *New York in the Revolution as Colony and State*, compiled by the Office of the State Comptroller, 2 vols. (Albany, NY: J. B. Lyon, 1904), 1: 11.

15. The military struggle for the valley is explored in Lincoln Diamant, *Chaining the Hudson: The Fight for the River in the American Revolution* (New York: Fordham University Press, 2004); Mark V. Kwasny, *Washington's Partisan War, 1775–1783* (Kent, OH: Kent State University Press, 1996).

16. See Countryman, *A People in Revolution*, 15–34, 47–55, 72–85, 104–16, 149–50; Thomas J. Humphrey, *Land and Liberty: Hudson Valley Riots in the Age of Revolution* (DeKalb, IL: Northern Illinois University Press, 2004); Sung Bok Kim, "Impact of Class Relations and Warfare in the American Revolution: The New York Experience," *Journal of American History* 69 (1982): 326–46; Staughton Lynd, *Anti-Federalism in Dutchess County, New York: A Study of Democracy and Class Conflict in the Revolutionary Era* (Chicago, IL: Loyola University Press, 1962); Lynd, "Who Should Rule at Home?: Dutchess County, New York, in the American Revolution," in *Class Conflict, Slavery, and the United States Constitution*, ed. Lynd, 25–34, 55–61 (New York: Bobbs-Merrill, 1967); Thomas Wermuth, "The Central Hudson Valley: Dutchess, Orange, and Ulster Counties," in *The Other New York: The American Revolution beyond New York City, 1763–1787*, ed. Joseph S. Tiedemann and Eugene R. Fingerhut, 127–54 (Albany, NY: State University of New York Press, 2005).

17. Peter Force, ed., *American Archives*, 4th series, 6 vols. (Washington, DC: Government Printing Office, 1837, 1839, 1840, 1843, 1844, 1846), 3: 596–608;

Countryman, A People in Revolution, 150–51; James Smith, History of Dutchess County, New York (Syracuse, NY: D. Mason, 1882), 130–31.

18. The state responded in the early summer of 1776 and authorized the organization of two new companies in Dutchess (and one company in Westchester) to pacify the "sundry disaffected and dangerous persons," who disturbed the peace and threatened to take up arms against the American cause. See American Archives, 4th series, 3: 457–59, 466–67, 1312–14, 1719–20; 4: 187–88, 389–90, 403, 1117–18, 1719–20; 5: 291, 968, 1402, 1459; and 6: 1415, 1424–26, 1429; Countryman, A People in Revolution, 150–51; New York in Revolution as Colony and State, 2: 137, 141–42; Lynd, "Who Should Rule at Home?," 34–37.

19. American Archives, 4th series, 5: 898; Peter Force, ed., American Archives, 5th series, 3 vols. (Washington, DC: Government Printing Office, 1848, 1851, 1853), 1: 1542; 2: 663, 697, 950; 3: 215, 229, 316, 603.

20. American Archives, 5th series, 1: 355–57, 360, 1408.

21. American Archives, 5th series, 3: 231–32; Humphrey, Land and Liberty, 91–107; Cynthia A. Kierner, "Landlord and Tenant in Revolutionary New York: The Case of Livingston Manor," New York History 70 (1989): 133–52; Kim, "Impact of Class Relations and Warfare in the American Revolution," 326–46; Lynd, "The Tenant Rising at Livingston Manor, May 1777," in Class Conflict, Slavery, and the United States Constitution, 63–77; James Smith, History of Dutchess County, 130, 312–13; Philip Smith, General History of Dutchess County, 53–56, 326.

22. "Minutes of the Committee and of the First Commission for Detecting Conspiracies in the State of New York, December 11, 1776–September 23, 1778," 2 vols., Collections of the New-York Historical Society, vols. 57 and 58 (New York: New-York Historical Society, 1924, 1925); Countryman, A People in Revolution, 144, 151–54, 180–83; Humphrey, Land and Liberty, 107–10; James Smith, History of Dutchess County, 129–42, 175–76, 181–82, 312–13, 467, 510–11, 539, 546, 552, 558; Philip Smith, General History of Dutchess County, 120–24, 141, 155, 187–91, 196–97, 219–21, 229–31, 261–64, 267–73, 326, 345, 416, 442–43; Wermuth, "The Central Hudson Valley," 135–41.

23. Runaway advertisements were extracted from the New York Journal and the General Advertiser (1777–1783) and New York Packet and American Advertiser (1776–1783), both of which had been printed previously in New York City. In the wake of the British occupation of New York in the late summer of 1776, the Journal and the General Advertiser resumed publication first in Kingston and then in Poughkeepsie. Samuel Loudon, printer of the New York Packet, fled to Fishkill in 1776. Both newspapers returned to the city at the end of the war. Billy G. Smith examines more than 1,800 runaway advertisements from the Mid-Atlantic region during the war in Billy G. Smith, "Runaway Slaves in the Mid-Atlantic Region during the Revolutionary Era," in Transforming Hand of Revolution, 199–230.

24. For a discussion of the complicated motivations of runways during the Revolution, see Smith, "Runaway Slaves," 214–24; White, Somewhat More Independent, 126–31.

25. The black Loyalist experience is explored in Aptheker, The Negro in the American Revolution, 16–21; Quarles, The Negro in the American Revolution, 19–32,

111–81; Cassandra Pybus, *Epic Journeys of Freedom: Runaway Slaves of the American Revolution and Their Global Quest for Liberty* (Boston, MA: Beacon Press, 2006); Raphael, *People's History of the American Revolution*, 320–54; James W. St. G. Walker, *The Black Loyalists: The Search for a Promised Land in Nova Scotia and Sierra Leone, 1783–1870* (New York: African Publishing, 1976); Ellen Gibson Wilson, *The Loyal Blacks* (New York: Holmes and Maiers, 1976).

26. *New York Journal and General Advertiser*, May 1, June 5, June 12, July 17, and September 4, 1780; *New York Packet*, September 2, November 4, 1779; May 11, May 25, 1780; June 7, and June 28, 1781.

27. Judith L. Van Buskirk, *Generous Enemies: Patriots and Loyalists in Revolutionary New York* (Philadelphia, PA: University of Pennsylvania Press, 2002), 131, 138.

28. *New York Journal and General Advertiser*, July 17, 1780.

29. *New York Journal and General Advertiser*, May 1, 1780.

30. The experience of black Loyalists in the New York City region is explored in Graham Hodges, "Black Revolt in New York City and the Neutral Zone: 1775–1783," in *New York in the Age of the Constitution, 1775–1800*, ed. Paul A. Gilje and William Pencak, 20–47 (Rutherford, NJ: Fairleigh Dickinson University Press, 1992); Hodges, *Root and Branch*, 139–61; Hodges, *Slavery and Freedom in the Rural North: African Americans in Monmouth County, New Jersey, 1665–1865* (Madison, WI: Roman Littlefield, 1997), 91–112; Van Buskirk, *Generous Enemies*, 129–54.

31. *New York Packet*, September 2, 1779.

32. "Minutes of the Committee and First Commission for Detecting Conspiracies," 1: 57–59, 88–89, 271–72, 292; *Calendar of Historical Manuscripts Relating to the War of the Revolution*, 2 vols. (Albany, NY: Office of the Secretary of State, 1868), 2: 113–15, 120–25; Philip Smith, *General History of Dutchess County*, 262–63.

33. Whatever the instructions the woman provided, the plans evidently involved the use of counterfeit money. See "Minutes of the Committee and First Commission for Detecting Conspiracies," 2: 443–44.

34. "Minutes of the Committee and First Commission for Detecting Conspiracies," 1: 202; Quarles, *Negro in the American Revolution*, 105–108. For examples of African Americans arrested or incarcerated by the Committee and Commission for Detecting Conspiracies, see "Minutes of the Committee and First Commission for Detecting Conspiracies," 1: 57–59, 70, 88–89, 169, 178–79, 270, 271–72, 279, 287, 292; 2: 340–41.

35. Philip Smith, *General History of Dutchess County*, 262–63.

36. Van Buskirk, *Generous Enemies*, 139–41. See also Raphael, *People's History of the American Revolution*, 326–41. In some instances, the British reenslaved black Loyalists.

37. "Minutes of the Committee and First Commission for Detecting Conspiracies," 1: 265.

38. Henry D. B. Bailey, *Local Tales and Historical Sketches* (Fishkill Landing, NY: J. W. Spaight, 1874), 67–69; MacCracken, *Old Dutchess Forever!*, 128; Philip Smith, *General History of Dutchess County*, 199–200; and A. J. Williams-Myers, "The African (American) in the Mid-Hudson Valley before 1800: Some Historiographical Clues,"

in *Transformations of an American County: Dutchess County, New York, 1683–1983*, ed. Dutchess County Historical Society, 110 (Poughkeepsie, NY: Dutchess County Historical Society, 1986).

39. Aptheker, *Negro in the American Revolution*, 30–31; Quarles, *Negro in the American Revolution*, 7–18. New York allowed the substitution of slaves for those drafted into the state militia in 1776 and five years later provided for the emancipation of any slave who enlisted and served either for three years or until honorably discharged. See *Calendar of Historical Manuscripts Relating to the War of the Revolution*, 1: 489; *Laws of New York*, 4th session, chapter 32; *New York in Revolution as Colony and State*, 1: 11.

40. *New York in Revolution as Colony and State*, 1: 145, 187–88; Quarles, *Negro in the American Revolution*, 8–9; A. J. Williams-Myers, "The Arduous Journey: The African-American Presence in the Mid-Hudson Region," in *The African-American Presence in New York State History: Four Regional History Surveys*, ed. Monroe Fordham, 24–28 (Albany, NY: New York African American Institute, 1990); Benjamin Myer Brink, *The Early History of Saugerties, 1660–1825* (Kingston, NY: New York African American Institute, 1902), 349–52; Alphonso T. Clearwater, ed., *The History of Ulster County, New York* (Kingston, NY: R. W. Anderson, 1907), 297.

41. Aptheker, *Negro in the American Revolution*, 30.

42. *The History of Ulster County, New York*, 297.

43. *Calendar of Historical Manuscripts Relating to the War of the Revolution*, 1: 489; *Laws of New York*, 4th session, chapter 32; *New York in Revolution as Colony and State*, 1: 11.

44. Aptheker, *Negro in the American Revolution*, 30. African American military service in the cause for independence is examined in Aptheker, *Negro in the American Revolution*, 27–42; Foner, *Blacks in the American Revolution*, 54–74; W. B. Hartgrove, "The Negro Soldier in the American Revolution," *Journal of Negro History* 1 (1916): 110–31; Nell, *Colored Patriots of the American Revolution*; Quarles, *Negro in the American Revolution*, 7–18, 51–110; Raphael, *People's History of the American Revolution*, 281–92.

45. *New York Packet*, July 16, 1778.

46. Quarles, *Negro in American Revolution*, 94–100; Williams-Myers, "Arduous Journey," 28. Any member of the Dutchess County militia drafted to work on the erection of the Fishkill barracks could hire an able-bodied "Man or Negro" in his stead. See *Calendar of Historical Manuscripts Relating to the War of the Revolution*, 1: 489.

47. *New York Packet*, July 17, 1783.

48. Captain Archibald Anderson took out an advertisement in the *New York Packet* requesting the master of the boy to "come and pay the charges, and take him away." See *New York Packet*, September 17, 1778.

49. *New York Packet*, September 5, 1782.

50. Women, many of whom shouldered familial obligations that discouraged flight, would have been particularly vulnerable when alone on the roads in a region torn by partisan violence. The overwhelming preponderance of male fugitives from the Mid-Hudson River Valley was greater than the proportion of males in the downstate region. According to Shane White, males accounted for just over three quarters of all runaways in the New York City area during the Revolution.

The proportion of runaways age twenty-five and younger during the Revolution was even more pronounced in New York City and the surrounding region, where more than three quarters of runaways were less than age twenty-six; see White, *Somewhat More Independent*, 142–43. According to Billy G. Smith, approximately 10 percent of fugitives in the Mid-Atlantic region were female; approximately three quarters were between the ages of twenty and forty; see Smith, "Runaway Slaves," 210–11.

51. A variety of different and often competing personal, cultural, moral, religious, social, economic, and political considerations informed individual decisions. See Michael Kammen, "The American Revolution as a Crise de Conscience: The Case of New York," in *Society, Freedom, Conscience: The American Revolution in Virginia, Massachusetts, and New York*, ed. Richard Jellison, 125–89 (New York: Norton, 1976).

52. "Minutes of the Committee and First Commission for Detecting Conspiracies," 2: 376–87. Jonathan Clark also discusses the episode in "A Government to Form," 73–74.

53. *New York Journal and General Advertiser*, December 21, 1778; *New York Packet*, January 21, 1779; *New York Journal and General Advertiser*, February 14, 1782; *New York Packet*, June 19, 1783; *New York Journal and General Advertiser*, June 8, 1778.

54. *New York Journal and General Advertiser*, December 10, 1781; *New York Packet*, December 10, 1778.

55. *New York Journal and General Advertiser*, October 11, 1779.

56. *New York Packet*, June 17, 1779.

57. *New York Packet*, October 30, 1777; December 16, 1779.

58. *New York Journal and General Advertiser*, June 5, June 12, 1780; *New York Packet*, June 8, 1780. Slaves who ran away repeatedly must have been particularly incorrigible. When advertising for the apprehension of her slave Caesar in November 1777, the widow Margaret Poyer of Fishkill noted that Caesar had run away previously using an alias. See *New York Packet*, November 27, 1777. Tight, a young man in his mid-twenties, fled his master on Livingston Manor during the summers of 1778 and 1779. See *New York Journal and General Advertiser*, September 7, 1778; September 6, 1779; *New York Packet*, September 9, 1779. Perhaps it was one woman's repeated attempts to abscond from her owner or the fear that she would become a flight risk in the future that weighed on the mind of one slave owner in 1780. Seeking to sell the twenty-three-year-old woman, the seller explicitly stipulated that no purchaser within thirty to forty miles of Fishkill needed to apply, suggesting that "Any gentleman trading to Boston or Philadelphia may purchase her on reasonable terms." See *New York Journal and General Advertiser*, May 22, 1780.

59. *Calendar of Historical Manuscripts Relating to the War of the Revolution*, 1: 642–43.

60. Hodges, *Root and Branch*, 155–56; Van Buskirk, *Generous Enemies*, 174–75.

61. Graham Hodges, ed., *The Black Loyalist Directory: African Americans in Exile after the Revolution* (New York: Garland Press, 1996), 18, 22, 30, 37, 50, 51, 59, 95, 98, 99, 163, 164, 174, 188, 195, 211. Although younger men comprised an overwhelming majority of fugitive slaves during the war years, women constituted

more than 40 percent of black emigrants leaving the port of New York in 1783. See Hodges, *The Black Loyalist Directory*, xx.

62. The ordeal of black Loyalists after the war is explored in Mary Beth Norton, "The Fate of Some Black Loyalists of the American Revolution," *Journal of Negro History* 58 (1973): 402–26; Walker, *Black Loyalists*; Wilson, *The Loyal Blacks*.

CHAPTER 4

Northern Virginia's Quakers and the War for Independence

Negotiating a Path of Virtue in a Revolutionary World

A. Glenn Crothers

In early September 1777, the Revolutionary War was not going well for the new United States, for the British occupied the country's two largest ports, New York City and Philadelphia, and the Continental army seemed unable to halt its advance. The occupation of Philadelphia, in particular, provoked widespread alarm in Pennsylvania and the Chesapeake area. The government of Virginia, for example, called up the state militia. In Frederick County, located in the lower Shenandoah Valley, local militia officers, following a newly amended state law, made no allowance for religious groups who for reasons of conscience would not fight. As a result, on September 23, fourteen members of the Society of Friends (or Quakers) belonging to the Hopewell Monthly Meeting in Frederick County were drafted into service. "With drawn swords," the American officers, "pushed the Friends into rank, threatening they would have their blood if they did not comply." When the men refused "to handle any of the muskets," the officers ordered the weapons "tied to their bodies," and the group was forcibly marched to George Washington's army located outside of Philadelphia. The Friends also refused "to partake of the provision allotted to themselves," forcing a number to drop out of the ranks "from indisposition of body" and return home as best they could. Those who made it to Pennsylvania "were forced to stand . . . for many hours together." Only the intercession of Clement Biddle, a lapsed Quaker serving in the Continental army, secured their release. At Biddle's urging, Washington ordered the men freed and gave them "liberty to return home." Throughout the ordeal, Friends noted with satisfaction, the men "bore a steady testimony against all warlike measures."[1]

For northern Virginia's Quakers, such incidents became a common, if sporadic, feature of life during the Revolution. Many Patriots viewed Quakers' neutrality in a struggle to decide the new nation's fate as tantamount to Toryism, and the new state governments forced Friends throughout America to endure harassment, incarceration, financial hardships, and deep suspicion.[2] In Virginia, the government's repression of Friends came in two waves: in late 1776 and 1777, when fighting in Pennsylvania threatened the Chesapeake area; and after 1780, when Virginia itself faced British invasion. In other words, Quakers were harassed at precisely those moments that the state's leadership felt most threatened and the American cause appeared most in jeopardy. Historians have typically portrayed the Revolution in Virginia as a product of enlightened leaders who confidently led a united white population into revolt, but the experience of Friends reveals a different picture, one that highlights the anxieties of the state's elite and the racial and class tensions that plagued Virginia.[3]

At the same time, however, the Revolutionary War transformed the Quaker sect. Long-standing pacifist convictions led Friends to embrace a course of action that deeply alienated them from the broader American community, but the Revolutionary experience simultaneously persuaded Quakers to embrace a new activism that aimed to correct a variety of social injustices. These changes affected Quakers throughout America, including those settled in the slaveholding region of northern Virginia, which included the counties of Fairfax, Loudoun, Berkeley, and Frederick. In short, the American Revolution had a profound effect upon Friends, accelerating ongoing efforts to purify the sect and generating a new awareness among local Quakers that they must work to redeem the broader society. By war's end, northern Virginia's Quakers had largely ended slave ownership among their members, and in the 1780s and 1790s they began a campaign to aid newly freed African Americans and to abolish the institution of slavery. Similarly, during the 1770s and 1780s, Friends in Frederick County in the Shenandoah Valley sought to reimburse the Indians who once owned the land upon which their meetinghouse sat in an effort to do justice to another downtrodden group. And it was in the wake of the Revolution that the region's Quakers embraced temperance and began enforcing the sect's rules against frivolous and immoral behavior more strictly. Thus in response to their "sufferings," northern Virginia's Quakers, like their coreligionists throughout the United States, forged a tighter and more purified group that enhanced the Quakers' sense of identity and community and offered them an important moral role in the new American nation.[4]

Friends from Pennsylvania and New Jersey had first settled in northern Virginia in the 1730s; by 1776, almost 2,000 Quakers resided in Fairfax, Loudoun, Berkeley, and Frederick counties. As part of an elaborate system

Friends

Figure 4.1 Friends: The Locations of Quakers in the Revolution

of hierarchical yearly, quarterly, monthly, and preparative meetings, they remained in close contact with their coreligionists in the Middle Colonies and throughout America. In 1776, northern Virginia Friends belonged to the Philadelphia Yearly Meeting, the largest and most influential one in America. The yearly meeting ultimately decided the content of the Quaker testimonies and discipline, although decisions in such matters were arrived at slowly and only after reaching a consensus among the membership. Each yearly meeting consisted of a number of quarterly meetings that met for worship and business, and they in turn consisted of numerous monthly meetings, where Friends enforced the society's testimonies and disciplined members who violated them. Individuals who failed to uphold the sect's discipline could face a variety of sanctions, the most severe being "disownment" or removal from the society. Such decisions were not taken lightly. Only after lengthy "treating" and visiting with wayward Friends, a process that often took months, were unrepentant members expelled. In addition to their ties to the Philadelphia meeting, the two monthly meetings of northern Virginia—Fairfax located east of the Blue Ridge Mountains in Loudoun County and Hopewell in Frederick County in the Shenandoah Valley—maintained close contact with the Virginia Yearly Meeting so that Friends throughout the province "manifest[ed] a oneness in practice, as well as Principle." Living under the same civil authority, all Virginia Friends faced similar sanctions and problems.[5]

Such ties ensured that Friends throughout America remained faithful to their spiritual beliefs, including the rejection of violence and war. Quaker pacifism had deep roots, becoming a central component of the sect's creed shortly after its formation in mid-seventeenth-century England. Friends' pacifism arose from their conviction that, as Quaker founder George Fox put it, "every man was enlightened by the divine light of Christ" and was thus equally capable of receiving God's grace. All people, even those who had not been exposed to Christianity, could achieve salvation if they followed the prompting of the "inward light." From this belief in humanity's spiritual equality arose the Quaker embrace of the golden rule, "Whatsoever ye would that men should do to you, do ye even so to them," and of pacifism. Friends believed it was wrong to take a human life, because all individuals possessed a divinely inspired "light within" that if followed would enable them to become "children" of the light and achieve salvation. Moreover, "Dwelling in the light," Fox noted, "takes away the occasion of wars, and gathers our hearts together to God, and unto one another." Peace, then, was the natural consequence of following the light within. These beliefs were soon reflected in the sect's disciplines, or rules of behavior, established by the various North American yearly meetings, which required Friends to eschew the use of harsh or virulent language that might lead to violence, to refuse service in the military, and (eventually) to avoid complicity in war making, including taking sides or paying military taxes.[6]

The Quaker refusal to proclaim allegiances during war stood in contrast to their attitude toward government in times of peace. Believing government to be divinely inspired, they adhered to a policy of obedience to any secular authority that did not force them to act against their conscience. As Quaker writer Isaac Penington noted in 1681, Friends sought "universal liberty for all sorts to worship God," but even when they were denied such freedoms, he urged his coreligionists to "be still and quiet in your Minds." "We are not at all," he concluded, "against Magistracy, Laws, or Government, though we cannot flatter or bend to them in that which is selfish and corrupt." In eighteenth-century America, where Friends enjoyed widespread toleration, Penington's counsel became an important component of the Quaker testimony. As the Philadelphia Yearly Meeting noted in 1755, "it is well known" that early Friends complied "with the Laws of Government under which they lived in every Case not contrary to the Laws and Doctrines of our Supreme Lord." On those occasions when government violated their religious testimonies, the yearly meeting counseled Quakers to practice passive disobedience, just as early Friends had "patiently suffered" under similar circumstances. Such resistance, the yearly meeting stressed, must be nonviolent, because "the followers of Christ" must not use "force and violence to oppose the Ordinances of Magistrates." Friends, then, must bear the consequences of their actions as a form of peaceful protest.[7]

Adherence to the existing government, however, did not forestall Quaker participation in the largely nonviolent protests of the mid-1760s. Indeed, most Friends supported American remonstrations against the taxation measures of the British government, arguing with their fellow colonists that they could be taxed only by their elected provincial representatives. Likewise, Quaker merchants in Philadelphia participated in early nonimportation agreements, although they worked to moderate the coercive tactics employed to enforce such commercial arrangements. When this opposition threatened to turn violent, however, Friends began distancing themselves from the independence movement, arguing that Americans needed to employ less combative measures and appeal instead to the British conscience. When violence finally erupted, Friends broke entirely from the Patriot movement. Not only were Americans overthrowing a legally constituted government, a task Quakers believed was God's responsibility alone, but Patriots were employing military measures to do so. Adherence to their religious testimonies demanded that Quakers take no part in the revolutionary struggle.[8]

I

Virginia Quakers were largely untroubled by the course of events in the 1760s and early 1770s. In fact, they remained a respected, if curious, part of Virginia society for much of the late eighteenth century. Contemporaries often praised Friends for their farming and business acumen, even if they had little respect for their spiritual values. Quaker farming methods, for example, were highly regarded and increasingly imitated by their non-Quaker neighbors. By the 1770s, Friends in Loudoun County, most of whom had migrated from Pennsylvania after 1740, were employing the most advanced farming methods, including crop rotation and soil fertilization. David Stuart, whom George Washington had hired to survey the agricultural prospects of the region, reported in 1791 that Loudoun County, under the influence of Quaker and German farmers, had become "the best farming county in the State." Likewise, local Quaker merchants, who were settled in the region's growing urban places, particularly Alexandria and Winchester, were widely respected for their fair business practices. William Hartshorne, for example, established a successful mercantile firm in Alexandria in 1774, earning the praise of Virginia planter William Lee as a "a sharp[,] keen quaker merchant . . . who can be trusted with safety."[9]

But it was not just Quakers' fair dealing and efficient agricultural practices that garnered praise. In the 1770s, some Virginians, from both the elite and from the growing evangelical population, began questioning the institution of slavery and its economic and social impact on the colony. Quakers, who were in the midst of an often difficult struggle to end slavery within their own ranks, were heartened by these antislavery rumblings, in part because they needed the support of leading Virginians to change the state's laws to make manumission possible. In 1774, the Philadelphia Yearly Meeting decided, after years of debate, to disown any Friend who bought, sold, imported, or owned a slave, and that discipline was put into effect in 1776. The Virginia Yearly Meeting followed suit the same year. However, Virginia Quakers' efforts were stymied by the colony's, and later the state's, laws that made it illegal for slaveholders to manumit their human property except for some act of "meritorious service" by the slave. In response to this legal obstacle, Friends campaigned to change the statute, forging alliances with and winning praise from a number of the state's leading men. In the 1770s, for example, Patrick Henry regularly corresponded with Quaker Robert Pleasants, one of the leaders of the Virginia Yearly Meeting, commending Friends for their "noble effort to abolish slavery." Their efforts paid off in 1782, when the state responded to intensive Quaker lobbying and passed legislation that made it easier for slaveholders to free their slaves.[10]

Finally, Friends' support for the American cause, both in England and the colonies, in the early 1770s garnered praise. Between 1774 and 1776, the *Virginia Gazette* lauded the Society of Friends for their opposition to the measures of the British Parliament and their "truly benevolent and humane" relief efforts. In June 1774, the paper reported that English Friends "have prepared a most spirited petition to Throne" "in Defence of their Rights in the Colonies," and in August Virginians learned that "the ministry have been greatly alarmed at the conduct of the Quakers," because "that most honorable body" of "upright and independent Principles of *Oliverian Firmness*" have been "standing forth to support their American brethren." As late as July 1775, the paper assured Virginians that the "Quakers of England . . . all join in one voice against the Ministry and . . . are faithful to the people of America." American Quakers, the paper reported in 1774, "profess themselves ready to consent to every measure which promises to preserve the rights of American," though they "do not chuse to demonstrate their dissatisfaction in the noisy manner the less orderly . . . colonists have adapted." In May 1775, Virginians learned, incorrectly, that "upwards of 6,000" Philadelphia Quakers had voted with only twenty-six opposed to "take up arms in defence of American liberty," and that within a month Friends had raised four companies of soldiers. More accurately, the paper praised society members for their "very active" efforts to raise "contributions" for the inhabitants of Boston.[11]

II

However, American opinion changed when the Philadelphia Yearly Meeting issued a series of public statements in 1775 and 1776 that articulated the reasons Quakers must oppose the Revolutionary struggle. Probably most damning was a January 1776 pronouncement that contrasted the "calamities and afflictions which now surround us" with the "peace and plenty" Americans enjoyed under the British Crown. The address concluded that Quakers should "firmly unite in the abhorrence of all . . . measures" designed "to break off the happy connexion we have heretofore enjoyed with the kingdom of Great Britain, and our just and necessary subordination to the king." Although the statement aimed to explain the reasons for the Quaker doctrine of passive neutrality and to avert a final break between the colonies and Great Britain, in the increasingly polarized environment of early 1776 Patriots interpreted it as proof of Friends' Loyalist sentiments. Patriot newspapers immediately published a series of blistering attacks on the Society and warned Quakers not to give offense by "endeavoring to counteract the measures of their fellow citizens for the common safety." Some writers wondered how a group that professed neutrality could express support for the monarchy. As Samuel Adams pronounced, "If they would not *pull down Kings*, let them not support *tyrants.*"[12]

The most withering response, however, came from Thomas Paine, whose inflammatory and wildly popular *Common Sense* appeared the same month as the January 1776 Quaker epistle. Subsequent editions of his pamphlet appended an address, "To the Representatives of the Religious Society of People called Quakers," which accused Friends of "dabbling in matters which your professed . . . Principles instruct you not to meddle in." Paine argued that the Society could not claim that "the setting up and putting down of kings and governments is God's peculiar prerogative" and at the same time make political pronouncements that condemned Patriot actions. Instead, Quakers must, if they were to be true to their principles, "wait with patience and humility for the event of all public measures . . . receive *that event* as the divine will towards you," and not try to have a "share in the business." Paine told Friends that their attempts to influence public opinion revealed "that either ye do not believe what ye profess, or have not virtue enough to practise what ye believe." In short, the Society had "mistaken party for conscience," and such "mingling [of] religion with politics" should "*be disavowed and reprobated by every inhabitant of* AMERICA."[13]

The following year the society's public reputation sank even farther when a fabricated letter from the nonexistent "Spanktown Yearly Meeting" was widely republished in American newspapers. The note, which had allegedly been found in the papers of an American officer who had defected to the British, and which was later published by Congress, revealed the size and location of Washington's army in Pennsylvania. Informing Congress of the letter, American General John Sullivan condemned Friends as "the most Dangerous Enemies America knows & such as have it in their power to Distress the Country more than all the Collected Force of Britain." "Covered with that Hypocritical Cloak of Religion," Sullivan continued, "they have with Impunity . . . Long Acted the part of Inveterate Enemies of their Country," and have "Prostituted" "their Religious Meetings . . . to the Base purposes of betraying their Country." Though Friends repeatedly informed Congress and the public that there was "no meeting throughout our whole Society" called Spanktown, and that no such "letter, or any one like it, [was] ever written in any of our meetings," the widely publicized missive had done its damage. Appearing at a time when British General William Howe was threatening to take Philadelphia, the new nation's capital, many Americans agreed with Sullivan and saw the Quakers as a threat to the Patriot cause. In Virginia, Edmund Pendleton assumed that Friends, whom he labeled "the broad brims" after their distinctive dress, had great "hopes of How[e]'s success." The *Virginia Gazette* joined this chorus when it falsely reported in November 1777 that Philadelphia Friends had given "*friend* Howe a free gift of six thousand pounds on his entrance into" the city.[14]

In the face of growing hostility, the Philadelphia Yearly Meeting worked to clarify the sect's discipline and to ensure that Quakers throughout America responded to the situation in a unified fashion. In September 1776, it issued explicit instructions to its subordinate meetings, including Fairfax and Hopewell in northern Virginia, on how to enforce the Quaker peace testimony and maintain uniformity within the sect. All Friends, the Philadelphia meeting declared, must resign from any positions they held within the new governments, because these had been founded on violence. Friends were to refuse payment of any war tax and of any penalties or fines they might incur for not paying war taxes or serving in the military. Finally, they were to disengage from any war-related business or trade from which they could personally profit. These strictures were not offered as advice; violating any of these testimonies, the Philadelphia meeting stressed, was punishable by disownment from the society. In December the Philadelphia meeting issued another epistle to fortify "weak" and "wavering" Friends. Admitting that this was a "time of deep . . . affliction and difficulty," the epistle nonetheless urged Friends to "withstand and refuse to submit to the arbitrary injunctions and ordinances of men who assume to themselves the power of compelling others." Girded by the "truth" of the inner light, Quakers could do no less than "steadily . . . bear our testimony against every attempt to deprive us of it."[15]

III

As heartening as these words must have been for beleaguered Friends throughout America, they did not change the real hardships that members of the sect faced during the war years. Indeed, northern Virginia's Quakers saw firsthand the most repressive American measures when at the behest of Congress, the Pennsylvania Council arrested eighteen leading Philadelphia Friends, the so-called "Virginia exiles," and marched them to the Shenandoah Valley, where they were held without charge or a hearing for seven months. At first the prisoners were detained in a single house in Winchester, but over time the conditions of their confinement improved. They were allowed to receive visitors, hold biweekly religious services, and visit with local Friends. Indeed, the letters the exiles wrote home reveal just how much they relied on the support and friendship of local Quakers, all of whom were members of the Hopewell Monthly Meeting. Henry Drinker, for example, wrote his wife in October that local Friends Sarah Janney and Elizabeth Jolliffe had "been kindly to see us, justly thinking it would be a comfort to us." Some days later, Drinker reported that the exiles were receiving "daily supplies" and "fresh provisions & those very good" from neighboring Quakers. By month's end, Drinker and two of his fellow exiles were dining regularly at the home of local Friend Joseph Steer, whose "wife & Family," he reported, "have been very kind from our first coming here." Before the end of the year, county authorities permitted the exiles to move into the homes of local Friends, and Drinker reported that the exiles regularly "attended Hopewell Mo. Meeting." Exile Thomas Fisher's map of Winchester, completed in March 1778, reveals even more fully the prisoners' bonds to the local Quaker community. Aside from a few topographical features, the only landmarks he identified on his map were the homes of local Friends and preparative and monthly meetings.[16]

In April 1778, American authorities permitted the Philadelphians to return home, but not before two of the exiles had died in custody, an "apparent lesson to local Friends," who refused to support the Patriot cause.[17] But by this time northern Virginia's Friends had already experienced their own "sufferings" at the hands of the state government. Like American leaders in Philadelphia, Virginia's planters were deeply concerned about the fate of the Patriot cause in 1777, and local committees of safety subjected a number of Quakers to close questioning. In Petersburg, for example, the county committee threatened Quaker Edward Stabler with public identification as a traitor for refusing to support the Continental Association, the boycott of British trade that the Continental Congress had established in the fall of 1774. In response, some Virginia Friends, including Robert Pleasants, reluctantly decided to "submit to all regulations of trade," because doing so did not violate the peace testimony.[18] But Tories and Quakers were not the Virginia gentry's only or even chief concern, for planters worried that the Revolution might unleash the long-simmering class and racial tensions that plagued the state. Lashing out at Quakers was a symptom of these larger concerns.

Indeed, as historian Woody Holton has argued, the planter class reluctantly embraced revolution in part to forestall slave and class unrest. Loudoun County, home to one of Virginia's largest concentrations of Friends and the Fairfax Monthly Meeting, was the center of a renter's revolt that had erupted in 1775. As the war lengthened and the bankrupt state needed to raise more troops and supplies from an often unwilling populace, increasing class and racial tensions made the gentry's control more tenuous. White unrest peaked in early 1781, when a series of tax revolts swept through the state, most notably in Hampshire County in the lower Shenandoah Valley, next to Frederick County's significant Quaker population.

The Continental Congress's decision to house large, if fluctuating, numbers of British and German prisoners of war in the Shenandoah Valley after 1776, many of whom left their poorly guarded camps to work for local farm families, only added to the unease of Virginia's revolutionary leaders. Most frightening to slaveholding planters, Virginia Governor Lord Dunmore's 1775 proclamation promising freedom to all enslaved men who joined his small army, and the invasion of the state by British troops in 1780 and 1781, enabled large numbers of enslaved people to escape to British lines, at the same time that Quakers were working to free their slave populations. Under these dire circumstances, Virginia Friends' failure to support the American cause made them an increasingly suspect group, and their repression reveals the insecurity of the Virginia gentry during the Revolutionary era.[19]

The Loudoun riots that erupted in November 1775 were sparked by an ongoing salt shortage. According to Holton, however, the underlying cause was the tension between landlords and tenants, in a county where up to one third of white heads of households rented their land from large planters such as George Washington and Richard Henry Lee. A shortage of specie forced local employers and military recruiters to pay wages in paper money, but local landlords continued to demand rent payments in cash. In response, tenants in Loudoun and neighboring Fauquier, led by Washington's former employee James Cleveland, refused to pay their rents unless the Continental Association's nonexportation agreement (which effectively halted the flow of specie into Virginia) was lifted. Large numbers of Loudoun farmers also were upset by the disparity between wages paid to officers and common soldiers and the gentry's poor wartime leadership. At least one county resident, Richard Morlan, warned that "he would not muster, and if fined would oppose the collection of the fine with his gun." Unrest continued into May 1776.[20] Although there is no evidence that local Quakers, most of whom were landowners, joined the revolt, their refusal to serve or contribute to the war effort made them as traitorous to the cause as were the rioters. Indeed, county leaders may have concluded that Friends' noncompliance was in fact more dangerous, and thus a more obvious target for suppression, than the justifiable, if disturbing, insubordination of the region's disgruntled renters. The British invasion of Pennsylvania in mid-1777 compounded such anxieties and prompted the first significant repression of northern Virginia's Quakers.

Most notably, the state assembly passed legislation that required all pacifists to bear arms or hire a substitute, overturning a 1766 law that had for the first time in the colony's history entirely exempted Quakers from military service. Charged with putting the new legislation into effect, Frederick County officials forcibly recruited fourteen Hopewell Quakers in September 1777. One month later, eighteen Friends from the Fairfax meeting faced a similar fate when County Lieutenant Francis Peyton drafted them into the county militia to serve with the Continental army. Peyton soon released two of the men for health reasons, but the remaining sixteen were marched

176 miles north and arrived outside of Philadelphia in early November. Despite these efforts, after a day in camp they were "discharged by order of General Washington" and returned home in mid-November. Throughout "their Restraint," the Fairfax Monthly Meeting reported with satisfaction, the forced recruits "Consciously avoided taking any Provision provided by the Officers" and exercised "a good degree of patience and Resignation." The tactics of passive disobedience worked effectively to undermine such forced recruitment.[21]

In response to Quaker tactics, the state legislature in October 1777 changed its strategy for dealing with conscientious objectors and decided they could be excused from service if they hired a substitute in their place. For Quakers this measure was equally objectionable. Seeking to avoid complicity in war making in any way, they refused to hire substitutes or to pay fines for nonservice. Local authorities responded by distraining, or seizing, Friends' property in amounts comparable to the fines and taxes assessed by the state. In practice, however, county officials often took items, whose value exceeded the state requisitions, and they jailed those who owned nothing of value. Ultimately, the loss of property, most of it through distraint, was the biggest burden that northern Virginia's Quakers faced during the war. Both the Hopewell and the Fairfax Monthly meetings, at the behest of the Philadelphia Yearly Meeting, established their own Committee for Suffering Cases, which detailed the ordeals of all Friends who suffered for honoring the peace testimony. By 1784, these committees reported that Friends in northern Virginia had paid almost 2,400 pounds in Virginia currency (or approximately 3,000 pounds in Pennsylvania currency) in distraints, most of which was for refusing to hire substitutes.[22]

IV

The state had nevertheless been surprisingly slow to adopt the tactic of distraint, and it was not until 1780 and 1781, when a combination of external threat—the British incursions into Virginia that began in the fall of 1780—and internal dissent—most notably, a Loyalist uprising in Hampshire County in mid-1781—prompted local officials to begin seizing Quaker property in a systematic fashion. Indeed, by 1779, the state had seized only slightly more than £115 of property from fourteen Friends in the Fairfax Monthly Meeting. The Hopewell meeting reported no distraints before that year, though these figures may reflect the backwardness of the local meetings in recording their sufferings in a regular fashion before 1780.[23] Whatever the cause for the initial low numbers, the British incursions into Virginia beginning in the fall of 1780 and the state's subsequent scramble for men and materials led to widespread seizure of Quaker property and even the occasional forced recruitment.

Friends were not the only Virginians to suffer in this crisis. In 1779, the legislature had empowered state officials to seize private property needed for the war effort, paying farmers in state certificates redeemable in six months at 6 percent interest. The following year Virginia reinstated the draft to raise troops for the Continental army. These measures generated widespread discontent among small farmers, who received no concrete payment for produce seized by the state, and who could not afford to hire substitutes if drafted, and thus faced the prospect of abandoning their families.[24]

In a number of locations the state's actions sparked open revolt, most notably in Hampshire County in 1781. According to County Lieutenant Garrett Van Meter, the "dangerous insurrection" began in March 1781, when the county tax commissioner attempted to raise troops and collect supplies as required by "the late Acts of [the] Assembly." The leader of the revolt, John Claypole, gathered a force of close to 150 men consisting of local draft evaders and deserters and a few escaped British prisoners of war who "Drank King George the third's health (and Damnation to Congress)." When ordered to stand down by the county sheriff and his fifty armed men, they refused but offered to negotiate their grievances at a future date. In mid-June, General Daniel Morgan, who resided in Frederick County, marched a force of 400 men into Hampshire County. In the face of this show of force, the revolt collapsed with only one death and the arrest of forty-two individuals. More than a year later, the governor pardoned all of the participants involved in the uprising. However, in 1781, as British forces under Benedict Arnold were plundering their way through eastern Virginia and threatening the state government, revolutionary leaders deemed the revolt extremely serious.[25]

The involvement of British troops pointed to yet another danger. Since 1777, Congress had housed significant numbers of British and German prisoners outside of Winchester. Many of them worked for local farm families and could easily disappear into the countryside. Daniel Morgan, for one, believed that the combination of local Tories and the large number of poorly guarded British and German prisoners was a dangerous one. Even after the defeat of Lord Cornwallis's British forces at Yorktown, Morgan remained anxious about the prospect of internal dissent. In November and December 1781, he warned both Washington and Virginia Governor Benjamin Harrison that the "Chain of Tories Extending thence along the Frontiers of Maryland and Pennsylvania would rather assist than prevent" the "Escape" of troops housed near Winchester. He was particularly worried that the main body of prisoners was housed "in the only Tory Settlement in the County," some "five miles from Winchester." Though the exact location of these barracks is unknown, historians place it close to Apple Pie Ridge, home to the Hopewell meetinghouse and a large Quaker settlement.[26]

Morgan never explicitly identified who lived in his purported "Tory settlement," but in 1780 and 1781 county officials throughout northern Virginia considered Friends a suspect group. In all, 143 Quakers from the region suffered the distraint of property between 1775 and 1782 for their failure to support the war effort. However, of these individuals, 126 (almost 90 percent) had their property seized between November 1779 and October 1782. Indeed, only one Quaker had property seized before 1779—in April 1775 Loudoun County's Thomas Taylor had his still, valued at sixty-five pounds, seized—and only one after April 1782. In short, the vast majority of distraints took place during those years when the Patriot cause in Virginia was most in jeopardy from both external and internal threats. Moreover, the repression of Friends in the region was extremely systematic given the standards of the eighteenth century. Approximately 450 adult men in northern Virginia's Quaker community were subject to military service, and over 30 percent of them had their property seized for refusal to serve or support the war. Little wonder that Samuel Kercheval, the valley's first historian, concluded that Quakers "were the greatest sufferers by the war."[27]

Most Friends lost their property in repeated seizures that taken together were often costly. Samuel Canby of Loudoun County, for example, lost over sixty pounds of property in six distraints between May 1780 and May 1781. In the valley, the biggest sufferer was Allen Jackson, who lost almost ninety pounds of property in seven seizures between February 1781 and March 1782. Other Friends, including Robert Harris and Andrew McKay of the Hopewell meeting and Mahlon Janney in Loudoun County, all lost over eighty pounds. But county officials did not stop with the wealthiest men. Many Friends lost a variety of small household items needed by Virginia troops. William Daniel, for example, had a pair of boots, a hat and a cheese, a frying pan and pewter plates, altogether valued at just less than five pounds, taken from him between April 1779 and March 1781. County officials also took great coats, halters, and bridles for use by soldiers. In contrast, items such as silk handkerchiefs, coverlets, feather beds, and "delph dishes" were sold at auction, often enabling, as Samuel Kercheval later reported, "designing individuals to make profitable speculations." Most often, however, county officials took the animals, wagons, and produce that American military forces put to use immediately.[28]

In the face of such extensive public and official pressure, not all Friends honored their peace testimony. Between 1775 and 1783, for example, the Hopewell meeting disowned seven men for "consenting to serve in the station of a soldier." Further east, the Fairfax meeting disowned sixteen men for "bearing Arms" or "hiring a substitute and joining in the active part of the war." Most of these removals came early in the war, when a "martial spirit" swept the new nation, and the adventure of military life appealed to young men. Some Quakers may have been persuaded that military service was acceptable because of erroneous reports that significant numbers of Philadelphia Friends had joined the fighting. Though some Philadelphia-area Quakers did urge the yearly meeting to support the Revolutionary cause, the "Free Quakers," as they would later be known, were a small group. As historian Arthur Mekeel has noted, in the first years of the war fewer than thirty Philadelphia Friends were disowned for "enlisting as a soldier." In northern Virginia, the story was much the same; over the course of the war, the monthly meetings disowned fewer than 6 percent of the approximately 450 Quaker men eligible for military service. In short, what is most striking is that most northern Virginia Friends successfully resisted the public and economic pressures to bear arms.[29]

V

However, northern Virginia's Quakers, like their brethren throughout America, found it difficult to develop a unified policy concerning paying taxes in time of war or taking loyalty oaths to the state. For the first time in the sect's history, nearly all Friends agreed that paying war taxes, or money collected to support the military directly, constituted a violation of the peace testimony. Both the Philadelphia and Virginia Yearly Meetings made such payments grounds for removal. The vast majority of Friends also agreed that taxes earmarked for nonmilitary purposes should be paid. Quakers disagreed, however, over whether members should pay mixed or general taxes, in which a portion of the money was used to support the military effort. Opposition to the payment of such levies was most pronounced within the Philadelphia and Virginia Yearly Meetings, though neither meeting could reach a clear consensus on the issue.[30]

But it was not for lack of trying. To ensure that Virginia Quakers acted as one on the issue of war taxes, the Virginia Yearly Meeting asked Hopewell and Fairfax Friends to send representatives to their annual gathering in December 1775. Following traditional Quaker religious practice, the meeting waited for "the calming influence of our Father's heavenly love" to be "measurably witnessed among us." "In silence," the group considered two questions: the use of "papers bills of credit that are or may be issued for the purposes of carrying on War"; and "the propriety of Friends voluntarily paying or refusing to pay" a mixed tax. On the first issue, Virginia Friends followed the advice of the Philadelphia meeting and refused to accept Continental currency, making Virginia and Philadelphia the only meetings to do so. On the second issue, the payment of a mixed or general tax, the group could not agree and wrote to Philadelphia for advice. Unfortunately, Philadelphia Friends, equally divided on the matter, could offer no firm counsel beyond requesting that Friends take "care to avoid complying with the injunctions and requisitions made for the purpose of carrying on War."[31]

Only in 1779, largely at the behest of leading Friend Robert Pleasants, did the Virginia Yearly Meeting advise Friends not to pay a mixed tax. Recognizing the consequences of this radical decision, the meeting urged Friends "to leave all hope as to the outward" estate. Whether Quakers in northern Virginia followed this advice, and it was only advice, not a disownable offense, is unclear. In 1784, the Fairfax committee for sufferings debated whether Friends should pay general taxes now that the war was over. "Friends," they concluded, "may be left at liberty to act according to their freedom either in complying or declining it as they seem most easy to do." The matter, then, was one of individual conscience. The Hopewell and Fairfax meetings likely treated the issue in a similar fashion before 1783, for no members were disciplined during the war for paying general taxes. Still, "a considerable number of Friends" did get into legal difficulties, prompting the Fairfax meeting to appoint a committee of prominent members in 1779 "to attend Court on behalf" of local tax resisters. In short, if calls for broader tax resistance failed to generate unanimous support, then the American Revolution marked the first time Friends as a body refused to pay levies specifically earmarked for military purposes. As Robert Pleasants noted in 1779, Quakers cannot pay war taxes because "they make us parties to the destruction, violence and confusion consequent to such intestine commotion."[32]

Throughout the war, Friends in northern Virginia also were plagued with the problem of taking loyalty oaths. After the Declaration of the Independence each state required that inhabitants take a test oath or an affirmation in which they declared their allegiance to the new government and renounced their loyalty to the Crown. Those who refused to take such oaths were labeled "non-jurors" and could suffer serious consequences, including fines, the loss of civil rights, the distraint of property, and imprisonment. Quakers would not take oaths or affirmations because they believed that to do so was to participate, however tangentially, in pulling down the legally constituted government. Moreover, Friends asserted that if they pledged their loyalty to the new regimes, then they were in effect sanctioning the violence that helped create these governments.[33]

The consequence of this Quaker "scruple" soon became apparent. The Virginia legislature passed its first law requiring an oath or affirmation of allegiance from all males above age sixteen in May 1777. Those who failed to take the oath faced a variety of penalties, including exclusion from public office and jury duty and restricted access to the legal system. In October, the legislature imposed a double tax on nonjurors and a year later raised this to a treble tax. In response, the Virginia Yearly Meeting, following the lead of its Philadelphia counterpart, directed its subordinate meetings to disown any Friend who took the test oath. Paying the fine was equally inadmissible. In June 1778, the Warrington and Fairfax Quarterly Meeting (to which both Hopewell and Fairfax monthly meetings belonged) decided that Friends should not provide the state with accounts of their property because doing so would make it easier for the state to collect fines assessed for refusing to take the oath. The Hopewell and Fairfax meetings, despite some internal debate, adhered to this position throughout the Revolutionary War. In 1782, for example, the Fairfax meeting, after consultation with Hopewell Friends, decided that members could not pay such fines or give the state an account of their property, because the revenue so raised would "be applied to the support of warlike Measures."[34]

A number of northern Virginia Quakers failed to sustain this aspect of the peace testimony. The Hopewell meeting eventually disowned five members for taking loyalty oaths to the state. The problem was more serious in the Fairfax meeting, where sixteen individuals, including a number of the meeting's most prominent members, faced disciplinary action for either taking the loyalty oath or paying "a Tax or Fine in lieu of taking a Test." Northern Virginia Friends were less quick to disown members for taking the loyalty oath than they were for other violations of the peace testimony and in 1780 sought advice from the quarterly meeting on how to deal with offenders. After much discussion, the quarterly meeting decided that oath takers who displayed "evident marks of their sincere repentance" and were willing "wholly to recant the Test" should be allowed to return to the meeting in "full Unity." As a result, the Fairfax meeting generally placed offenders "under the care of the meeting" for an extended period of time in an effort to convince them of their wrongdoing. Ultimately, this lenient tactic worked with all but six members. Isaac Votaw, for example, was at first "not sure in his own mind that he was wrong" but kept "under care" for almost two years until he finally admitted his "error" in 1781. Likewise, William Hartshorne, whose oath taking was reported in 1779, came under the care of the meeting for nearly four years before he acknowledged his backsliding.[35]

VI

Friends' more lenient enforcement of this aspect of their peace testimony should not obscure the fact that the sect was once again willing to take an unpopular stand in defense of their peace testimony and to pay the economic consequences for doing so. But equally important, the suffering

Friends experienced during the war led them to embrace another line of conduct: aid to their fellow sufferers. After the arrest of the Virginia exiles, for example, Virginia Quaker Warner Mifflin was moved to consider anew the suffering of African American slaves, who likewise endured an arbitrary power. "I was brought," he remembered later, "into renewed sympathy with our oppressed African brethren," because like the exiles they were "exposed to the uncontrolled power of man, without any tribunal on earth whereunto they can appeal for redress of grievances." The Fairfax and Hopewell meetings shared Mifflin's sympathies and continued their active campaign, started years before the war began at the behest of the Philadelphia Yearly Meeting, to convince all local Friends to free their slaves. Elders concerned about the spiritual welfare of slaveholding Friends "treated" with them at length, while preparative and monthly meetings formed committees to visit members who repeatedly refused to manumit their bondsmen.[36]

As early as 1762, the Fairfax meeting cautioned member Thomas Taylor that his recent "purchase of a Negroe" was "directly contrary to the Judgment of the Yearly Meeting." He did not, however, relent. Despite "having been much laboured with" over the course of the next fifteen years, he was "fixed to keep Slaves," and in November 1777 the Fairfax meeting, acting at the behest of the Quarterly Meeting, decided to disown him. But this was not the end of the story. After the intercession of Isaac Zane Jr., a prominent local Quaker, the meeting reinstated Taylor when he promised to free his slaves by 1780. The meeting exercised similar patience with other local slaveholders. In 1774, it issued an unequivocal statement addressed to "such Friends that have any . . . Slaves in their possession," stating that "we Apprehend [that] they [slaves] have a Natural Right to freedom and Equal Justice as those of our own Color." Still, various committees appointed to treat with slaveholders reported limited progress. A 1774 committee, for example, reported that only "one Friend . . . Signified to us he would" free his slaves. The problem still festered in 1778, when at the behest of the Quarterly Meeting a new committee was appointed "to take some further care to obtain Manumissions" of slaves. Manumission in northern Virginia went slower than elsewhere in the Philadelphia Yearly Meeting, because the colony's laws made it difficult to free enslaved property. Virginia statutes of 1723 and 1741 declared it illegal for masters to free their slaves "except for some meritorious services, to be adjudged and allowed by the governor and council . . . and a licence thereupon first had and obtained." Despite the legal problems, by 1779 enough slaves had been emancipated that the Warrington and Fairfax Quarterly Meeting urged the monthly meetings to establish a new committee to ensure that Friends continued to provide aid to those they had freed.[37]

A few Patriot leaders praised the Quakers' emancipation schemes, but as the threat posed to human property by the war became apparent, most slaveholders viewed Friends' efforts as ill timed at best and treasonous at worse. Whenever the British army appeared in Virginia, thousands of slaves fled to the British lines, posing a grave threat to the continued stability of the institution. Indeed, Thomas Jefferson estimated that the state lost 30,000 slaves in 1781 alone, though recent historians have charged him with exaggerating this figure. Still, Jefferson's numbers point to the perceptions of slaveholders, their sense that slavery itself was under siege during the Revolutionary War. As Anglican minister and Tory Jonathan Boucher put it, the war forced Virginia slaveholders to confront the fact that "we have within ourselves an enemy fully equal to all our strength."[38] In this context, Quaker racial philanthropy posed one more threat to the precarious social order of the state. Thus it was little wonder that Patriot authorities focused on Friends when the state was under siege in the period 1780–1781.

Still, for northern Virginia's Quakers, racial philanthropy, though ultimately among their most striking and significant concerns, was part of a larger effort to secure a new public role for themselves. For local Friends, service to the broader community became a central way to put into action their spiritual principles of nonviolence and respect for all humanity while at the same time enabling them to make a positive contribution to the new civil society taking shape in Virginia. This could mean embracing unpopular causes. In 1778, Hopewell Friends, concerned that the first Quakers to settle in the valley had never properly reimbursed Native Americans for the land on which their meetinghouse sat, raised money for the benefit of the dispossessed Indians. "It becomes us as a religious society," the meeting noted, "to demonstrate that testimony of justice and uprightness which we have ever held forth." By June the meeting had raised £665 for distribution among the Indians, but neither Philadelphia nor Hopewell Friends could discover or agree upon which Indian nation lived on the land before Europeans moved into the region. Still, Quakers did not let the matter drop. During treaty negotiations with the U.S. government in the fall of 1794, the Tuscarora claimed to have resided in the Shenandoah Valley in the early eighteenth century. When Friends investigated the Indians' "ancient maps and documents," however, they remained unconvinced. Nonetheless, in 1796, the Baltimore Yearly Meeting—to which Friends in northern Virginia now belonged—gave a "considerable sum" to the Tuscarora, because they "entertained strong expectations of receiving a donation." More important, the Baltimore meeting used the remainder of the money raised by the Hopewell meeting to create a permanent committee assigned to work "for the service, & benefit of other Indians." Over the next fifty years the Indian committee provided money, agricultural supplies, and legal and practical advice to a number of Native American nations in upstate New York and the Old Northwest.[39]

Friends also realized, of course, that if such generosity were directed toward more popular causes, then it could help restore the good image of the society. Thus despite their economic problems, Friends generously provided aid to those who faced hardship as a result of the fighting or for other reasons. These efforts began almost as soon as violence erupted. In November 1775, after the British occupied Boston, the Philadelphia Yearly Meeting, to which Fairfax and Hopewell Friends belonged, sent almost 2,000 pounds to New England, to be distributed to all who suffered because of the conflict. Likewise, in April 1776, after the royal governor, Lord Dunmore, ordered his small military force to destroy Norfolk, local Quakers "collected . . . Provisions" for the "Use of such poor inhabitants" of the town "as may stand in need." Similar aid was extended by northern Virginia Quakers throughout the war. In the midst of their own suffering, then, northern Virginia Quakers turned their concerns outward, concurring with their brethren in North Carolina, who in 1779 concluded, "We hold it the duty of true Christians at all times to assist the distressed."[40]

After the war ended, providing aid to those who suffered remained a central theme of Quaker life in northern Virginia and throughout the nation. Out of the gauntlet of war, Friends achieved a new unity and strengthened their internal discipline. Forced by outsiders to define more clearly the meaning of their testimonies, particularly the peace testimony, they did so with vigor, disciplining and disowning those who failed to measure up. More important, Friends forged for themselves a novel role in the new United States. Once the Revolution ended, northern Virginia Quakers accepted the new state and federal governments, just as they had accepted British rule before 1776. But building on the precedent of their efforts during the war, they set as their task to become "a holy army" to fight for the good of the state and the nation by spreading virtue. This meant, of course, maintaining a strong peace testimony. But it also meant establishing schools that accepted the poor and free African Americans, providing social services for and defending the interests of the new nation's Indian population, and working to end slavery and to aid enslaved African Americans in northern Virginia and throughout the nation. Out of the social tensions of Virginia and the stresses of war, then, Quakers found for themselves a new public role: a conscience for the state and the nation.[41]

Notes

1. This incident is recorded in a variety of sources; see Thomas Gilpin, ed., *Exiles in Virginia: With Observations on the Conduct of the Society of Friends during the Revolutionary War* (Philadelphia, PA: Published for Subscribers, 1848), 181; Arthur J. Mekeel, *The Relation of the Quakers to the American Revolution* (Washington, DC: University Press of America, 1979), 264; Jay Worrall Jr., *The Friendly Virginians: America's First Quakers* (Athens, GA: Iberian, 1994), 214.

2. Other local studies of Quakers in the Revolution conclude that, with the exception of a small number of individuals, Friends' neutrality did not amount to Loyalism; see, for example, Dorothy Gilbert Thorne, "North Carolina Friends and the Revolution," *North Carolina Historical Review* 38 (1961): 323–40; Roger E. Sappington, "North Carolina and the Non-Resistant Sects during the American War of Independence," *Quaker History* 60 (1971): 29–47; Robert F. Oaks, "Philadelphians in Exile: The Problem of Loyalty during the American Revolution," *Pennsylvania Magazine of History and Biography* 96 (1972): 298–325; Steven Jay White, "Friends and the Coming of the Revolution," *The Southern Friend* 4 (1982): 16–27; Joseph S. Tiedemann, "Queens County, New York Quakers in the American Revolution: Loyalists or Neutrals?," *Historical Magazine of the Protestant Episcopal Church* 52 (1983): 215–27; Karen Guenther, "A Crisis of Allegiance: Berks County, Pennsylvania Quakers and the War for Independence," *Quaker History* 90 (2001): 15–34.

3. For an excellent summary of what historians have called a "consensus" view of the Revolution in Virginia, see John E. Selby, *The Revolution in Virginia, 1775–1783* (Williamsburg, VA: Colonial Williamsburg Foundation, 1988). For recent scholarship that emphasizes the divisions within Virginia society and the anxiety of the colony's gentry leaders, see Woody Holton, *Forced Founders: Indians, Debtors, Slaves, and the Making of the American Revolution* (Chapel Hill, NC: University of North Carlina Press, 1999); Michael A. McDonnell, "Popular Mobilization and Political Culture in Revolutionary Virginia: The Failure of the Minutemen and the Revolution from Below," *Journal of American History* 85 (1998): 946–81; McDonnell, "Class War? Class Struggles during the American Revolution in Virginia," *WMQ*, 3rd ser., 63 (2006): 305–44. For an older, "progressive" account that emphasizes the divisions within white Virginia society during the Revolution, see H. J. Eckenrode, *The Revolution in Virginia* (New York: Houghton Mifflin, 1916; rept., Hamden, CT: Archon Books, 1964), esp. 232–60.

4. This argument follows Sydney V. James, *A People among Peoples: Quaker Benevolence in Eighteenth-Century America* (Cambridge, MA: Havard University Press, 1963), esp. 240–334, and James, "The Impact of the American Revolution on Quakers' Ideas about Their Sect," *WMQ* 19 (1962): 360–82.

5. Worrall, *The Friendly Virginians*, 123–32, 203, 255–56, 263–64; Mekeel, *The Relation of the Quakers*, 2–3; Stephen Weeks, *Southern Quakers and Slavery: A Study in Institutional History* (1896; rept. New York: Berghman, 1968), 96–100, 328–44; William Wade Hinshaw, *Encyclopedia of American Quaker Genealogy*, 6 vols. (Ann Arbor, MI: Edwards Brothers, 1950), 6: 357–60, 463–66, 589, 609–14, 725–28; Howard Beeth, "Outside Agitators in Southern History: The Society of Friends, 1656–1800" (PhD dissertation, University of Houston, 1984), 19–95; Epistle of Virginia Friends to the Philadelphia Meeting for Sufferings, December 22, 1775, Philadelphia Meeting for Sufferings, Minutes, 1775–1785, 66, Friends Historical Library, Swarthmore College, Swarthmore, Pennsylvania (hereafter FHL).

6. George Fox, quoted in Thomas D. Hamm, *The Transformation of American Quakerism: Orthodox Friends, 1800–1907* (Bloomington, IN: Indiana University Press, 1988), 2; Fox, quoted in Frederick Tolles, *Meeting House and Counting House: The Quaker Merchants of Colonial Philadelphia, 1682–1763* (Chapel Hill, NC: University of

North Carolina Press, 1948), 9. See also Howard H. Brinton, *The Religious Philosophy of the Quakerism* (Wallingford, PA: Pendle Hill, 1973), 5–7; Peter Brock, *Pioneers of the Peaceable Kingdom: The Quaker Peace Testimony from the Colonial Era to the First World War* (Princeton, NJ: Princeton University Press, 1968), xi–xvi; Mekeel, *The Relation of the Quakers*, 2–3.

7. Isaac Penington, "A Brief Account of What the People Called Quakers Desire, in Reference to Civil Government," in *Works of the Long-Mournful and Sorely-Distressed Isaac Penington*, ed. B. Clark, 326–27 (London, 1681); Philadelphia Yearly Meeting, quoted in Mekeel, *The Relation of the Quakers*, 2–3, 9, n. 5; James, *A People among Peoples*, 243; Brock, *Pioneers*, xi–xvi. Obedience to secular governments remained a part of the Quaker discipline into the nineteenth century; see Baltimore Yearly Meeting Minutes, October 13–18, 1806, 244–45, FHL (Quakers in northern Virginia became part of the Baltimore Yearly Meeting in the mid-1780s).

8. The best overview of Quakers before the Revolution is Mekeel, *The Relation of the Quakers*, 1–83; see also Brock, *Pioneers*, 141–44.

9. Gertrude R. B. Richards, ed., "Dr. David Stuart's Report to President Washington on Agricultural Conditions in Northern Virginia," *Virginia Magazine of History and Biography* 61 (1953): 289; William Lee to Samuel Thorp, April 15, 1793, William Lee Letterbook, May 1792–May 1793, Virginia Historical Society, Richmond, Virginia (hereafter VHS). See also Worrall, *The Friendly Virginians*, 187–88, and A. Glenn Crothers, "Quaker Merchants and Slavery in Early National Alexandria, Virginia: The Ordeal of William Hartshorne," *Journal of the Early Republic* 25 (2005): 47–77.

10. Jean R. Soderlund, *Quakers & Slavery: A Divided Spirit* (Princeton, NJ: Princeton University Press, 1985); Thomas E. Drake, *Quakers and Slavery in America* (New Haven, CT: Yale University Press, 1950), 1–99; William Walter Hening, ed., *The Statutes at Large; Being a Collection of All the Laws of Virginia, from the . . . the Year 1619*, 13 vols. (Richmond, NY, and Philadelphia, PA: Samuel Pleasants, 1809–1823), 4: 132, 6: 112, 11: 39–40; Peter Joseph Albert, "The Protean Institution: The Geography, Economy, and Ideology of Slavery in Post-Revolutionary Northern Virginia" (PhD dissertation, University of Maryland, 1976), 168–74; Patrick Henry to Robert Pleasants, January 18, 1773, in Roger Bruns, ed., *Am I a Man and a Brother: The Antislavery Crusade of Revolutionary America, 1688–1788* (New York: Chelsea House, 1977), 221–22; Selby, *The Revolution in Virginia*, 321–22. As Selby notes, the act was progressively restricted until 1806, when the legislature required that manumitted slaves leave the state within a year of obtaining their freedom.

11. *Virginia Gazette*, February 10, 1774 (Rind), June 9, 1774, August 4, 1774 (Purdie and Dixon), July 7, 1775 (Purdie), September 29, 1774, May 18, 1775 (Pinkey), and June 16, 1775 (Purdie), July 29, 1775 (Dixon). Of course not all reports from these years were favorable. A May 1775 dispatch derided a pro-American Quaker petition to the king for "being couched in terms the most humiliating, breathing nothing but passive obedience, abject submission, and an utter aversion to justifiable resistance"; see *Virginia Gazette*, May 5, 1775 (Purdie).

12. The four major pronouncements of the Philadelphia Yearly Meeting, dated January 5 and 24, 1775, and January 20 and December 20, 1776, are most readily found in Gilpin, *Exiles*, 282–93; the second was reprinted in the *Virginia*

Gazette, March 2, 1775 (Pinkey). Samuel Adams, quoted in Mekeel, *The Relation of the Quakers*, 93–96, 136–40 (the quote is on p. 138, emphases in original); Brock, *Pioneers*, 144–47.

13. Thomas Paine, *Common Sense*, in *Thomas Paine: Collected Writings*, ed. Eric Foner, 54–59, emphases in original (New York: Library of America, 1995).

14. Testimony of the Philadelphia Yearly Meeting, October 4, 1777; Extract of a Letter from General Sullivan to Congress, August 25, 1777, in Gilpin, *Exiles*, 57–59, 61–62, 299; Sullivan to John Hancock, August 24, 1777, quoted in Mekeel, *The Relation of the Quakers*, 173–74; Pendleton to William Woodford, September 13, 1777, in *The Letters and Papers of Edmund Pendleton*, 2 vols., ed. David John Mays, 1: 223 (Charlottesville, VA: University Press of Virginia, 1967); *Virginia Gazette*, November 14, 1777 (Purdie), emphasis in original.

15. Mekeel, *The Relation of the Quakers*, 162–63; Brock, *Pioneers*, 147–48, 189–90; Philadelphia Meeting for Sufferings, "To Our Friends and Brethren in Religious Profession," December 20, 1776, in Gilpin, *Exiles*, 291–93.

16. Henry Drinker to Elizabeth Drinker, October 4, 14, 17, 23, November 4, and December 10, 1777, in Letters of Henry Drinker, Quaker Collection, Haverford College, Haverford, Pennsylvania. The full story of the Virginia exiles is told by Gilpin, *Exiles*, Oaks, "Philadelphians in Exile," 298–325 (map, pp. 319–20), and Mekeel, *The Relation of the Quakers*, 173–88.

17. Stephen L. Longnecker, *Shenandoah Religion: Outsiders and the Mainstream, 1716–1865* (Waco, TX: Baylor University Press, 2002), 53.

18. Edward Stabler to Israel Pemberton, May 16, 1775, Pemberton Papers, 1641–1880, Historical Society of Pennsylvania, Philadelphia; *Virginia Gazette*, February 11, 1775 (Dixon); Henrico Quarterly Meeting, February 2, 1775, quoted in Mekeel, *The Relation of the Quakers*, 103. For a good account of the effectiveness of the county committees of safety in Virginia, see Eckenrode, *The Revolution in Virginia*, 38, 96–122.

19. Holton, *Forced Founders*; McDonnell, "Popular Mobilization," "Class War?" Holton and McDonnell's scholarship builds on a variety of works focusing on the anxieties of the eighteenth-century Virginia gentry and the class and racial tensions that gripped the colony; see, for example, Rhys Isaac, *The Transformation of Virginia, 1740–1790* (Chapel Hill, NC: University of North Carolina Press, 1982); Isaac, *Landon Carter's Uneasy Kingdom: Revolution and Rebellion on a Virginia Plantation* (New York: Oxford University Press, 2004); T. H. Breen, *Tobacco Culture: The Mentality of the Great Tidewater Planters on the Eve of Revolution* (Princeton, NJ: Princeton University Press, 1985); James Titus, *The Old Dominion at War: Society, Politics, and Warfare in Late Colonial Virginia* (Columbia, SC: University of South Carolina Press, 1991); Kathleen M. Brown, *Good Wives, Nasty Wenches, and Anxious Patriarchs: Gender, Race, and Power in Colonial Virginia* (Chapel Hill, NC: University of North Carolina Press, 1996); Allan Kulikoff, *Tobacco and Slaves: The Development of Southern Cultures in the Chesapeake, 1680–1800* (Chapel Hill, NC: University of North Carolina Press, 1986). For black unrest in Virginia during the Revolution, see Sylvia Frey, *Water from the Rock: Black Resistance in a Revolutionary Age* (Princeton, NJ: Princeton University Press, 1991), 53–56, 63–64, 143–171; Benjamin Quarles, *The Negro in the American Revolution* (Chapel Hill, NC: University of North

Carolina Press, 1961), 19–32, 115–19, 111–33, 140–42. For detailed accounts of the British and German prisoners in the Shenandoah Valley, see Lion G. Miles, "The Winchester Hessian Barracks," *Winchester-Frederick County Historical Society Journal* 3 (1988): 19–63; George W. Knepper, "The Convention Army, 1777–1783," PhD dissertation, University of Michigan, 1954, 137–266.

20. Holton, *Forced Founders*, 175–88 (the Morlan quote is on p. 181); McDonnell, "Popular Mobilization," 970; Willard F. Bliss, "The Rise of Tenancy in Virginia," *Virginia Magazine of History and Biography* 58 (1950): 427–41.

21. Hening, *The Statutes at Large*, 8: 242–44; 9: 139, 345; A Narrative of the Sufferings of Members of the Hopewell Monthly Meeting, August 2, 1778, and A Narrative of . . . the Sufferings of Members of the Fairfax Monthly Meeting, August 25, 1779, both in Philadelphia Meeting for Sufferings, Miscellaneous Papers, 1770–1790 (unpaginated), FHL.

22. Hening, *The Statutes at Large*, 10: 261–62, 314–15, 334–35, 360–61, 417–18; Fairfax Monthly Meeting Minutes, December 27, 1777 (established committee on sufferings); Hopewell Monthly Meeting Minutes, January 5, 1778 (established committee on sufferings), FHL. The total figure is derived from the following reports: "An Account of Sufferings in the Fairfax Monthly Meeting," August 28, 1779; "An Account of Friends Sufferings in Loudoun County," May 26, 1781; "An Account of the Sufferings of Friends Belonging to Fairfax Monthly Meeting in Loudoun County, Virga," August 25, 1781; "An Account of the Sufferings of Friends Belonging to the Fairfax Mo. Meeting," February 23, 1782; "An Account of Friends Sufferings Belonging to and within the Verge of Hopewell Monthly Meeting," September 3, 1781; and "An Account of Friends Sufferings Belonging to Hopewell Monthly Meeting," May 30, 1782, all in Philadelphia Meeting for Sufferings, Miscellaneous Papers, 1771–1780, 1781–1790 (unpaginated), FHL. Mekeel, in *The Relation of the Quakers*, 263–65, reports a figure of over 5,000 pounds, but he presumably counts all of the meetings within the Fairfax and Warrington Quarterly Meeting, which included some Maryland and southern Pennsylvania monthly meetings. See also Worrall, *The Friendly Virginians*, 201–203.

23. "An Account of Sufferings in the Fairfax Monthly Meeting," August 28, 1779, Philadelphia Meeting for Sufferings, Miscellaneous Papers, 1771–1780 (unpaginated); and "An Account of the Sufferings of Friends at Fairfax Monthly Meeting," September 21, 1780, Philadelphia Meeting for Sufferings, Minute Book, 1775–1785, 290–91, FHL. On the problems of obtaining a "proper & explicit Account" of Friends' sufferings in Fairfax and Hopewell meetings, see Philadelphia Meeting for Sufferings, Minute Book, 1775–1785, February 1, 1781, 299, and September 18, 1784, 430–32. According to the Philadelphia meeting, Hopewell submitted a summary of sufferings between 1777 and 1779, but it is not extant in the records.

24. McDonnell, "Popular Mobilization," 974–81; McDonnell, "Class War?," 337–39. The legislature's failing at raising troops and supplies in 1779 and 1780 is documented in Selby, *The Revolution in Virginia*, 204–85.

25. Garrett Van Meter to Thomas Jefferson, April 11, 14, 20, June 16, 1781; Van Meter to Thomas Nelson, July 28, 1781; Peter Hog to Thomas Nelson, August 2, 1781, in *Calendar of Virginia State Papers and Other Manuscripts, from April 1,*

1781 to December 31, 1781, Preserved at the Capitol at Richmond, vol. 2, ed. Sherwin McRae, 28–29, 40–41, 58–59, 163–64, 262–63, 284–85 (Richmond, VA: Secretary of the Commonwealth of Virginia and State Library, 1881). See also Eckenrode, *The Revolution in Virginia*, 246–48; Samuel Kercheval, *A History of the Valley of Virginia*, 4th ed. (Strasburg, VA: W. N. Grabill, 1925), 144–46; James Graham, *The Life of General Daniel Morgan, of the Virginia Line of the Army of the United States* (New York: Derby and Jackson, 1859), 378–81.

    26. Daniel Morgan to George Washington, November 25, 1781, George Washington Papers at the Library of Congress, 1741–1799: Ser. 4, General Correspondence, 1697–1799, http://www.memory.loc.gov/; Morgan to Benjamin Harrison, December 11, 1781, *Calendar of Virginia State Papers*, 2: 646–47. On the fluctuating number of British and German prisoners outside of Winchester and the location of the barracks, see Miles, "Hessian Barracks," passim. Frederick County had no record of widespread Loyalism. As historian Freeman H. Hart noted, "There were few . . . actual Tories" in the county or the Valley, and thus few groups other than the Quakers who fit Morgan's description; see Hart, *The Valley of Virginia in the American Revolution* (Chapel Hill, NC: University of North Carolina Press, 1942), 107.

    27. This and the following paragraph are based on "An Account of Sufferings in the Fairfax Monthly Meeting," August 28, 1779; "An Account of Friends Sufferings in Loudoun County," May 26, 1781; "An Account of the Sufferings of Friends Belonging to Fairfax Monthly Meeting in Loudoun County, Virga," August 25, 1781; "An Account of the Sufferings of Friends Belonging to the Fairfax Mo. Meeting," February 23, 1782; "An Account of Friends Sufferings Belonging to and within the Verge of Hopewell Monthly Meeting," September 3, 1781; and "An Account of Friends Sufferings Belonging to Hopewell Monthly Meeting," May 30, 1782, all in Philadelphia Meeting for Sufferings, Miscellaneous Papers, 1771–1780, 1781–1790 (unpaginated), FHL; Kercheval, *A History of the Valley of Virginia*, 148.

    28. Kercheval, *A History of the Valley of Virginia*, 148.

    29. Hopewell Monthly Meetings, 1775–1783, passim; Fairfax Monthly Meetings, 1775–1783, passim (both FHL); *Virginia Gazette*, June 16, 1775 (Purdie); Mekeel, *The Relation of the Quakers*, 131–32, 283–93; Worrall, *The Friendly Virginians*, 194–96, 203.

    30. Mekeel, *The Relation of the Quakers*, 192, 266; Brock, *Pioneers*, 167–69, 171–72.

    31. Epistle of Virginia Friends to Philadelphia Meeting for Sufferings, December 22, 1775; Epistle of the Philadelphia Meeting for Sufferings to the Virginia Yearly Meeting, March 25, 1776, in Philadelphia Meeting for Sufferings Minute Book, 1775–1785, 60, 71–73; Letter from the Virginia Yearly Meeting and Fairfax Monthly Meeting Regarding the Payment of War Taxes and Use of Continental Currency, December 22, 1775, Philadelphia Meetings for Sufferings, Miscellaneous Papers, 1771–1780 (unpaginated), FHL, see also Mekeel, *The Relation of the Quakers*, 150–51; Worrall, *The Friendly Virginians*, 196.

    32. Fairfax Monthly Meeting, May 22, 1784, February 27, 1779 (FHL); Worrall, *The Friendly Virginians*, 217–18; Weeks, *Southern Quakers*, 189; Brock, *Pioneers*, 168–69, 172–73; Mekeel, *The Relation of the Quakers*, 192; Pleasants, quoted in

Adair P. Archer, "The Quaker's Attitude towards the Revolution," *The WMQ*, 2nd ser., 1 (1921): 179.

33. Brock, *Pioneers*, 162–64; Mekeel, *The Relation of the Quakers*, 189–90, 193, 271–72, 336.

34. Hening, *The Statutes at Large*, 9: 281–83, 351, 549; Warrington and Fairfax Quarterly Meeting, June 22, 1778 (FHL); Fairfax Monthly Meeting, March 23, 1782 (FHL).

35. Hopewell Monthly Meeting, September 4, 1780–November 3, 1783, passim; Fairfax Monthly Meeting, March 27, 1779–February 22, 1783, passim (FHL).

36. Mifflin, quoted in Brock, *Pioneers*, 212; Fairfax Monthly Meeting, March 25, 1775–September 28, 1782, passim (FHL).

37. Fairfax Monthly Meeting, June 26, July 31, 1762, October 25, November 22, December 27, 1777, February 28, March 28, April 25, May 23, 1778 (Taylor); August 27, 1774 (statement against slavery); July 25, 1778 (lack of progress); Hening, *The Statutes at Large*, 4: 132, 6: 112. For a fuller discussion of the efforts of northern Virginia's Quakers to end slavery within their meetings see Crothers, "Quaker Merchants."

38. Frey, *Water from the Rock*, 53–56, 63–64, 68, 143–71, 222, n. 22; Thomas Jefferson to Alexander McCaul, April 19, 1786, in Julian P. Boyd et al., eds., *The Papers of Thomas Jefferson*, 32 vols. (Princeton, NJ: Princeton University Press, 1950–2007), 9: 388–90; Boucher quoted in Carl Degler, *Place over Time: The Continuity of Southern Distinctiveness* (Baton Rouge, LA: Louisiana State University Press, 1977), 28. See also Quarles, *Negro in the Revolution*, 19–32, 115–19, 111–33, 140–42; Holton, *Forced Founders*, 133–63. For a critical look at Jefferson's numbers, see Cassandra Pybus, "Jefferson's Faulty Math: The Question of Slave Defections in the American Revolution," *The William Mary Quarterly*, 3rd ser., 62 (2005): 243–64. Pybus estimates that together Virginia and Maryland slaveholders lost approximately 6,000 slaves between 1775 and 1781 (258–59).

39. James, "Impact of the Revolution," 369–77; *The Life and Travels of John Pemberton, A Minister of the Gospel*, in *The Friends' Library: Comprising Journals, Doctrinal Treatises, and Other Writings of Members of the Religious Society of Friends*, 14 vols. (Philadelphia, PA: Joseph Rakestraw, 1837–1850), 6: 294; *Hopewell Friends History, 1734–1934: Records of the Hopewell Monthly Meetings and Meetings Reporting to Hopewell* (Strasburg, VA: Shenandoah, 1936), 123–24; Samuel Janney, *History of the Religious Society of Friends, From Its Rise to the Year 1828*, vol. 3 (Philadelphia, PA: T. Ellwood Zell, 1867), 440–41 (quote); *A Journal of the Life, Travels and Religious Labours of William Savery, a Minister of the Gospel of Christ, in the Society of Friends, Late of Philadelphia*, in *Friends' Library*, 1: 354, 363–66; Gerald T. Hopkins, *A Mission to the Indians, from the Indians, from the Indian Committee of Baltimore Yearly*.

40. Mekeel, *The Relation of the Quakers*, 294–313; *Virginia Gazette*, April 13, 1776 (Dixon); Fairfax Monthly Meeting, March 25, 1775–September 28, 1782, passim (FHL); Thorne, "North Carolina Friends," 339 (quote).

41. James, "Impact of the Revolution," 377–82.

CHAPTER 5

"Faithful Allies of the King"

The Crown's Haudenosaunee Allies in the Revolutionary Struggle for New York

Robert W. Venables

The Indians were a free People Subject to no Power on Earth, that they were the faithful Allies of the King of England, but not his Subjects.[1]

The American Revolution was a civil war for the Haudenosaunee, just as it was for the colonists. During the Revolutionary War in New York, most of the Indian allies of the Crown were warriors from the Haudenosaunee—the "Six Nations" or "Iroquois Confederacy" (Mohawks, Oneidas, Onondagas, Cayugas, Senecas, and Tuscaroras). But there were Haudenosaunee on the Patriot side as well, primarily Oneidas and Tuscaroras. Moreover, many Haudenosaunee, including most of the Onondagas and a large number of Cayugas, remained neutral until 1779, when Patriot invasions of Haudenosaunee country impelled them to choose the British side.

This chapter examines the events and forces that influenced those Haudenosaunee who sided with the British either during the early years of the war or by the end of 1779. These Haudenosaunee were caught up in a frontier war that often resulted in horrific violence carried out by both sides. This was especially true following the brutal Battle of Oriskany, which took place on August 6, 1777, at the western end of the Mohawk Valley. Both sides subsequently perceived the other as an implacable enemy. Inevitably, noncombatants on the eastern frontier of the Haudenosaunee—the New York frontier—increasingly became victims to the war's ferocity. The Patriots claimed that the pro-British Haudenosaunee began the killing of noncombatants. But the situation, as this chapter will show, was more complicated. As happens in most, if not all, wars, the combatants on both sides became convinced that their actions were rational responses to events, and that "the other side" had been the first to commit atrocities. Historian Howard Swiggett, in his 1933 *War Out of Niagara*, summarized his view of the atrocities committed during what he called "the partisan fighting" on the Haudenosaunee frontier by placing that frontier war within the broader context of human history: "It certainly may be stated that frontiersmen in all wars and countries sanction conduct against colored races which they religiously condemn and ruthlessly take revenge for when employed against themselves."[2]

English historian John Buchan, in his preface for *War Out of Niagara*, candidly noted how difficult it can be for any nation's citizens to understand the perception of those who lost a major war against their nation, and how civil wars are even more difficult to frame historically: "In a civil war the loser is in a worse case, for the cause he opposed has become the cherished loyalty of a nation, and opposition to it is felt to carry a moral as well as an intellectual stigma."[3]

During the Revolution, no Haudenosaunee faction was ever entirely defeated. Although those Oneidas, Tuscaroras, and others who fought on the Patriot side were driven from their homes by pro-British Haudenosaunee

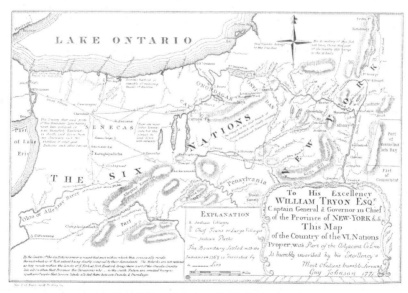

**Figure 5.1 Map of the Province of New York, 1771,
Showing the Country of the Six Nations**

Figure 5.1 Map of the Country of the VI Nations, 1771

in 1780, they reoccupied their homelands.[4] Even the Patriots' devastating invasions of Haudenosaunee country in 1779, under General John Sullivan, ended in the Patriots' withdrawal from all of the Haudenosaunee territory they had invaded. The Patriots also failed to capture Fort Niagara, the British base that supplied the pro-British Haudenosaunee. Pro-British warriors continued fighting until the end of the war, at which time the Patriots did not occupy any Haudenosaunee lands west of the line drawn by the British at the Treaty of Fort Stanwix (1768), the treaty that both the British and the Haudenosaunee believed had established the western boundary of New York.[5] Nevertheless, the terms of the 1783 Treaty of Paris stated that the new United States could claim the right of preemption over the entire Haudenosaunee homeland.[6] "Preemption" was not synonymous with "sovereignty" but meant only that the United States had the exclusive right, superceding the claims of any European nation, to negotiate land transactions with the Indians located in the geographical limits defined in the 1783 Treaty of Paris. By the end of 1797, both pro-Patriot Haudenosaunee and pro-British Haudenosaunee had been forced to give up almost all of their lands in what is now New York State.[7]

Why Were Many Haudenosaunee "Faithful Allies of the King"?

The Haudenosaunee who sided with the Crown were motivated by some of the same reasons shared by those whites and blacks who also fought for King George III. But those Haudenosaunee who sided with Britain had additional reasons, reasons that white and black Loyalists did not share:

1. Haudenosaunee national interest: The British were perceived to be more inclined to be willing to stop illegal white settlement, whereas the Patriots appeared to be more likely to violate treaties and to permit illegal settlers to continue to encroach on Haudenosaunee lands, including those in New York, in north central and western Pennsylvania, and in eastern Ohio.[8]

2. The Covenant Chain: This was the metaphor for the economic, political, and military alliance the Haudenosaunee had forged first with the Dutch and then with the English. The term "Covenant Chain" was used from 1677 onward.[9]

3. Economics: The British could supply more trade goods than the Patriots.[10]

4. Friendship: Prewar personal friendships between British Indian Department officials and the Haudenosaunee reinforced wartime loyalty to the Crown. Among the influential whites were Sir William Johnson, superintendent of Indian affairs until his death in 1774; Sir William's son, Sir John; Sir William's nephew, Guy; Daniel Claus; and John Butler.[11]

5. The Patriot invasions of 1779: The "Sullivan campaign" destroyed neutral as well as pro-British Haudenosaunee towns and impelled the neutrals to ally with the British.[12]

Haudenosaunee Society at the Outbreak of the Revolution

Haudenosaunee towns were originally composed of multifamily longhouses of arched saplings and bark coverings. Within each longhouse, everyone was related directly or by marriage to the eldest female resident. By the Revolution, these longhouses had virtually disappeared and had been replaced by smaller cabins, primarily because the Haudenosaunee realized that living in multifamily buildings spread epidemic diseases such as smallpox far too quickly. The few longhouses that survived were primarily for religious ceremonies and political meetings. The first cabins were made of bark mounted on a lattice of saplings, but they were eventually constructed of horizontally placed logs, not unlike those of their white frontier neighbors.[13]

Although Haudenosaunee society had been complex before white contact, it was even more so after the introduction of European trade goods. Guns and kettles were the obvious trade goods that changed daily life. But other goods had a more subtle effect on Haudenosaunee culture. For example, by 1634, the Mohawk longhouses had "interior doors made of split planks furnished with iron hinges."[14] These additions undoubtedly altered the personal interactions of the traditional extended family that lived within each longhouse. Spiritual worldviews also became more complex with the introduction of Christianity. By the time of the Revolution, most Mohawks were Christian: Catholic, if they lived in the St. Lawrence Valley, and Anglican, if they lived in the Mohawk Valley. Most of the Onondagas, Cayugas, and Senecas still followed the traditional religion of their ancestors. Many Oneidas and Tuscaroras were Presbyterians. In many cases, those Haudenosaunee who held Christian beliefs also maintained at least some traditional religious teachings.

Haudenosaunee warriors could not march into war without the women's support because agriculture was primarily the domain of the women who grew the crops and preserved the meats and other foods vital to war parties. The Haudenosaunee landscape was a balance. Women tended "The Clearings," which included the towns, homes, and extensive communal fields. Men hunted in "the Woods."[15] The Haudenosaunee, whether traditional or Christian, were matrilineal, and the women alone selected the male civil or "peace" chiefs. The powers of the male civil chiefs were balanced by those of the clan mothers, prominent female leaders who could, after consulting with the other women in their respective clans, veto the chiefs and even remove a chief from office. War chiefs were temporary positions held by outstanding warriors such as the Mohawk Joseph Brant (Thayendanegea), whose leadership was dependent upon recognition by both the women and the warriors. Joseph Brant's power was enhanced by the influence of his sister, Molly (Mary) Brant (Konwatsitsiaienni, meaning "Someone lends her a flower"), the wife of the late Sir William Johnson, superintendent of Indian Affairs.[16]

During the Revolution the pro-British Haudenosaunee were defending an agricultural lifestyle based on extensive cornfields, a lifestyle that represented more than 1,000 years of maize (corn) agriculture. Moreover, this agricultural lifestyle was knitted to Haudenosaunee traditional religion, which included specific ceremonies that marked the agricultural cycle from planting to harvest. When Patriot armies invaded Haudenosaunee country in 1779, the soldiers were amazed to see the extensive and flourishing fields in a fine countryside.[17] There also were clear adaptations of European life: apple and peach orchards, small herds of cattle, and horses. The interiors of Haudenosaunee cabins, from the Mohawk Valley westward to Seneca country, included tables, chairs, and beds, much like their white frontier neighbors. Archaeological excavations of eighteenth-century Seneca town sites in what is now western New York have unearthed German stoneware bottles as well as Delft-styled ceramics from both the Netherlands and England. The furnishings also reflected traditional Haudenosaunee culture and included objects such as beautifully carved wooden ladles and spoons as well as religious items such as turtle rattles.[18]

An extensive range of trade goods was described in 1761 as goods "usually sold to the Indians." In addition to muskets, metal tomahawks, knives, and rum, these goods included "Pewter Spoons"; "Gilt Gill [four-ounce] Cups"; "Red Leather trunks"; "Brass & tinn Kettles large & Small"; "Linnens & ready made Shirts, of all Sizes"; "Calicoes"; "Women & Childrens Worsted and Yarn Hose with [an ornamental pattern known as] Clocks"; silver broaches and other ornaments; both fine and coarse woolen blankets; needles; awls; "Jews Harps small & large"; "Brass Wire different Sizes"; "Scizars & Razors"; "Looking Glasses"; clay tobacco pipes; and "Tobacco, & Snuff boxes."[19]

Trade items had become necessities, not luxuries. In 1770, General Thomas Gage, the British commander in chief, reported that "Our

Manufactures are as much desired by the Indians, as their Peltry is sought for by us; what was originaly [sic] deemed a Superfluity or a Luxury to the Natives is now become a Necessary; They are disused to the Bow, and can neither hunt nor make war, without Fire-Arms, Powder, and Lead."[20]

The Onondagas, the Cayugas, and the Senecas all lived in towns west of the 1768 colonial boundary of New York. But some Oneidas and virtually all of the Mohawks in the Mohawk Valley were interspersed among more numerous white settlements in a checkerboard settlement pattern.[21]

Since the early decades of the seventeenth century, the Mohawks had been boldly experimenting, altering their society by continually adapting European technology and ideas (including Christianity).[22] Among the Mohawks in the Mohawk Valley, there were a few stone houses in addition to the usual log cabins. Because the Mohawks were surrounded by whites, who had extensive cattle herds, the Mohawks had begun to fence in their cornfields to protect them from the cattle. Rather than planting corn, beans, and squash in the small mounds of earth that was a Haudenosaunee tradition, they adapted the white agricultural custom of plowing their lands, with the men assuming this responsibility.[23] Mohawk Joseph Brant ran a store to sell and trade European goods to both Indians and whites. His sister, Molly Brant, also was a trader and had a home at Canajoharie furnished with items such as twelve black chairs, fine ceramic tableware, and linen. She possessed silk dresses and jewelry of gold and silver. She also owned four black slaves—two men and two women. Her wealth, which included a herd of cattle, was a reflection of her status as the wife of the late Sir William Johnson, and she may also have been a clan mother.[24]

A Sovereign People

The Haudenosaunee also were defending their firm belief that they were a sovereign people, thus those who sided with the British considered themselves "allies," not "subjects," of George III. The British also considered them allies, not subjects. Prior to the Revolution, on October 7, 1772, General Thomas Gage wrote to Sir William Johnson, the Indian superintendent for the northern colonies: "As for the Six Nations having acknowledged themselves Subjects of the English, that I conclude must be a very gross Mistake and am well satisfied were they [the Haudenosaunee] told so, they would not be well pleased. I know I would not venture to treat them as Subjects, unless there was a Resolution to make War upon them, which is not very likely to happen, but I believe they would on such an attempt, very soon resolve to cut our Throats."[25]

Reinforcing this sense of Haudenosaunee sovereignty was the fact that most Haudenosaunee lands lay west of the colony of New York. At the Treaty of Fort Stanwix (1768), Sir William Johnson and negotiators for the Haudenosaunee had specifically defined the western boundary of colonial New York as a line running from Fort Stanwix south to the northern border of Pennsylvania, then to the southwest, and then along almost the entire length of the Ohio River. British officials made it very clear that the treaty was intended to separate New York from most of the Haudenosaunee lands. On August 17, 1768, General Gage wrote to Lord Hillsborough: "The Congress with the Six Nations, and Indians of Ohio, for the Settlement of the general Boundary, is expected to be held sometime next Month . . . so as to form Limits between the Six Nations, and [the] Province of New-York, [otherwise] the Indians will not be Secure, and the Affair of the Boundary defeated, in its principal Object."[26]

Because the Haudenosaunee regarded themselves as sovereign, most initially attempted to remain neutral when the Revolution began. Even after many warriors joined the British in 1777, Haudenosaunee leaders maintained that the confederacy was sovereign. They believed they were adhering to an old political and economic alliance that had been established more than a century earlier: the Covenant Chain. Mohawk leader Joseph Brant recalled in 1803 how the pro-British Haudenosaunee had "reflected upon the covenant of our forefathers as allies to the King, and said, 'It will not do for us to break it, let what will become of us.' "[27]

The Struggle for Neutrality

In 1775, although many young Haudenosaunee were ready for battle, the Haudenosaunee as a confederacy remained neutral. On the one hand, Haudenosaunee diplomats assured Guy Johnson, the superintendent of Indian Affairs for the northern colonies, of their loyalty to the king in a conference at Oswego in July 1775. Then, at conferences in Albany during September and at Fort Pitt in October, Haudenosaunee delegates assured Patriot commissioners that they would remain neutral. For the moment, most Haudenosaunee chose to see the conflict as the Continental Congress viewed it, as a "family quarrel" in which they had no real interest.[28]

A major problem, however, was that the Patriots would not abide by the Treaty of Fort Stanwix (1768) or the Treaty of Pittsburgh (1775). White frontiersmen, who also claimed to be Patriots, continued to seize Haudenosaunee lands in western Pennsylvania and Ohio. In addition, old tensions continued between Mohawk Haudenosaunee and Patriot families, such as the land-grabbing Klock family in the Mohawk Valley. But not all of the impetus was toward the British. For example, the Reverend Samuel Kirkland sowed pro-Patriot fervor among the Oneidas. When the Patriot armies of Richard Montgomery and Benedict Arnold invaded Canada in August and September 1775, some Kahnawake Catholic Mohawks helped the Patriots, while some Protestant Mohawks from the Mohawk Valley fought on the British side, including William of Canajoharie (Tagawirunte), the son of Molly Brant and the late Sir William Johnson. The Patriots failed to take Canada during the winter of 1775–1776, and a British counteroffensive was launched during the summer and fall of 1776. British negotiations with some of the Haudenosaunee at Fort Niagara in September 1776 clearly indicated that many of them were pro-British. But all would depend upon the success or failure of the British counteroffensive under Sir Guy Carleton that moved southward onto Lake Champlain, an area the British recognized legally as a part of Mohawk territory. Some Mohawks were among the Indian contingent that accompanied the British, who won victories at Valcour Bay on October 11 and at Split Rock on October 13. However, these actions slowed the British advance, and Carleton chose not to attempt to capture Fort Ticonderoga, let alone Albany. Although the Patriots had abandoned Crown Point, the British withdrew further north to St. John's on the Richelieu River. Because neither the British nor the Patriots were able to gain a clear advantage, most Haudenosaunee continued their neutrality during the second winter of revolution, 1776–1777.[29]

In the early months of 1777, the British secured the support of most of the Mohawk and Seneca warriors, partly because members of the northern Indian Department—including ardent Loyalists such as Guy Johnson, Sir John Johnson, John Butler, and Daniel Claus—had earned the Haudenosaunee' friendship and respect after years and even decades of personal contact. Personalities, however, were not the only factor in the Haudenosaunee decision. Most Haudenosaunee, despite their hopes of neutrality, were induced to enter into an alliance with the British because of their need for European trade goods. During the summer of 1776, after the Patriot armies had been driven from the St. Lawrence Valley, the Haudenosaunee were still not receiving sufficient British supplies to meet their needs, because most British ships arriving in Canada brought only military reinforcements. The Patriots also were unable to supply adequate goods to the Haudenosaunee, because the Continental Congress remained short of funds. The Patriots were placed in an even worse commercial position in September 1776, when General William Howe captured New York City, the major port of entry for the Haudenosaunee trade. During the winter of 1776–1777, the Haudenosaunee situation became desperate. They needed clothing, and they needed food because they had no powder and lead for hunting. The British

found themselves in an excellent position to use trade and presents to bring
the Haudenosaunee to their side. By now the British completely controlled
the St. Lawrence route to the Haudenosaunee from Quebec to Fort Niagara.
In addition, many Mohawk Haudenosaunee were already committed to the
British and proved to be useful persuaders. Early in 1777 the British were
able to distribute a few articles to the Haudenosaunee by appropriating some
of the military supplies brought over to help secure Canada. These supplies
were not sufficient to fill the Indians' needs, but because the Patriots could
offer even less, the British consignment was enough to retain the Haudenosaunee. The British also promised future deliveries of blankets and guns.
In exchange, they did not ask for furs; they requested military assistance,
and individual Haudenosaunee responded.[30]

Between 1775 and 1776, individual warriors took opposite sides. Then,
in the winter of 1776–1777, an epidemic swept through the Confederacy's
capital, Onondaga, killing ninety, including three chiefs. The surviving chiefs
covered the Confederacy's council fire at Onondaga in January 1777, signify-
ing that individual warriors and women throughout the entire Confederacy
could make their own choices of alliance.[31] Because of the "confederate"
nature of the Haudenosaunee, the warriors and their supporters had this
right to choose. Therefore, legally and literally, the Confederacy remained
politically neutral, even as increasing numbers of warriors and women chose
a particular side.

1777: Turning Points

More than a century of political treaties, the economic ties of the "Covenant Chain," and a dependence upon European trade goods were evoked
by British officials who sought to bring the Haudenosaunee into the war.
Indian Superintendent Guy Johnson had spent the winter of 1775–1776 in
London learning how the Privy Council expected him to use Indian allies.
With him on this mission was one of the most important Haudenosaunee
leaders, Joseph Brant, educated at the Reverend Eleazar Wheelock's Indian
mission school in Lebanon, Connecticut, where he had studied Hebrew,
Greek, Latin, the sciences, the arts, and European manners. Brant was literate in both Mohawk and English, and he was a Mason in the lodge located
in Johnson Hall. Brant and Johnson were told to utilize Indians only in
formal military expeditions.[32]

The first opportunity to use large numbers of pro-British Haudenosaunee
came during the summer of 1777. In order to capture all of New York and
split the colonies, an army led by General John Burgoyne marched south
from Canada to capture Albany and the upper Hudson Valley. At the same

time, an army under Colonel Barry St. Leger was to march on Albany from
the west, moving from Oswego and then eastward down the Mohawk Valley.
One thousand Haudenosaunee and Canadian Mississaugas joined St. Leger's
army of 700 regulars, German mercenaries, and Loyalists at Oswego. These
Haudenosaunee and Mississaugas, as well as a few from other Canadian
Indian nations, were led by their various chiefs, by Joseph Brant, and by
John Butler, an experienced Indian Department officer. Their first objective
was Fort Stanwix, the major Patriot defense guarding the western approach
to the Mohawk Valley (and ironically the site of the 1768 treaty that drew
a firm boundary line between colonists and the Haudenosaunee). During the
ensuing siege, the Haudenosaunee warriors were accompanied by their wives
and other female relatives. The warriors intended to serve mainly as scouts
and spectators to a great victory brought about by the soldiers and their
artillery. Then, on August 5, three days after the siege began, a Patriot relief
column of 800 militia under General Nicholas Herkimer was reported to be
marching toward the fort. Herkimer's Patriots were accompanied by about
sixty Oneida Haudenosaunee scouts. The Oneida Haudenosaunee presence
on the Patriot side and the formidable number of other Haudenosaunee
on the British side were clear declarations that conflicting debates within
the Confederacy had resulted in conflicting choices. Joseph Brant's sister,
Molly, sent messengers from her home at Canajoharie in the Mohawk Valley, warning of the approaching Patriots. The warriors decided to fight the
Patriot reinforcements in order to save the campaign.[33]

On August 6, 1777, about 450 Haudenosaunee, plus Hanau Jägers,
Loyalist Rangers, and Loyalist infantry, executed an ambush at Oriskany. They
might have wiped out the Patriot relief force had the trapped Patriots not
been stubborn and courageous fighters. The Battle of Oriskany underscored the
fact that the Revolution also had become a Haudenosaunee civil war. While
about 450 Haudenosaunee warriors were allied with the Crown (primarily
Mohawks and Senecas, along with a few Cayugas and Onondagas), about
sixty Oneida Haudenosaunee warriors fought alongside the Patriots.[34]

The fighting was horrific. Decades after Oriskany, the Seneca, Théwonyas (Chainbreaker, after 1812 known as Blacksnake), dictated his rec-
ollections to a younger Seneca, Benjamin Williams, who wrote down the
old man's words in the young Seneca's own imperfect English. Describing
the Battle of Oriskany, Théwonyas noted that the warriors had decided to
begin the battle by firing one volley at the Patriot militia and then "run
amongst them . . . while we [were] Doing of it, feels no more [than] to Kill
the Beast . . . [but I was nearly killed] by the Speare in the End of musket
[bayonet], that I had to Denfended mysilfe. . . . During all the afternoon, But
take tomehawk and knifes and Swords to cut Down men with it, there I
have Seen the most Dead Bodies all it over that I never Did see, and never

will again I thought at that time the Blood Shed a Stream Running Down on the Decending ground."[35]

After a terrible slaughter, the warriors believed that they had both inflicted and suffered enough casualties. They pulled back, followed by their allies. The Patriot forces gathered their survivors and likewise retreated. The Battle of Oriskany ended in an exhausted stalemate. The Haudenosaunee and their white allies had accomplished their objective and prevented the Patriot army from reaching the fort. However, the Haudenosaunee had not expected such stout resistance. Though the Patriots suffered higher casualties with at least 200 killed, Haudenosaunee losses were about sixty-five, including some favorite warriors and chiefs.[36] When the Haudenosaunee learned that another Patriot relief column was coming toward them, they refused to continue the siege of Fort Stanwix and withdrew westward toward Lake Ontario. Without Indian allies, British Commander Barry St. Leger was forced to retreat.

After Oriskany, pro-Patriot Oneidas and Tuscaroras, together with a few Onondagas, traveled east to fight the British army of General John Burgoyne.[37] On October 27, pro-Patriot Oneida warriors arrived at the Confederacy's capital of Onondaga with the news that Burgoyne's army had been defeated and had surrendered at Saratoga. This encouraged the considerable neutral faction among the Onondagas. The Onondaga chief, Black Cap (Tehonwaghsloweaghte), a friend of the pro-Patriot missionary among the Oneidas, the Reverend Samuel Kirkland, sent a message to the Patriot commander, General Horatio Gates, who had accepted Burgoyne's surrender at Saratoga: "We have long expected it would be his [Burgoyne's] fate, as he talked very proudly among all the Indians, and told what he would do to the Americans—he despised them. The army [St. Leger's] he sent against Fort Schuyler [the Patriot name for Fort Stanwix] spake [sic] very insolently—quite too proud— . . . but now the proud are brought low: this is right."[38]

Strikes and Counterstrikes

For the remainder of the war, both the pro-British and the pro-Patriot Haudenosaunee remembered their losses at Oriskany with vendetta fervor.[39] Furthermore, after Oriskany, the pro-British Haudenosaunee had no choice but to fight a guerilla war, because the British refused to assign a major regular army to fight alongside them. Seneca raids into Pennsylvania from September to December 1777 killed a number of Pennsylvania settlers near Ligonier and on the upper Susquehanna near Wyalusing in raids that further inflamed Patriot sentiments against all Indians.[40]

After 1777, the British encouraged the Haudenosaunee to conduct raids on civilian areas with the justification that the civilians produced foodstuffs that fed Patriot troops. The Patriots also were ready, if not quite able, to destroy Haudenosaunee civilian areas on the New York frontier. Philip Schuyler was finally able to hold a council in Johnstown in March 1778, but no Senecas attended, and only a few Cayugas were present. Demanding that the Haudenosaunee maintain neutrality, Schuyler warned that the Patriots would avenge any future hostilities by attacking Haudenosaunee country, a speech that was authorized by the Continental Congress. After the council, Schuyler wrote to the president of the Continental Congress, Henry Laurens, on March 15, 1778. He suggested that in order to prevent Indian raids on Patriot settlements, the Patriots should strike first, attacking Haudenosaunee towns. He believed that this first strike would not require any more troops than would otherwise be necessary to defend the frontier settlements. The Patriot dilemma became vivid when a Loyalist and Haudenosaunee raid, led by Joseph Brant, struck Cobleskill on May 30, 1778, destroying eleven houses and killing many of the settlement's civilian militia as well as some Patriot Continental soldiers. In June, Congress appropriated funding—about $932,743—for two major expeditions. The first would be launched against the Senecas and commanded by Horatio Gates. The second would attack the British post at Detroit. Even though the appropriations were made, no expeditions were actually launched.[41] Thus in the summer and fall of 1778, only the pro-British Haudenosaunee were able to carry out their extensive plans. When Patriot expeditions were finally launched in 1779, the actions took on the appearance of justified retaliations, when actually the Patriots would have been just as willing to have initiated such warfare.

The British hoped to prevent civilian casualties by having rangers fight alongside the Indians. On September 15, 1777, official approval was given to a corps of white rangers under Colonel John Butler, a corps that had already served at Oriskany in August.[42] The May 1778 raid on Cobleskill had already resulted not only in the deaths of Patriot Continental soldiers but also of Patriot civilians who were under arms as militia. Were the Patriot civilians who died defending their homes civilians or combatants? The question is as old as warfare and as recent as today's headlines.

The Battle of Wyoming

Haudenosaunee leaders such as Joseph Brant were determined to do their best to prevent casualties among noncombatant civilians. But the major test of the British-Haudenosaunee strategy to coordinate Haudenosaunee and white fighters and to prevent as many civilian casualties as possible came in the summer of 1778. Intent on destroying a major Patriot wheat crop, 400 Haudenosaunee and 100 Loyalist rangers swept down on the Wyoming Valley in the Susquehanna River region of Pennsylvania in July 1778. Among the Haudenosaunee were Gahkoondenoiya (Onondaga), Ojagehte (Juggeta, Fish Carrier, Cayuga), Sagwarithra (Tuscarora), Seqyudonquee (Little Beard, Seneca), Sagoyewatha (Red Jacket, Seneca), and Gyantwahia (Cornplanter, Seneca). Another present was Ganeodiyo (Ganiodaio, Handsome Lake, Seneca, also referred to as Skananiateriio) who would, between 1799 and 1815, become a major spiritual leader and the teacher of the Gai'wiio (the Good Word, inspired by spiritual messengers). Historian Paul Lawrence Stevens noted how the invasion of the Wyoming Valley was more than just a military expedition: "The Senecas, Cayugas, and [the allied] Delawares had long-standing grievances with the methods by which the whites had obtained the valuable farming and hunting lands along the Susquehanna [in a 1754 illegal transaction] and the manner in which they had stepped over the 1768 treaty line."[43]

The raid on Wyoming was led by the Loyalist ranger, Colonel John Butler. The valley was populated by more than 1,000 white families living in seven scattered settlements, each with its own fort. On July 1, two small forts capitulated immediately, when the families and soldiers inside were guaranteed quarter, with the soldiers promising not to serve in the Patriot cause again.[44] But on July 3, Forty Fort, larger and garrisoned by over 500 militia, would not surrender. When John Butler realized that the fort could not be taken without the loss of a great number of men, he sent Loyalists and the Haudenosaunee to nearby abandoned farms to gather cattle and burn all buildings. Although the women and children were safe within the fort, the militiamen in Forty Fort were not content to watch their homes go up in smoke, and about 500 of them sallied out. "This pleased the Indians highly," noted John Butler.[45] Butler deliberately pulled his men back as the militia approached the farms that the raiders were burning. Then, choosing a good defensive position, the Rangers and the Haudenosaunee lay flat on the ground in a line across the militia's path. The 500 militiamen realized their enemy's strategy and formed for an attack. The Patriots came through the woods, firing a volley at 200 yards. The raiders did not stir. The militia marched on, firing two more volleys without drawing a response. When they were within 100 yards, the Senecas and Rangers began shooting. "Our fire was so close, & well directed," Butler reported, "that the affair was soon over, not lasting above half an hour, from the time they gave us the first-fire till their flight."[46] "Their flight"—hundreds of men running terrified with screaming Indians in pursuit—became a slaughter. Of the 500 militiamen, 302 were killed; only five were taken prisoner. Butler's losses were one Indian and two Rangers killed and eight Indians wounded. Later, Butler explained why no mercy was shown: "The Indians were so Exasperated with their loss Last year near Fort Stanwix (Oriskany) that it was with the greatest difficulty I could save the lives of those few."[47] At the next settlement, Westmoreland, the fearful inhabitants surrendered and were spared, although most of their homes were burned to the ground.[48]

Butler reported that his raiding party had destroyed eight abandoned forts after the defenders had surrendered, burned 1,000 buildings, and killed or driven off 1,000 cattle. Patriot evidence proves that this was no exaggeration. "But what gives me the Sincerest Satisfaction," Butler wrote, "is, that I can with great truth assure you that in the destruction of the Settlement not a Single person has been hurt of the Inhabitants but such as were in arms, to those indeed the Indians Gave no Quarter."[49] Was this a "massacre"? Anthropologist Thomas S. Abler summarized his extensive research: "It is not unusual to see the Battle of Wyoming described as a "massacre. . . . Those who died there, however, were under arms and had marched out to give battle. Throughout the history of warfare, troops who panic and run have suffered losses comparable to those at Wyoming. A fairer description of the battle would be a one-sided victory resulting from the steadiness, courage, and tactics of a larger veteran force of Indians and Rangers over a smaller untried force of frontiersmen." Furthermore, "despite myths that have grown up around the Battle of Wyoming, there is no evidence that prisoners or civilians were harmed."[50]

Although rumors of noncombatant deaths spread quickly among the Patriots, it is significant to recall that entire garrisons chose to surrender, promised never to fight in the war again, and left their forts unharmed.[51] After the expedition the Haudenosaunee maintained that the Patriots "falsely accused the Indians of cruelty at Wyoming"—a statement that was given, as will be seen later, by Loyalist leader Walter Butler (the son of John Butler) in the aftermath of the noncombatant deaths at Cherry Valley.[52]

Battle and Massacre at Cherry Valley

Although the Battle of Wyoming did not result in any noncombatant casualties, that was not the case in subsequent events, exemplified by the attack on Cherry Valley, New York. On November 6, five days before the actual attack occurred, a pro-Patriot Oneida warned Cherry Valley's inhabitants that an attack was imminent. This information had initially been provided by a pro-Patriot Onondaga—yet one more indication of the divisions within the Confederacy that paralleled the white colonists' own factions. In response to the warning, Cherry Valley's families asked the local commander, Colonel Ichabod Alden, if they could take refuge in the fort. But he believed the report to be a rumor and refused to allow the civilians to enter the fort. As for the colonel, he remained in comfortable quarters in a private home outside the walls of the fort. On November 11, 1778, the Loyalist Haudenosaunee and their white allies attacked the settlement, the last target of that long year of expeditions. Well outside the town, a settler was wounded by one member of the attacking party. Though wounded, the settler rode into the settlement to warn the colonel. The colonel did nothing.[53]

The warriors approaching Cherry Valley were already infuriated because some of the Wyoming Patriot soldiers, whom they had allowed to surrender on the specific condition that they not fight again, had again taken up arms and attacked Indian towns.[54] Thus the Haudenosaunee were not inclined to show Patriot soldiers any future mercy. Furthermore, the Haudenosaunee had learned that fantastic, fictional stories had been invented about Haudenosaunee atrocities against civilians at Wyoming.[55]

All combatants—Patriots, Haudenosaunee, and Loyalists—had become ensnared in a sequence of retaliations, each of which was more violent than its predecessor.[56] The facts of this escalating violence help explain how the New York frontier was consumed with fury. Back in September, Haudenosaunee and Loyalist raiders attacked German Flats in the Mohawk Valley. Patriot Peter Bellinger reported that "the enemy burned 63 Dwelling houses, 57 barns, with grain and fodder, 3 grist mills, 1 saw mill, took away 235 horses, 229 horned cattle, 269 sheep, killed and destroyed hogs and burned a great many outhouses. Two white men, 1 negro killed."[57] In October, a Patriot expedition retaliated by attacking and burning Unadilla, Onaquaga, and several smaller Haudenosaunee settlements, all of which were on the Upper Susquehanna River.[58] The Patriot commander noted that the towns included homes made of stone, with brick chimneys and glass windows, "the finest I have ever seen."[59] This time, however, the escalation of frontier violence took on a new horror: three Patriot soldiers raped and killed a young Haudenosaunee woman.[60]

Because Haudenosaunee leaders such as Joseph Brant realized that their Patriot adversaries would use the deaths of noncombatants to rally support, they made great efforts to keep the warriors working closely with the white Loyalist Rangers and regular troops.[61] But this system disintegrated at Cherry Valley with tragic results. As many as 470 Haudenosaunee, 300 Loyalist volunteers, 150 Rangers, and 50 British regulars were led by John Butler's son, Walter, and by Haudenosaunee leaders, such as Cornplanter and Joseph Brant. During the march toward Cherry Valley, Walter Butler insulted Joseph Brant by attempting to usurp his leadership among the Indians and the 300 white volunteers loyal to him. The Mohawk warriors persuaded Brant to forget the insult and to concentrate on the expedition; however, ninety of the white volunteers left in disgust, refusing to serve with the arrogant Walter Butler. Other whites and Indians also may have left at this time. Because of the incident, Brant and Butler did not work closely during the raid. Butler separated the white and Indian forces, attaching only fifty-three Rangers to the Indians. Brant, although he did his best, was unable to prevent some warriors from scattering across the countryside. These warriors slaughtered at least thirty-three white men, women, and children. Also killed were sixteen soldiers, including the hapless Colonel Alden, who had been twice warned of the attack. Seventy were taken prisoner and marched away, although about forty were released, including twelve who turned out to be Loyalists.[62]

Interview with a Haudenosaunee War Leader

One Haudenosaunee leader, probably a Seneca—his name is uncertain—left an interesting account of the 1778 and 1779 campaigns, including Wyoming and other Haudenosaunee-British expeditions in 1778 (probably including Cherry Valley) as well as raids in early 1779. He was the son of a Haudenosaunee woman and an Englishman who migrated to America and found work as a blacksmith among the Haudenosaunee. Evidently this Englishman's son was adopted by the Haudenosaunee, and because the Haudenosaunee are matrilineal, his status came from his mother. During the war he was "chosen" by the Haudenosaunee to be a war leader. Patriots captured him, but he escaped to the Hudson Valley where, a year after Wyoming and other battles, he was interviewed by a Hessian officer, Captain Johann Ewald on June 4, 1779. The interview, which Captain Ewald recorded in his diary, reveals interesting details of a Haudenosaunee column on the march on raids into Pennsylvania as far south as Maryland and in New York. The interview reveals how this mixed-blood war leader, while adopted by the Haudenosaunee, still saw himself as somewhat apart from them, even as he also demonstrates a thorough acceptance of the spirit of Haudenosaunee warfare and refers to Haudenosaunee beliefs as "our customs and laws."

> "How strong is the corps under Colonel [John] Butler?"—"When I was captured it consisted of fifty English regulars, a number of loyalists, and four to five hundred Indians."
> "How did you obtain your food in the wild country?"—"In the beginning we lived on the wild game that is found in plenty there, which the savages shot and shared with others. But as soon as we reached the borders of Pennsylvania and Maryland, we found flour and meat—provisions in abundance—but we could not get salt and strong drink any more."

"How did you treat the disaffected [Patriot] subjects and prisoners?—"Man, woman, and child were either cut down or carried off with us; the dwellings plundered, devastated, and burned. In the first action which we had with the rebels on the Susquehanna [the Battle of Wyoming], two whole brigades were massacred, of which the greater part were scalped half-dead, and in such misery lost their lives."

"Have you also scalped, since no Indians are allowed to keep such trophies? [In fact, scalps were kept.]—"Oh, yes!"—(whereat a wild laugh expressed in his features indicated his delight at the recollection)—"In the same affair [Wyoming] I had worked so hard with my tomahawk and scalping knife that my arms were bloody above the elbows. I was born and brought up among these people, and am trained in their customs. This piece of trousers I am wearing here, which they gave me in prison, is the first that I have worn in my life. He who lives with the Indians and wants to enjoy their friendship must conform to them in all respects, but then one can depend upon these good people. They are indeed good, sincere people."[63]

"Good, sincere people" who can also commit cruelties—within this context, Captain Ewald notes: "From this story of a people, one perceives that all our acts depend upon our upbringing and customs."[64]

Torture and Adoption

Although torture and adoption appear to be inconsistent actions, in the Haudenosaunee worldview they were the consequence of the same spiritual belief. This perspective is useful in understanding, but not in justifying, Haudenosaunee warfare and culture. At Oriskany (1777) and Wyoming (1778) some Patriot soldiers captured in battle were tortured to death. While this was clearly revenge, the Haudenosaunee also believed that because they had lost so many warriors at Oriskany in 1777, their individual and communal spiritual strengths, their "orenda," had been thrown out of balance.[65] The torture replicated the pains that their slain warriors had endured in battle. The spiritual essence of the tortured Patriots thus rebalanced the spiritual forces that gave strength to the Haudenosaunee. The Haudenosaunee considered the spiritual essence of their enemies equal and therefore of equal value in contributing to the communal orenda. This sense of equality was also why far more white prisoners were adopted than were tortured. Because the spiritual force of each human was equal, adopted prisoners replaced lost relatives—both the physical and the spiritual presence of those who had died in battle, epidemics, or other circumstances. This belief also explains why the Haudenosaunee were offended when they learned that whites rarely took prisoners. Outright killing wasted the spiritual potential of a human, who could be adopted or tortured to rebalance the world.[66]

The Patriot Campaign of 1779:
Rape, Massacre, and Total War

The Haudenosaunee successes of 1778 frustrated George Washington, who was determined to reverse the collapsing morale on the frontier and to end the destruction of the wheat crops needed to feed his soldiers. In 1779 he ordered expeditions under the overall command of General John Sullivan, with the assistance of General James Clinton, to march into the Haudenosaunee country of western New York, to knock the Haudenosaunee out of the war, and to capture Fort Niagara. In April 1779, the first assault of this campaign began, when 558 Patriot soldiers, under Colonel Goose Van Schaick, marched westward from Fort Stanwix at the western end of the Mohawk River and destroyed most of the Onondaga Haudenosaunee communities, including those that were neutral or pro-Patriot.[67] It is important to note that there had been no rapes of white women at Cherry Valley or at any other frontier settlement, for as General James Clinton noted, "Bad as the Savages are, they never violate the chastity of any women, their prisoners."[68] Not so for the Patriots. In an atrocity far worse than any at Cherry Valley, the Patriots raped and then butchered some of the Onondaga women. These atrocities burned deep into Haudenosaunee hearts. During a council in Niagara on December 11, 1782, Tioguanda, an Onondaga chief, recalled: "When They came to the Onondaga Town (of which I was one of the principal Chiefs) They put to death all the Women and Children, excepting some of the young Women that they carried away for the use of their Soldiers, and were put to death in a more shameful and Scandalous manner; Yet these Rebels calls themselves Christians."[69]

The instructions that General Washington sent to Sullivan on May 31, 1779, were explicit in calling for the destruction of Haudenosaunee towns and for the capture of men, women, and children, perhaps to use as hostages during any future prisoner exchanges:

> Sir: The expedition you are appointed to command is to be directed against the hostile tribes of the six nations of Indians, with their associates and adherents. The immediate objects are the total distruction [sic] and devastation of their settlements and

the capture of as many prisoners of every age and sex as possible. It will be essential to ruin their crops now in the ground
& prevent their planting more. . . . parties should be detached
to lay waste all the settlements around, with instructions to do
it in the most effectual manner, that the country may not be
merely *overrun* but *destroyed*.[70]

The main Patriot army, under General Sullivan, defeated the Haudenosaunee
and their Delaware allies at Newtown (Elmira), New York, on August 29,
1779. For the Haudenosaunee, the earlier Patriot rape of Onondaga clearly
signaled that no matter what battles they might fight with the Patriots,
their first priority had to be the protection of their women and children.
Thus when the Sullivan expedition, aided by Oneida and Tuscarora scouts,
marched into Haudenosaunee country, it found the towns abandoned. General Sullivan reported that his army burned forty towns and many lesser
settlements evacuated by the Senecas and Cayugas. The general also noted
that the Patriots destroyed corn that "must amount to 160,000 bushels,
with a vast quantity of vegetables of every kind."[71] During the campaign
Sullivan ignored Cayuga and Oneida pleas that some of the Cayuga towns
he planned to attack were in fact neutral, and that the corn there would aid
pro-Patriot Onondagas.[72] Sullivan did not attack Niagara and turned back
in the middle of September because of the lateness of the season. In the
meantime, another Patriot army, under Colonel David Brodhead, marched
north from Pittsburgh and burned Haudenosaunee towns along the Allegheny
River. The Haudenosaunee were furious with the British for their failure to
provide more assistance during the various Patriot assaults. But with their
homes and food supplies destroyed, they had no recourse but to accept what
little Britain would give them. More than 5,000 Haudenosaunee arrived at
Fort Niagara during the last two weeks of September 1779, seeking food,
clothing, and the protection of the fort. This was at least a third of the
total Haudenosaunee population. As for the Oneidas who scouted for the
Patriots, the commander at Fort Niagara, Colonel Mason Bolton, noted
that the pro-British Haudenosaunee "have given no quarter to those of that
Nation who fall into their hands."[73]

Haudenosaunee refugees remained at Fort Niagara or dispersed to Ohio,
Ontario, and other locations. Others attempted to return to their towns
and territories to hunt and survive as best they could. However, starvation
affected many. Mary Jemison, a white who had been adopted into the Seneca
Nation, recalled how life among the Senecas had changed after the Sullivan
campaign had destroyed so many towns. These circumstances were made all
the more severe by the winter of 1779–1780, which Jemison described as
"the most severe that I have witnessed since my remembrance. The snow fell

about five feet deep, and remained so for a long time, and the weather was extremely cold; . . . almost all the game upon which the Indians depended for subsistence, perished, and reduced them almost to a state of starvation through that and three or four succeeding years. When the snow melted in the spring [of 1780], deer were found dead upon the ground in vast numbers; and other animals, of every description, perished from the cold also, and were found dead, in multitudes. Many of our people barely escaped with their lives, and some actually died of hunger and freezing."[74]

Retaliations continued as pro-British Haudenosaunee struck all along the New York frontier. In 1780, pro-British Haudenosaunee destroyed the Oneida and Tuscarora settlements because those nations had provided scouts for the Sullivan campaign in 1779. The Oneidas and Tuscaroras were forced to take refuge near Schenectady. Frontier warfare continued through 1781, and then faded as all sides realized that peace was likely. Loyalists and British at Fort Niagara learned about the Peace of Paris on April 23, 1783, when four Loyalist Rangers returned with the news from a winter-long spying mission, during which they had approached within eighteen miles of George Washington's camp in the Hudson Highlands. Corroboration of these terms came during the first days in May when other spies brought in copies of Philadelphia newspapers. The newspapers confirmed that the treaty gave the Continental Congress the right of preemption over the entire Haudenosaunee country. The pro-British Haudenosaunee were also angry that the Patriots usually killed Haudenosaunee prisoners of war. In contrast, the Haudenosaunee not only spared, but they did not torture, the vast majority of prisoners. At the end of the war, according to Haudenosaunee custom, captives were allowed to declare whether they wanted to remain as adopted members of a community or whether they preferred to be returned to the white communities. On April 2, 1783, again at Niagara, the aged Seneca Sayenqueraghta noted that the Patriots had given the Haudenosaunee "great Reason to be revenged on them for their Cruelties to us and our Friends [i.e., Indians on other frontiers], and if we had the means of publishing to the World the many Acts of Treachery & Cruelty committed by them on our Women & Children, it would appear that the title of Savages would with much greater justice be applied to them than to us."[75]

Aaron Hill (Kanonaron), a Mohawk chief, had fought alongside the British since the Battle of Oriskany in 1777. During a May 1783 meeting with the commander at Niagara, he expressed amazement that the British could even think of breaking their honor and the 1768 Treaty of Fort Stanwix by giving the Patriots the right of preemption over Haudenosaunee lands. According to British commander Allan Maclean "exactly as translated":

They told me they never could believe that our King could pretend to Cede to America What was not his own to give, or that the Americans would accept from Him, What he had no right to grant. That . . . in the Year 1768 . . . a Line had been drawn from the Head of Canada Creek (near Fort Stanwix) to the Ohio, that the Boundaries then Settled were agreeable to the Indians & the Colonies. . . . That the Indians were a free People Subject to no Power upon Earth, that they were faithful Allies of the King of England, but not his Subjects. . . . it was impossible . . . to imagine, that the King of England Should pretend to grant to the Americans, all the Whole Country of the Indians Lying between the Lakes and the fixed Boundaries, as settled in 1768 between the Colonies and the Indians. . . . That if it was really true that the English had basely betrayed them by pretending to give up their Country to the Americans Without their Consent, or Consulting them, it was an act of Cruelty and injustice that Christians *only* were capable of doing, that the Indians were incapable of acting So . . . to friends & Allies, but that they did believe We had Sold & betrayed them.[76]

Peace

Although the Confederacy was shaken to its roots, it was not destroyed. In 1784, immediately prior to opening negotiations with the United States at what became known as "the Second Treaty of Fort Stanwix," the Haudenosaunee reaffirmed the cohesiveness of their Confederacy through a traditional Haudenosaunee ceremony at Fort Stanwix. After this ceremony, they opened negotiations with U.S. representatives that would conclude with a mutual declaration of peace with the U.S., the Second Treaty of Fort Stanwix. As recorded by a white observer, "We were witnesses of the reconciliation of the Oneidas with their [Haudenosaunee] enemies. Although both dwelt, for several days, near the fort, and in spite of the cessation of hostilities, communication had not been reestablished between them. The "Great Grasshopper" [an Oneida leader] . . . followed by five other savages . . . went to the cabins of the Senecas" representing the pro-British Haudenosaunee. "They walked stiffly, and stopped from time to time. The chief of the Senecas came out and went to receive them at some distance. They sat on the grass and compliments were exchanged by the two chiefs. They smoked the pipe of peace and separated. The next day the visit was returned by the Senecas to the Oneidas with . . . the same formalities."[77]

Conclusion

After the Revolution, many Haudenosaunee fled to what is now Ontario, where their descendants reside today. The Confederacy's council fire, for centuries at Onondaga, was transferred to the safer location of Buffalo Creek, in what is now western New York. Then, in 1847, the fire was returned to Onondaga.[78] There at Onondaga, the Confederacy still meets.

Notes

1. Aaron Hill at Fort Niagara, May 18, 1783, Allan Maclean to Sir Frederick Haldimand, May 18, 1783, in the Haldimand Papers (232 volumes, hand copied for the Library and Archives of Canada from the originals in the British Museum, the Library and Archives of Canada, Ottawa), Haldimand Papers, B.103: 177.

2. Howard Swiggett, *War Out of Niagara: Walter Butler and the Tory Rangers* (reprint of 1933 edition; Port Washington, NY: I. J. Friedman, 1963), 144.

3. John Buchan, "Preface," in Swiggett, *War Out of Niagara*, vii.

4. John MacDonnell to Colonel Mason Bolton, July 1, 1780, in Haldimand Papers, B.100: 418–19; Colonel Mason Bolton to Frederick Haldimand, August 8, 1780, in Haldimand Papers, B.100: 446; Barbara Graymont, *The Iroquois in the American Revolution* (Syracuse, NY: Syracuse University Press, 1972), 242.

5. General Thomas Gage to Lord Hillsborough, August 17, 1768, in Clarence Edwin Carter, ed., *The Correspondence of General Thomas Gage with the Secretaries of State, 1763–1775*, 2 vols. (New Haven, CT: Yale University Press, 1931–1933), 1: 185.

6. Richard B. Morris, *The Peacemakers: The Great Powers and American Independence* (New York: Harper and Row, 1965), 321–22; Treaty of Peace with Great Britain [Treaty of Paris], September 3, 1783, Articles I and II, in Henry Steele Commager, ed., *Documents of American History*, 9th ed. (Englewood Cliffs, NJ: Prentice Hall, 1973), 117–18.

7. State of New York, Report of the Special Committee Appointed By the Assembly of 1888 to Investigate the "Indian Problem" of the State [Whipple Report] (Albany, NY: Kessinger Publishing, 1889), 15–20; see also 190–382.

8. General Thomas Gage to Lord Hillsborough, August 17, 1768, in Carter, *The Correspondence of General Thomas Gage,* 1: 185.

9. "The Onnodagoes [sic] Ansr. To ye propasitones [sic] made to ym the 20 of July 1677," in Lawrence H., Leder, ed., *The Livingston Indian Records, 1666–1723* (Gettysburg, PA: Pennsylvania Historical Association, 1956), 43; cf. Francis Jennings, William N. Fenton, Mary A. Druke, and David R. Miller, eds., *The History and Culture of Iroquois Diplomacy: An Interdisciplinary Guide to the Treaties of the Six Nations and Their League* (Syracuse, NY: Syracuse University Press, 1985), 116–17.

10. Guy Johnson, August 9, 1776, letter to Daniel Claus, Claus Papers, the Library and Archives of Canada, Ottawa, Canada, C-1478, I, 216; Graymont, *The Iroquois in the American Revolution*, 122.

11. Lois M. Huey and Bonnie Pulis, *Molly Brant: A Legacy of Her Own* (Youngstown, NY: Old Fort Niagara Association, 1997), 127–32, and passim.

12. Thomas S. Abler, *Complanter: Chief Warrior of the Allegany Seneca* (Syracuse, NY: Syracuse University Press, 2007), 49–53.

13. William Engelbrecht, *Iroquoia: The Development of a Native World* (Syracuse, NY: Syracuse University Press, 2003), 164; Peter Nabokov and Robert Easton, *Native American Architecture* (New York: Oxford University Press, 1989), 76–90.

14. Harmen Meyndertsz van den Bogaert, *A Journey into Mohawk and Oneida Country, 1634–1635: The Journal of Harmen Meyndertsz van den Bogaert*, translated and edited by Charles T. Gehring and William A. Starna, with word list and linguistic notes by Gunter Michelson (Syracuse, NY: Syracuse University Press, 1988), 4.

15. Horatio Hale, *The Haudenosaunee Book of Rites*, with an introduction by William N. Fenton (1883; Toronto: Forgotten Books, 1963), 116–19, 200, 210; Hazel W. Hertzberg, *The Great Tree and the Longhouse: The Culture of the Iroquois* (New York: Macmillan, 1966), 23–24.

16. Huey and Pulis, *Molly Brant*, 13, 45–61; William L. Stone, *Life of Joseph Brant—Thayendanegea, including the Indians Wars of the American Revolution*, 2 vols. (New York: J. Munsell, 1838) 1:18; Isabel Thompson Kelsay, *Joseph Brant, 1743–1807: Man of Two Worlds* (Syracuse, NY: Syracuse University Press, 1984), 227.

17. Graymont, *The Iroquois in the American Revolution*, 216. See also Lieutenant John Jenkins, *Journal*, in Frederick Cooke, ed., *Journals of the Military Expeditions of Major General John Sullivan against the Six Nations of Indians in 1779 with Records of Centennial Celebrations* (Auburn, NY: Knapp, Peck, and Thomson, 1887), 173–76. In another journal, Dr. Jabez Campfield noted, "From French Catherin's [Catherine's Town, south of Seneca Lake] to this place [Genesee River], 95 miles at least, is undoubtedly the best land, and capable of the greatest improvement, of any part of the possession's of the U. States." In Cooke, *Journals*, 60.

18. German stoneware and Delft-styled ceramics are in the collections as well as the exhibit "The Western Door," Rochester Museum and Science Center, Rochester, New York. Examples of ladles and other finely carved utensils can be found in the collections of the New York State Historical Association's Fenimore Art Museum, in Cooperstown, New York, and in the National Museum of the American Indian, Washington, D.C.

19. Sir William Johnson, February 12, 1761, to General Jeffrey Amherst, enclosure: "A List of Such Merchandise as is Usually sold to the Indians," in James Sullivan et al., eds., *The Papers of Sir William Johnson*, 14 vols. (Albany, NY: University of the State of New York, 1921–1965) 3: 334–35.

20. General Thomas Gage to the Earl of Hillsborough, November 10, 1770, in Carter, *The Correspondence of General Thomas Gage*, 1: 278.

21. Huey and Pulis, *Molly Brant*, 15–17.

22. Ibid., 19.

23. Report of Expenses, Sir William Johnson, October 5, 1764, manuscript in the Papers of Sir William Johnson, Archives of the State of New York, Albany.

24. Huey and Pulis, *Molly Brant*, 44–45; H. Pearson Gundy, "Molly Brant—Loyalist" *Ontario History* 54 (1953): 97–108.

25. General Thomas Gage, October 7, 1772, to Sir William Johnson, in Sullivan et al., *The Papers of Sir William Johnson*, 12: 995.

26. General Thomas Gage to Lord Hillsborough, August 17, 1768, in Carter, *The Correspondence of General Thomas Gage*, 1: 185.

27. Joseph Brant, 1803, quoted in Stone, *Life of Joseph Brant*, 1: 89.

28. Randolph C. Downes, *Council Fires on the Upper Ohio* (Pittsburgh, PA: University of Pittsburgh Press, 1940), 182–83.

29. Paul Lawrence Stevens, "His Majesty's 'Savage' Allies: British Policy and the Northern Indians during the Revolutionary War. The Carleton Years, 1774–1778," PhD diss., State University of New York at Buffalo, 1984, 374–85, 526–27, 773–814; Christopher Ward, *The War of the Revolution*, edited by John Richard Alden, 2 vols. (New York: Macmillan, 1952), 1: 384–97.

30. Stevens, "His Majesty's 'Savage' Allies," 1: 686–87, and passim.

31. Speech of the Oneida Chiefs, January 19, 1777, in Stone, *Life of Joseph Brant*, 1: 176.

32. Kelsay, *Joseph Brant*, 71–77, 165–75.

33. Gavin K. Watt, *Rebellion in the Mohawk Valley: The St. Leger Expedition of 1777* (Toronto: Dundurn Press, 2002), 120–34.

34. The Oneidas fought under leaders such as Honyery Tewahangaraghkan (Thawengarakwen, also known as Honyery Doxtader) and his wife, Senagena. The Senecas allied with the Crown at Oriskany included Cornplanter (Kiantwhauka, or Gayentwahga); Théwonyas (Chainbreaker; after 1812 known as Blacksnake); and Sagoyewátha (Red Jacket). The pro-British Cayugas included the leader Ojagehte (Juggeta, Fish Carrier), and one of the Onondaga leaders was Tioguanda (Teaqwanda). The Mohawks at Oriskany included Tagawirunte (also known as William of Canajoharie and as William Johnson), the son of the late Sir William Johnson and Molly Brant; Aaron Hill (Kanonaron) and Joseph Brant (Thayendanegea). Some Haudenosaunee women who had accompanied their husbands were back in the camps the British forces had erected as part of the siege of Fort Stanwix. See Stevens, "His Majesty's 'Savage' Allies," 1: 233; Watt, *Rebellion in the Mohawk Valley*, 122, 159, 177, 193, 195; Graymont, *The Iroquois in the American Revolution*, 132–35.

35. Théwonyas [Chainbreaker, known after 1812 as Governor Blacksnake, a Seneca leader], *Chainbreaker: The Revolutionary War Memoirs of Governor Blacksnake as Told to Benjamin Williams*, edited and with an introduction by Thomas S. Abler (Lincoln, NE: University of Nebraska Press, 1989), 129–30.

36. Watt, *Rebellion in the Mohawk Valley*, 195.

37. John Butler to Frederick Haldimand, December 14, 1777, in Haldimand Papers, B.105: 4.

38. Stevens, "His Majesty's 'Savage' Allies," 1,470.

39. Colonel Mason Bolton to Guy Carlton, January 31, 1778, in B. 100: 11.

40. Stevens, "His Majesty's 'Savage' Allies," 1,467–1,468.

41. Stevens, "His Majesty's 'Savage' Allies," 1,711–1,714; Graymont, *The Iroquois in the American Revolution*, 162–67; Alexander C. Flick, *New Sources on the Sullivan-Clinton Campaign in 1779* (reprinted from *Quarterly Journal of the New York State Historical Association* 10 (1929): 185–224, 265–317 [Albany, NY: New York

State Historical Association, 1929?]), 26–27. Flick refers to the plans of 1778 as "The Forgotten Campaign of 1778" (p. 26).

42. Guy Carleton to General John Burgoyne, September 15, 1777, in B.40: 8; Guy Carlton to Lieutenant Colonel Mason Bolton, September 16, 1777, in Haldimand Papers, B.18: 178.

43. Stevens, "His Majesty's 'Savage' Allies," 1,724–1,725. Cf. Oren Lyons in an interview with Huston Smith, "Redeeming the Future: The Traditional Instructions of Spiritual Law," in Huston Smith, *A Seat at the Table: Huston Smith in Conversation with Native Americans on Religious Freedom*, edited and with a preface by Phil Cousineau (Berkeley, CA: University of California Press, 2006), 183.

44. Stevens, "His Majesty's 'Savage' Allies," 1,727–1,728.

45. John Butler to Colonel Mason Bolton, July 8, 1778, in Haldimand Papers, B.100: 38.

46. Ibid. 39.

47. Ibid.

48. Ibid., 40.

49. Ibid..

50. Abler, *Cornplanter*, 46. Abler's statement is significant, because eight years earlier he had thoroughly analyzed the possibility of noncombatant deaths at Wyoming. In Abler, ed., *Chainbreaker*, 97–101, 135–37.

51. Stevens, "His Majesty's 'Savage' Allies," 1,735; Graymont, *The Iroquois in the American Revolution*, 172, 167–74, 181; William R. Nester, *The Frontier War for American Independence* (Mechanicsburg, PA: Stakepole Books, 2004), 202–203. Cf. John Grenier, *The First Way of War: American War Making on the Frontier* (New York: Cambridge University Press, 2005), 166. Grenier maintains that civilians were killed. However, the evidence Grenier cites—the diary of Captain Johann Ewald—seems to refer to a raid somewhere other than Wyoming, as is explained later in this chapter.

52. Walter Butler to Colonel Mason Bolton, November 17, 1778, in Haldimand Papers, B.100: 86.

53. Abler, *Cornplanter*, 48; Stone, *Life of Joseph Brant*, 1: 371–73.

54. Walter Butler to Colonel Mason Bolton, November 17, 1778, in Haldimand Papers, B.100: 86. Cf. Stone, *Life of Joseph Brant*, 1: 384–86.

55. John Butler to Colonel Mason Bolton, c. June 24, 1779, in Haldimand Papers, B.100: 173.

56. "The stupid sequence of retaliation" is how events on the New York frontier were described by Howard Swiggett in his *War Out of Niagara*, 144.

57. Colonel Peter Bellinger, September 19, 1778, quoted in Swiggett, *War Out of Niagara*, 143.

58. Glenn F. Williams, *Year of the Hangman: George Washington's Campaign against the Iroquois* (Yardley, PA: Westholm, 2005), 168–71.

59. William Butler, quoted in Swiggett, *War Out of Niagara*, 143.

60. Ibid., 144.

61. George Forsyth and William Taylor to Daniel Claus, November 15, 1778, in *The Claus Papers*, Microfilm, 4 vols. (Ottowa: Public Archives of Canada), C-1478, 2: 67.

62. Walter Butler to Colonel Mason Bolton, November 17, 1778, in Haldimand Papers, B.100: 86. Historian Barbara Graymont summarized the impact of Cherry Valley: "Until this bloody affair, the Indian-Tory incursions had been fairly humane, as wars go. With some scattered exceptions, noncombatants had not previously been attacked." See Graymont, *The Iroquois in the American Revolution*, 189.

63. Captain Johann Ewald, entry for June 4, 1779, in *Diary of the American War: A Hessian Journal*, translated and edited by Joseph P. Tustin (New Haven, CT: Yale University Press, 1979), 166–67.

64. Ibid., 167.

65. William Engelbrecht summarizes "orenda" as "the spiritual power inherent in existence . . . all natural entities have spirits, and hence inherent power or *orenda*." See Engelbrecht, *Iroquoia*, 5. See also Arthur C. Parker, *Seneca Myths and Folk Tales*, with an introduction by William N. Fenton (1923; Lincoln, NE: University of Nebraska Press, 1989), 3–4.

66. An excellent survey of Haudenosaunee torture and its relationship to spirituality is in Engelbrecht, *Iroquoia*, 4–6, 42–45, 161–63. See also Graymont, *The Iroquois in the American Revolution*, 17–19.

67. Théwonyas [Chainbreaker] *Revolutionary War Memoirs*, 143–44.

68. Stone, *Life of Joseph Brant*, 1: 404.

69. Tioguanda [Tiahogwando], Onondaga leader, December 11, 1782, speech to Allan Maclean, in Haldimand Papers, B.102: 250. Cf. Colonel Bolton, January 13, 1778, to Guy Carleton, Haldimand Papers, B.100: 11; Daniel Claus, June 18, 1781, to James Blackburn in London, Claus Papers, Microfilm, 4 vols. (Ottawa: Public Archives of Canada), C-1478, 3: 29; Colonel Bolton, October 12, 1778, to Governor Haldimand, in Haldimand Papers, B.100: 58. Many Onondagas settled among the Senecas at Canandaigua. John Butler to Colonel Mason Bolton, May 28, 1779, in Alexander C. Flick, *The Sullivan-Clinton Campaign in 1779: Chronology and Selected Documents* (Albany, NY: University of the State of New York, 1929), 90.

70. George Washington to John Sullivan, May 31, 1779, in Flick, *The Sullivan-Clinton Campaign*, 90, 91, emphases in original. An electronic version is available at http://www.etext.virginia.edu/toc/modeng/public/WasFi15.html.

71. General John Sullivan, Report to the Continental Congress, September 30, 1779, in Cooke, *Journals*, 303.

72. Major Jeremiah Fogg, *Journal*, in Cooke, *Journals*, 99–100. Cayuga leaders had discouraged Cayuga warriors from assisting John Butler and Joseph Brant in what became the Battle of Newtown, noted in Joseph Brant to Colonel Mason Bolton, August 19, 1779, in Flick, *The Sullivan-Clinton Campaign*, 130.

73. Colonel Mason Bolton to Frederick Haldimand, October 2, 1779, in Haldimand Papers, B.100: 286. The Sullivan campaign is discussed in detail in Williams, *Year of the Hangman*, 240–96, and in Graymont, *The Iroquois in the American Revolution*, 192–222.

74. Mary Jemison, *A Narrative of the Life of Mrs. Mary Jemison* (1824; New York: Corinth Books, 1963), 75.

75. Sayenqueraghta, speech, April 2, 1783, in Haldimand Papers, B.104: 42.

76. Aaron Hill, speech, in Allan Maclean to Frederick Haldimand, May 18, 1783, Haldimand Papers, B.103: 177–79, emphasis in original.

77. Eugene Parker Chase, ed., *Our Revolutionary Forefathers: The Letters of François, Marquis de Barbé Marbois* (New York: Duffield, 1929), 205. From the internal evidence, it appears that the reconciliation took place sometime between October 2 and 11. The Confederacy tacitly accepted the 1784 treaty but never ratified it. See Anthony F. C. Wallace, *The Death and Rebirth of the Seneca* (New York: Aldred A. Knopf, 1969), 152.

78. Harold Blau, Jack Campisi, and Elisabeth Tooker, "Onondaga," in *Northeast*, ed. Bruce G. Trigger, 496 (Vol. 15 of the *Handbook of North American Indians*, William C. Sturtevant, general editor; Washington, DC: Smithsonian Institute).

PART 3

People

CHAPTER 6

The Ordeal of John Connolly

The Pursuit of Wealth through Loyalism

Doug MacGregor

John Connolly, a determined Pennsylvanian who would become a Virginia land speculator, spent much of his life in the backcountry, and by 1774 he believed he had succeeded in capitalizing on his familiarity with the fertile lands along the Ohio River. He utilized his knowledge of the Ohio Valley's interior to impress many visitors to the frontier, including George Washington, and finally to engage in a plan to acquire from Virginia a valuable tract of land at the Falls of the Ohio (present-day Louisville, Kentucky). His knowledge of the land would not be all that he needed to secure his title. To obtain his grant he agreed to enforce Virginia's control over the Fort Pitt (or Pittsburgh) area, which Pennsylvania also claimed. At Fort Pitt the Allegheny and Monongahela rivers flow together to form the Ohio River, which was at the time the primary route to the Illinois Country and the Mississippi Valley. The colony that possessed Fort Pitt controlled the main route to the West. Connolly also sought to extinguish Native American claims to the Ohio River Valley. Connolly was succeeding in these ventures when the outbreak of the American Revolution posed a new problem. His title to the land could only survive with the support of Lord Dunmore, Virginia's governor. Connolly consequently maintained his loyalty to his "King and Country" and fled Pittsburgh to join Dunmore in exile off the coast of Virginia. Without the governor and without royal government, Connolly would lose his land and his chance to rise above the "common sort." However, because of his loyalty, he lost not only his land but his family, health, property, and right to return to the United States.

Although John Connolly would later clash with Pennsylvanian officials, while trying to establish Virginia's control over the contested area, he had

161

been born near Wright's Ferry in Lancaster County, Pennsylvania. His exact year of birth is unknown but is believed to have been between 1742 and 1744. He was the only child of John Connolly, a surgeon in the British army, who died in 1747, and Susanna Howard Ewing, who died in 1753. She also had two other sons by another marriage, one of whom was James Ewing, who would become a general in the Continental army.[1]

Upon Susanna's death, her son John was placed under the care of James Wright, who apprenticed him to be a doctor. However, it was his "ambition to be a soldier," and in 1762 he found his opportunity in the global struggle of the Seven Years' War (known in the United States as the French and Indian War, 1754–1763) and became a surgeon's mate. In 1764, he briefly joined the British forces under Colonel Henry Bouquet as a volunteer for the march into the homelands of hostile Native American nations.[2]

Connolly claimed he made his way west to the backcountry at this time to "make myself worthy to serve my King and country on future occasions." Sometime before 1767, he was living in the frontier village of Pittsburgh, where he married Susannah, a daughter of Samuel Sample, a tavern keeper.

Figure 6.1 Portrait, Probably of John Connolly (*Filson Historical Society*)

Connolly soon found himself in debt in Pittsburgh and left for the British forts in the newly acquired Illinois country. There, Connolly followed the footsteps of his prominent uncle, George Croghan, and entered into trade with Native Americans in 1769. Lacking the skills required to make the business a success, Connolly left the Illinois Country in greater debt and was back in Pittsburgh by the autumn of 1770. He had not amassed the fortune he had sought in the trade with Native Americans, but he had gained an intimate knowledge of the land and waterways of the frontier.[3]

In Pittsburgh Connolly spent much of his time at his father-in-law's tavern, which attracted many visitors and land speculators, including George Washington, who dined with Connolly and "other Gentlemen" at Sample's on November 22, 1770. He was impressed by Connolly's knowledge of the lands to the west and described him as "a very sensible Intelligent man who had travell'd over a good deal of this Western Country both by land and water." Following a trip to the Illinois Country, Connolly wrote Washington on June 29, 1773, asking for help in securing from Virginia 2,000 acres at the Falls of the Ohio. Anticipating success in obtaining a title, he had the tract surveyed. The land at the Falls was valuable, because travelers on the Ohio River unloaded their watercrafts to portage around the cascade. This necessity ensured that every traveler on the river would be diverted through any town built at the site, making it an ideal location for settlement and a source of profit to the proprietor of the land. Possession of this location would be the key to wealth as people moved west.[4]

Although Connolly hoped Washington would help him get the lands, a brighter prospect appeared at Fort Pitt in the person of John Murray, Fourth Earl of Dunmore and governor of Virginia. In the summer of 1773, Dunmore toured the Ohio River Valley, seeking land for investment. There he met Connolly, who must have impressed the governor, for Connolly was invited to Williamsburg the following December. That meeting set in motion armed strife between Virginia and the Native Americans for possession of the Ohio Country and between Virginia and Pennsylvania for possession of the Fort Pitt area. Patrick Henry was at the meeting, and in September 1774 he relayed the details to Thomas Wharton of Philadelphia, as both the war with the Native Americans and the colonial boundary dispute were approaching the boiling point. Connolly had described the richness of the lands in the Ohio Country to Dunmore, who stated that he intended to move his family to America. The governor wished to build a fortune by driving out the Native Americans, primarily the Shawnee, from this territory, securing it for Virginia, and then selling the land at a profit.[5]

At the meeting Dunmore granted Connolly 4,000 acres at the Falls. In doing so, Dunmore relied upon Virginia's second charter of 1609, which claimed much of the land as far west as the "Western Sea," including Fort

Pitt and the Ohio River Valley. The Proclamation of 1763 had barred settlement west of the Appalachian Mountains. However, complaints from land-hungry colonials led Britain in the Fort Stanwix Treaty (1768) to allow them to purchase additional lands west of the Appalachians from the Iroquois Confederacy, which claimed sovereignty over much of the area. The Shawnee, Delaware, and Mingo nations, who actually lived in this region of the Ohio River Valley, protested the Iroquois claim and the sale. They had not been involved in the negotiations and had received none of the proceeds. The British government instructed Virginia not to issue any grants in the area to prevent confrontation with the disgruntled nations. Dunmore ignored these instructions and gave Connolly his 4,000-acre grant. Other colonists whose applications were rejected made "a great deal of Noise." William Preston, surveyor of Fincastle County, noted to George Washington that it was "the Opinion of many good Judges that the Patents [which Dunmore granted were] altogether illegal." Even though the grant at the Falls may have been dubious, Connolly returned to Fort Pitt to assert Virginia's authority over the region.[6]

In 1772 General Thomas Gage, commander in chief of His Majesty's Forces in North America, ordered that Fort Pitt be abandoned, leaving the settlement undefended. This created a power vacuum that allowed Pennsylvania to sell land in the region pursuant to the Fort Stanwix purchase. As settlers flowed westward, Pennsylvania created new western counties—Bedford in 1771 and Westmoreland in 1773—to govern them. At the same time Dunmore was evading royal instructions prohibiting the creation of new counties in western Virginia by claiming that the Fort Pitt area lay in the District of West Augusta, in Augusta County, which had been created in 1738.[7]

On January 6, 1774, Connolly posted a notice proclaiming himself "Captain Commandant of the Militia of Pittsburgh and its Dependencies" and ordered the Virginia militia to muster on January 25. Arthur St. Clair, a magistrate in Westmoreland County, Pennsylvania, quickly informed Governor John Penn of the situation and arrested Connolly. Connolly was soon released, but his imprisonment marked the beginning of often violent civil disturbances that continued until the settlement of the boundary between Pennsylvania and Virginia in 1780. However, during 1774, Connolly found great support among Pittsburgh residents and easily filled the ranks of his militia. At this time the opposing officials began arresting each other's supporters and pulling down homes to intimidate their rivals.[8]

Almost immediately after Connolly's announcement of his captaincy in January 1774, Virginian settlers violently attacked the Native Americans living in the region. When they retaliated, Connolly issued a circular letter in April that frontier inhabitants regarded as a declaration of war against the

Shawnee and Mingo nations. This development led to the brutal massacre of the family of Mingo leader Logan. When Logan retaliated, Dunmore and the Virginians used these attacks as a pretext to mount a military campaign against the Shawnee and Mingo nations. Arthur St. Clair thought the violent conduct of the Virginians was "part of the Virginia plan," or "at least part of Mr. Connolly's plan," and he "hoped some of the devilish schemes that have been carrying on here will come to light." The *Pennsylvania Gazette* asserted that "it appears that a scheming party in Virginia . . . mostly land jobbers, would wish to have those lands." While carrying out this supposedly "devilish scheme" of driving out all rivals to Virginia's claim to the Ohio Valley, Connolly advertised lots for sale at the Falls.[9]

Dunmore's visit to the area in September 1774 reinforced Virginia's claim to the region. He arrived at Fort Pitt at the head of the contingent of troops that Virginia had raised to confront the hostile Native American nations of the Ohio Country. The Virginia forces were divided into two groups: one under Dunmore and the other under Andrew Lewis. On October 10, 1,000 Shawnee warriors attacked Lewis's force at Point Pleasant along the Ohio River. The result was a draw, but the Shawnee withdrew toward Chillicothe to counter the second force under Dunmore. Facing a numerically superior enemy on two fronts, the Shawnee sued for peace. Dunmore held a peace conference, at which final peace negotiations were scheduled for the following summer at Fort Pitt.[10]

Because of Virginia's victory and Lord Dunmore's presence in the region, the Virginia faction grew stronger and the boundary dispute more bitter. Virginia officials kept up their harassment of Pennsylvanians, claiming they held invalid land grants. They formed a jury of twelve men to try each Pennsylvania land-grant holder. On May 3, 1775, Connolly confiscated the land of Devereaux Smith, a leading Pennsylvania official in the Fort Pitt region.[11]

In 1775, the struggle halted not through the diplomatic efforts of governors Penn or Dunmore but in a manner neither side could have imagined. Around May 1, news of the battles of Lexington and Concord reached Pittsburgh. As a result, even though there had been no previous agitation in the region against Britain's policies, Virginia and Pennsylvania settlers called an emergency meeting on May 16 at Fort Pitt, which created a committee of correspondence for West Augusta, Virginia. It began mobilizing a militia, securing ammunition, and cultivating a "friendship with the Indians." The same day, residents of Westmoreland County met at Hannastown, the county seat, to give their support to the American cause.[12]

The Virginians and Pennsylvanians had thus put aside their land disputes and joined together by signing their names to fight for liberty. Virginian support for Dunmore disappeared, although only a few weeks earlier many Virginians had sent an address thanking him for his help against the Shawnee and repudiating a rumor that the governor had deliberately incited them to war. Their resolves of May 16 to create a Revolutionary committee reversed this position and instead blamed the "wicked minions of power to execute our ruin, added to the menaces of an Indian War, likewise said to be in contemplation, thereby thinking to gain our attention, and divert it from that still more interesting object of liberty and freedom."[13]

The majority of frontier inhabitants appeared to favor the American cause. The English traveler, Nicholas Cresswell, a young aristocrat in search of wealth through land speculation, often found himself in trouble and was even threatened with a tarring and feathering. Cresswell noted that the frontier population was "Liberty mad," thinking of nothing but war, and that "the best riflemen" were prepared to go to Boston "for the humane purpose of killing the English officers." Pittsburgh Patriots showed their solidarity and support in August 1775 by confiscating and burning tea at a Liberty Pole in a local version of Boston's "Tea Party." There were, however, some who were troubled by the prospect of war. Arthur St. Clair, who would later become a major general in the Continental army and Pennsylvania's highest-ranking citizen, wrote in the days after his regions' mobilization for war that he was "as much afraid of success in this contest as of being vanquished."[14]

The Revolution's onset led all involved in the western land disputes to change their priorities. In Williamsburg, Dunmore was busy combating the Patriotic fervor. On May 21, he infuriated Virginians by moving the colony's store of gunpowder to a British warship. In response, Patrick Henry raised a company of militia, and Dunmore fled to a British warship in the Chesapeake Bay, but only after issuing a final order disbanding all Virginia troops, including those at Fort Pitt. On July 25, Pennsylvanians from the Fort Pitt area forwarded a request to the Continental Congress for a temporary boundary. However, Virginia and Pennsylvania delegates to the Congress, including Benjamin Franklin, John Dickinson, Patrick Henry, and Thomas Jefferson, jointly asked that the troubles of the Pittsburgh area be forgotten "for the defense of liberties in America." The boundary could be settled later.[15]

In May 1775, when most of the inhabitants of Pittsburgh had agreed to favor the Patriots, John Connolly had already decided whom he would support. In reply to a letter from Connolly, George Washington informed him that matters between the colonies and Great Britain "wear a disagreeable aspect," and that the "minds of men are exceedingly disturbed at the measures of the British government." Washington ended with the ominous thought that "a little time must now unfold the mystery, as matters are drawing to a point." Connolly now "resolved to exert every faculty in defense of the royal cause." He feared his land grants would be worthless if the Americans won the struggle. He had come too far to abandon his dreams. He needed Governor Dunmore to stay in power. At the start of 1775, Pittsburgh had seemed to be firmly under Virginia's control, and it appeared to be only a matter of time before he would reap a substantial profit from his land at the Falls of the Ohio River. Without Lord Dunmore, Connolly's claim to the Falls was tenuous at best. All of the other land grants that Virginia had issued between the Fort Stanwix purchase in 1768 and Lord Dunmore's arrival in 1772 had been dismissed by the Privy Council, including those held by Patrick Henry, Thomas Jefferson, and George Washington, as they intended in enforcing the Proclamation of 1763. Dunmore's grant to Connolly, which had not been dismissed, was an anomaly and considered "altogether illegal" in "the Opinion of many good Judges." When Lord Dartmouth learned of Dunmore's actions, he ordered him to cease further land grants.[16]

Eventually, in 1779, Pennsylvania and Virginia agreed to appoint commissioners to determine a permanent boundary. Pennsylvania won the dispute after surveys revealed that the region was within the area originally granted to Pennsylvania; the Mason-Dixon line was extended westward to its present location. The matter came to a close on September 23, 1780, when both states ratified the solution. Pittsburgh was now permanently under Pennsylvania's control.[17]

However, in 1775, as the Revolution was beginning, Connolly had received orders from Dunmore to disband the Virginia militia at Fort Pitt and to lead the negotiations with the Native Americans that spring in Dunmore's absence. His mission was to enlist their support for the Royal cause. Connolly also took it upon himself secretly to find out who else in Pittsburgh would remain loyal to the king. He immediately undertook to persuade the Ohio Indians to join the British. The negotiations held at Fort Pitt in 1775 had major implications for the war developing in the east. Connolly was determined that the Ohio Indians should support the Crown, and the American Patriots were equally determined that they should not.[18]

Between May 19 and 21, 1775, Connolly issued invitations to the Shawnees, Mingoes, and Delawares to attend a conference in Pittsburgh on June 20. Pittsburgh Patriots sent word to the Continental Congress about the forthcoming negotiations, asking that it send a representative. Whig leaders in Virginia appointed a committee to attend the conference as well. James Wood, chairman of this Virginia Committee, set out for Pittsburgh on June 25.[19]

Pennsylvania officials arrested Connolly on the evening of June 21 and moved him fifty miles east to Ligonier. In captivity, Connolly was informed that he had been imprisoned because he was a "dangerous person and a Tory, an appellation lately revived" as well as being "suspected of an intention to raise a body of men to act against the liberties of America."

Originally Connolly was to be sent to Philadelphia to stand trial before the Continental Congress. However, he was not sent there. The Virginia officials of West Augusta suspected his arrest was actually another maneuver in the boundary dispute, and not a preventive measure in the war with Great Britain. Consequently, they arrested three Pennsylvania magistrates and sent a "spirited" letter to the Westmoreland County, Pennsylvania, Committee, demanding Connolly's release. St. Clair avoided any potential violence by releasing Connolly.[20]

Meanwhile, the council with the Ohio Indians had already begun without Connolly. Upon his release, he joined the conference and took an active role until its close on July 6. The conference was productive, and all of the attending Native American nations as well as all of the whites left satisfied, desiring peace. Connolly did not complete the alliance that Dunmore sought; however, that did not stop him from boasting that he had done so, when he applied after the Revolution to a parliamentary commission for Loyalist claims for compensation in London. Even the committee appointed by Virginia's revolutionary government to oversee the conference was pleased with Connolly's performance. On July 9, James Wood, the Virginia commissioner appointed to the conference, commended Connolly on his "most open and candid manner."[21]

Now that negotiations were over, Connolly was free to leave Pittsburgh to join Lord Dunmore, who had been in exile since July 25 aboard a British warship stationed off of the Virginia coast. While making preparations to leave, Connolly carefully sought out the men in Pittsburgh who remained loyal to the king. He composed a list of their names, which he later submitted to Lord Dunmore.[22]

With three Shawnees and Alan Cameron, a fellow Loyalist, he traveled to Williamsburg under the pretense that the Shawnees wished to meet with Virginia's Revolutionary leaders. Pittsburgh Patriots sent warnings ahead, alerting officials to his presence. At Warm Springs, Virginia, local officials detained Connolly, intending to investigate further. However, the committee appointed to do so never materialized, and Connolly left in a hurry. Near Winchester, his party was detained again because of similar warnings, one of which came from the West Augusta Committee. As the local committee inspected Connolly and his entourage, a messenger arrived declaring that the West Augusta Committee desired Connolly's presence in Richmond. The kind words that James Wood had written about him had changed the Winchester Committee's attitude toward him. It congratulated Connolly on his service to America and sent him on his way. The following day he sent the Shawnees to Richmond, but he continued to Dunmore's warship.[23]

Connolly stayed with Dunmore for two weeks, discussing a plan of war he had developed to defeat the American cause. On August 9, Connolly wrote to John Gibson, whom he believed to be a trustworthy Pittsburgh Loyalist. Connolly enclosed a message from Dunmore to the Ohio Indians and asked Gibson to translate it. In exchange for their neutrality, Dunmore promised that the king would protect their land. The message never made it to the intended recipients, for Gibson turned it over to the West Augusta Committee of Correspondence.[24]

Following the letter to Gibson, Connolly and Dunmore completed their plan of attack, which they hoped would crush the rebellion. Connolly's scheme relied upon the assistance of the Ohio Indians and the Pittsburgh Loyalists, whom he had identified before departing. The plot called for Connolly to start in Detroit and to lead Native American and Loyalist troops to Pittsburgh, gathering additional men along the way. After seizing Fort Pitt, Connolly's force was to proceed to Alexandria, Virginia, where they would meet Dunmore's troops, successfully cutting the colonies in half. With this plan, Connolly traveled to Boston. He met General Gage, received his approval, and immediately left for Virginia. He began his journey to Detroit in late November with Alan Cameron, who had accompanied him from Fort Pitt.[25]

Connolly's party did not get very far. Upon reaching Hagerstown, Maryland, Connolly met a man who had been a private under his command while in Pittsburgh. The private recognized and publicly addressed him as "Major." This alerted some Patriots, and Connolly left immediately before anyone questioned him. Meanwhile, the private headed for the local tavern. The Continental Congress had already informed the Virginia Committee of Safety of Connolly's activities. The committee ordered that he be secured. With the private's help, the colonel of the Hagerstown militia now realized that Connolly was a wanted man. The committee set out after him and captured Connolly's party on November 23. The committee searched the group's baggage and found a copy of Dunmore's instructions, explicitly implicating Connolly in the Loyalist military plot.[26]

Connolly and his comrades were held until further instructions were obtained from Congress, which notified Washington of his arrest. On December 8, Congress ordered that the prisoners be jailed in Philadelphia. Washington was pleased that Connolly was now in prison and no longer a threat. He reported to Joseph Reed, who would become Pennsylvania's radical constitutionalist president, that he was "exceeding [sic] happy to find that villain Connolly is seized" and hoped that he would "meet with the punishment due to his demerit and treachery."[27]

While in confinement with Cameron, Connolly managed to write warnings to those involved in his plot. He wrote to Alexander McKee in Pittsburgh, asking him to send a warning to the British officers on the frontier. He also wrote to Captain Richard Beringer Lernoult, the commanding officer at Detroit, and Captain Hugh Lord, commander at Illinois, informing them of his failed plot. These letters were given for delivery to a Dr. John Smyth, who was part of Connolly's party but who had escaped on December 29, just before the group was moved to Philadelphia.[28]

The trip to Philadelphia was difficult for Connolly and Cameron. They spent the first day of 1776 being paraded through Yorktown, Pennsylvania, at the head of a "Rogue's March," during which they were ridiculed by the townspeople, who sarcastically wished them a Happy New Year. From York, they were taken to Wright's Ferry, Connolly's birthplace. There, his half brother, James Ewing, watched as he was taken to prison, making it a very "melancholy" experience for the prisoner. They arrived in Philadelphia on January 3 and were brought before the Continental Congress, which handed them over to the Pennsylvania Committee of Safety, which then confined them in a miserable, makeshift prison that Connolly described as nothing more than a "dirty room."[29]

Although Connolly had been captured, he hoped that the warnings Dr. Smyth had smuggled out would alert the British to the failure of his plot and thereby possibly salvage the plan without him. However, Smyth had been captured on January 10, just before he reached Pittsburgh. Not only did Connolly's letters fail to reach and alert the British, but they also encouraged the Patriots to keep a close watch on suspected Loyalists, including Connolly's friend, Alexander McKee.[30]

Soon after being imprisoned, Connolly sought parole from the Pennsylvania Committee of Safety. He wrote on January 26, 1776, promising to remain idle in "the present unhappy contest." However, the committee found him to be too dangerous and denied his request. The jail's deplorable conditions began to affect Connolly's health. In February he wrote to the Continental Congress and the Pennsylvania Committee of Safety, notifying both of his deteriorating condition and asking to be exchanged in order to save his health. Dr. Benjamin Rush examined him and prescribed exercise, particularly riding a horse and exposure to fresh air. Instead, Congress modified his incarceration by allowing him to walk the prison yard.[31]

Even from jail, Connolly did what he could to support the British cause and to warn the western posts of a possible American attack. He found an opportunity when the Pennsylvania Committee of Safety began to grant paroles to British and Loyalist prisoners, who would take an oath to remain passive throughout the war. Connolly persuaded a fellow inmate to take the oath and then to transmit messages to Pittsburgh, where other Loyalists would pass them on to the British posts. However, Congress discovered the plan and revoked his prison yard walking privileges.[32]

In February 1776, Connolly suffered a more substantial loss—all of his land. In his role as Virginia's agent, he had amassed a large debt in rebuilding

Fort Pitt. His creditors had been frustrated when he left Pittsburgh in the summer of 1775 to join the British, but they were overjoyed in January 1776 when they heard that he was in the Philadelphia jail. They took advantage of his imprisonment to collect the debts he owed. Among his creditors were Alexander Ross and the firm of Simon and Campbell. The latter reached an agreement with Connolly, giving John Campbell 2,000 acres at the Falls of the Ohio. Connolly mortgaged the remaining 2,000 acres to the firm of Simon and Campbell. Alexander Ross also visited Connolly in jail. They resolved a portion of the debt owed to Ross, but a larger amount went unpaid. Losing these parcels of land strengthened Connolly's attachment to the British cause. He seemed to have reasoned that only through the restoration of British rule would he regain his lands.[33]

Connolly's next scheme came in late March 1776, when his father-in-law, Samuel Sample, visited him in his Philadelphia cell. Connolly shared with him a plan he hoped would free all of the Loyalists imprisoned in Philadelphia. The details are not known, but Congress once again discovered the plot, placed Connolly in solitary confinement, and even contemplated imposing a harsher punishment on him in retaliation for the conditions American prisoners endured in British prisons.[34]

On May 13, Susannah Connolly came to see her husband but after five days asked Congress to let her leave. Her application was denied, and she was directed not to depart the city without permission. They feared her husband might have given her information to transmit to Pittsburgh Loyalists. Throughout the summer and fall, Susannah repeatedly and unsuccessfully applied to Congress for permission to leave. In November 1776, she reported to Congress that her husband was planning to escape. They investigated immediately but could find no evidence to support the claim. She then complained to Congress that her husband had been mistreating her since she had revealed the plot, and it was now impossible for her to stay with him. She was finally granted permission to depart; she now had the freedom to leave Philadelphia and her husband for good.[35]

The approach of the British army into New Jersey in 1776 induced Congress to vacate Philadelphia and move to Baltimore in December. On December 12, it ordered Connolly to be sent there, but the order was not carried out. Connolly then requested that he be moved to a remote jail in the country, where he might regain his health, but this request was denied. He remained in Philadelphia, where his half brother, General James Ewing of the Continental army, soon took command. Ewing was a veteran of the French and Indian War and a member of the Pennsylvania Assembly from 1771 to 1775. He was appointed a brigadier general in 1776. In mid-January 1777, he obtained permission for Connolly to stay at his farm, near Wrightsville, Pennsylvania. However, in mid-February Connolly was ordered to return to prison. On February 26, he again complained of ill health, and on March 9, Dr. Benjamin Rush examined him and once more concluded that Connolly could only be cured by living where fresh air was available. On March 29, James Ewing presented Connolly's case to Congress and vowed to take responsibility for him. Congress referred the matter to the Pennsylvania Committee of Safety, which on April 2 accepted Ewing's offer of responsibility for Connolly, released him on 2,000 pounds' bail, but limited his freedom. Now that Ewing was responsible for Connolly, the Pennsylvania Committee would not have to worry about him, and the bail money was greatly needed for the war effort. Connolly enjoyed his time on Ewing's farm, where he improved his health and refocused his attention on being exchanged. He remained on the Ewing farm until October 14, 1777, when he was forced to return to prison because of Sir William Howe's advance on Philadelphia. Connolly was moved to the jail in Yorktown, Pennsylvania, where he again complained of his confinement. In May 1778, he and his fellow inmates informed Congress of the horrible conditions and asked for parole, if they could not be exchanged. Congress investigated the claims and concluded on May 23 that the accusations were groundless and recommended that the jailers be stricter with the prisoners. Connolly's next request for an exchange also failed, and he was returned to the Philadelphia jail in early August after the British had retreated from Philadelphia. He again campaigned for release, but the congressional committee created to hear his case denied his parole for fear he would join with the Loyalist and British forces on the frontier and because he had been arrested as a spy. This accusation surprised Connolly, and he bitterly denied he was a spy. He argued that he was a commissioned officer under Lord Dunmore, and that America had not even been an independent nation when he was captured, therefore, there was no country to spy against at the time. The committee promised to consider his request for parole if an exchange could not be achieved.[36]

On November 12, the committee reported its findings to Congress and argued that Connolly should be treated as a spy guilty of repeatedly attempting to escape. The committee was upset, too, with his frequent complaints of ill treatment, news of which had reached British ears. Joshua Loring, the British Commissary of Prisoners, had written to the Continental Congress threatening to retaliate against American prisoners of equal rank if his conditions did not improve. Congress wrote to Loring, advising him of Connolly's status as a spy rather than as a prisoner of war and of the groundlessness of such complaints.[37]

Congress then appointed another committee to handle Connolly's case. It reported to Congress on July 14, 1779, that Connolly was indeed a commissioned officer, not a spy, and suggested parole. Congress rejected the recommendation. On August 24 and again on October 14 Connolly petitioned Congress to follow the suggestions of the committee. These petitions were forwarded to the Board of War, which quickly tired of his complaints and referred his case back to Congress with the suggestion that he be exchanged for an American officer of equal rank. By November 17, 1779, Congress believed Connolly's release would pose no danger to the war effort and agreed to exchange him.[38]

Connolly was granted parole, and in July 1780 he traveled to New York City to exchange himself for Lieutenant Colonel Nathaniel Ramsey. This exchange indicates the importance of Connolly, as Ramsey was one of the heroes of the 1778 Battle of Monmouth. The deal was completed on October 25, 1780. As part of his exchange, Connolly pledged that he would do nothing to harm the United States. However, he immediately began to design a second scheme to destroy the new nation. He also evidently hoped to regain his land in the Ohio Valley. To accomplish these goals he presented British General Sir Henry Clinton with a plan similar to his original one. He would lead British troops across Lake Erie, take Fort Pitt, and proceed toward the Potomac River, where he would join British troops coming from the east. General Clinton liked the idea and hoped to implement it later in 1781. However, by late March 1781, Washington had already received intelligence of the plot and warned Fort Pitt. British troops on the frontier outposts did not learn of the plan until September 1781, and by then it was too late to carry it out.[39]

Realizing the plan was no longer feasible, Clinton sent Connolly to join Lord Cornwallis in the South. Connolly was placed in charge of Royalists from Virginia and North Carolina, as well as the Loyal York Volunteers. Before he could organize these troops, Connolly was ordered to Yorktown, Virginia, to counter the recent arrival of the French fleet. Connolly fell ill and received permission on September 21 to travel to the countryside to regain his health, but he was captured instead. Eventually, he was brought before General Washington, whom he foolishly believed remained his friend. Much to his dismay, Connolly lamented that the "friendly sentiments that he once publicly professed for me no longer existed." Washington ordered him back to prison, where he stayed until March 1782, when he was released and allowed to go to British-occupied New York City for his voyage to Europe.[40]

In that year Connolly left New York for London, where he survived on his pay as an army officer. While there, he requested compensation for his losses in service of his king. In 1783, he published "A Narrative of the Transactions, Imprisonment, and Sufferings of John Connolly, an American Loyalist and Lieut.-Col. in His Majesty's Service," in which he chronicled his actions.[41]

To compensate Loyalists for their losses in the Revolution, Parliament created a special commission to evaluate their pleas for recompense. Among the committee's standards in compensating Loyalists was that payment would not be granted for uncultivated lands. Most of Connolly's claim was of this type. On February 2, 1784, he presented his case to the commission, claiming a loss of £6,849 for the 4,000 acres at the Falls of the Ohio, for other lots he owned elsewhere, and for his wages, while in the service of Virginia. After reviewing the case, the commission allowed him £793 in compensation. The loss of his wife, family, and health went uncompensated.[42]

By the winter of 1787–1788, Connolly had moved to Quebec, from where he was sent to Detroit to act as lieutenant governor in 1788. While in Detroit, he sought to regain the Falls of the Ohio and the Kentucky territory for Great Britain. Also, he sought to secure for himself the lands Dunmore had previously granted him. By this time settlers had moved near the Falls in the Kentucky territory of Virginia, naming the place Louisville. The following year Louisville settlers petitioned the Virginia Assembly, asking that Connolly's claim be forfeited, that their town be established, and that titles be granted to inhabitants for plots of land. The Virginia Assembly complied with this request the following year, completing Connolly's loss. To counter this act he set out in September 1788 for Louisville, where he told his old partner, John Campbell, that he had come to estimate the value of the land, and he also offered to help seize New Orleans from Spain. Campbell felt Connolly posed no threat, as he was too "obnubilated" by alcohol.[43]

By 1788, the Kentuckians wished to separate from Virginia because they were too remote from the capital to be adequately represented there. They held a constitutional convention, at which they decided to become an independent member of the United States. Virginia approved this resolution, but before Kentucky's situation could be discussed in the Continental Congress, the U.S. Constitution was adopted, and Kentucky's statehood was postponed. Connolly used this opportunity to make a public offer to the people of Kentucky to join Great Britain. He suggested that the king would supply them with men and arms so that they could secure the Mississippi River and the port at New Orleans, which would provide access for shipping. Kentucky's settlers rejected his offer and forced him to flee.[44]

Little is known of Connolly's activities over the next few years. By 1798, he was at L'Assomption, Montreal, Canada. He wrote to his half brother, James Ewing, and suggested that the war raging in Europe would eventually involve the United States in a war with Spain. Surprisingly, he offered to assist the Americans in such a war.[45]

Connolly's final attempt to obtain a position of importance came with the death of his old friend, Alexander McKee, Deputy Superintendent General of Indian Affairs at Detroit. With the aid of the Duke of Kent, Connolly was appointed to the vacancy in December 1799. However, the position had already been promised to Captain William Claus, the grandson of Sir

William Johnson, the famous Indian agent of the mid-eighteenth century. Claus obtained the aid of Canada's Lieutenant Governor Peter Hunter, who wrote to the British ministry, which forced Connolly out by July 1800. Writing from Montreal to his half brother, James, Connolly noted that "the repeated disappointments I have met with in my life, & the late unexpected shock has brought on me complaints which I much fear. My old nervous disorder is much increased accompanied with others of a serious nature." Little is known of his life following this letter, but after suffering a "long and painful illness," he died at about age seventy in Montreal on January 30, 1813. According to his then-wife Margaret, his final years were spent mulling over the many frustrations and disappointments that had filled his life.[46]

Only death could bring an end to the pain and frustrations that plagued John Connolly. He had made grandiose plans throughout his life, hoping they would bring him wealth. He failed as a trader with the Native Americans on the frontier and lacked the skills necessary to succeed in business. He came closest to success through his valuable grant at the Falls of the Ohio. To obtain this title, he promoted a vicious interprovincial dispute and a war with Native Americans. These ventures nearly made him a wealthy man. But he was stymied by the Revolution, which displaced the government that would have granted his wishes. He chose to support Governor Dunmore and the British to achieve his dream of making a fortune, but Britain and he lost the Revolution. In failure, he moved to Canada with neither land nor wealth. Not only had he lost his dreams, he had lost his health, his family, and his property.

Notes

Doug MacGregor wishes to thank the editors of this collection of chapters and Karen W. MacGregor, Wayne Bodle, Charles Cashdollar, Michelle Wagner, and David Dixon for all of their help and support.

1. F. R. Diffenderfer gives either 1742 or 1743 as the year of Connolly's birth in F. R. Diffenderfer, "Col. John Connolly: Loyalist," *Lancaster County Historical Society Publications* 7 (1903): 109.

2. John Connolly, "A Narrative of the Transactions, Imprisonment, and Sufferings of John Connolly, an American Loyalist and Lieut.-Col. in his Majesty's Service," *Pennsylvania Magazine of History and Biography* (PMHB) 12 (1888): 310.

3. Connolly, "A Narrative," 311; Charles Hanna, *The Wilderness Trail*, 2 vols. (New York: G. P. Putnam's Sons, 1911), 2: 84; Clarence Walworth Alvord, ed., *Trade and Politics, 1767–1769*, vol. 16 of *Collections of the Illinois State Historical Library, British Series*, vol. 3 (Springfield, IL: Illinois State Historical Library, 1921), 519–20; Franklin Ellis and Samuel Evans, *History of Lancaster County, Pennsylvania* (Philadelphia, PA: Everts and Peck, 1883), 954.

4. Donald Jackson, ed., *The Diaries of George Washington*, 6 vols. (Charlottesville, VA: University Press of Virginia, 1976), 2: 322–33; Stanislaus M. Hamilton, ed., *Letters to Washington and Accompanying Papers*, 5 vols. (New York: Houghton Mifflin, 1901–1902), 4: 208.

5. "Letters of Thomas Wharton, 1773–1783," *PMHB* 33 (1909): 445–46.

6. "[John Connolly land grant], December 10, 1773," Reuben T. Durrett Misc. MSS, University of Chicago Library, Special Collections Research Center; "William Preston to George Washington, March 7, 1774," Hamilton, *Letters to Washington*, 4: 345–47. See also Patricia Johnson, *William Preston and the Allegheny Patriots* (Pulaski, VA: B. D. Smith, 1976), 114.

7. See John W. Huston, "The British Evacuation of Fort Pitt, 1772," *Western Pennsylvania Historical Magazine (WPHM)* 48 (1965): 317–29: Donna B. Munger, *Pennsylvania Land Records* (Wilmington, DE: Scholarly Resources, 1991), 63; Woody Holton, "The Ohio Indians and the Coming of the American Revolution," *Journal of Southern History* 60 (1994): 457–71; Thomas P. Abernathy, *Western Lands and the American Revolution* (New York: D. Appleton-Century, 1937), 94.

8. William Smith, ed., *The St. Clair Papers*, 2 vols. (Cincinnati, OH: R. Clarke, 1882), 1: 272, 279, 309; Boyd Crumrine, ed., *Virginia Court Records in Southwestern Pennsylvania* (Baltimore, MD: Genealogist Publishing, 1974), 18.

9. Anne M. Ousterhout, *A State Divided: Opposition in Pennsylvania to the American Revolution* (New York: Greenwood, 1987), 250–53.

10. Nicholas B. Wainwright, "Turmoil at Pittsburgh, Diary of Augustine Prevost, 1774," *PMHB* 85 (1961): 118, 131.

11. Samuel Hazard, ed., *Pennsylvania Archives*, ser. 1, 12 vols. (Philadelphia, PA: J. Severns, 1853–1856), 4: 625–26.

12. Edward G. Williams, "Fort Pitt and the Revolution on the Western Frontier," *WPHM* 59 (1976): 131, 133–35; Peter Force, ed., *American Archives*, ser. 4, 5 vols. (Washington, DC: Government Printing Office, 1837–1844), 2: 612–15.

13. Ousterhout, *A State Divided*, 253; Force, *American Archives* ser. 4, 2: 612–15; also found in Williams, "Fort Pitt and the Revolution," 133–35.

14. Nicholas Cresswell, *The Journal of Nicholas Cresswell, 1774–1777* (New York: Dial Press, 1924), 74, 97–99; "The Pittsburgh Tea Party," *PMHB* 39 (1915): 230–31; Smith, *The St. Clair Papers*, 1: 353–54.

15. Williams, "Fort Pitt and the Revolution," 27–31, 32–33, 131.

16. Connolly, "A Narrative," 314–15; "William Preston to George Washington, March 7, 1774," Hamilton, *Letters to Washington*, 4: 345–47; Holton, "The Ohio Indians," 467–473. See also Johnson, *William Preston and the Allegheny Patriots*, 114.

17. Williams, "Fort Pitt and the Revolution," 52; Percy B. Caley, "Lord Dunmore and the Pennsylvania-Virginia Boundary Dispute," *WPHM* 22 (1939): 100; J. W. F. White, "The Judiciary of Allegheny County," *PMHB* 7 (1883): 153.

18. Connolly, "A Narrative," 315.

19. Robert L. Scribner and Brent Tartar, eds., *Revolutionary Virginia: The Road to Independence*, 8 vols. (Charlottesville, VA: University Press of Virginia, 1983), 3:148–55; Hazard, *Pennsylvania Archives*, ser. 1, 4: 629; "Virginia Legislative Papers," *Virginia Magazine of History and Biography* 14 (1907): 56.

20. "Virginia Legislative Papers," 60–61; Connolly, "A Narrative," 318, 320, 356–57.

21. Connolly, "A Narrative," 315; Scribner and Tartar, *Revolutionary Virginia*, 3: 272.

22. Hanna, *The Wilderness Trail*, 2: 79–80.

23. Connolly, "A Narrative," 321, 322–23.

24. Force, *American Archives*, ser. 4, 3:72, 72–73; Louise Kellogg and Reuben Gold Thwaites, *The Revolution on the Upper Ohio, 1775–1777* (Madison, WI: Wisconsin Historical Society, 1908), 71.

25. Connolly, "A Narrative," 410.

26. Ibid., 413–14; Scribner and Tartar, *Revolutionary Virginia*, 4: 262.

27. Force, *American Archives*, ser. 4, 4: 155, 201, 216; John C. Fitzpatrick, ed., *The Writings of George Washington*, 39 vols. (Washington, DC: Government Printing Office, 1931), 4: 167.

28. Force, *American Archives*, ser. 4, 4: 479–80, 617; Connolly, "A Narrative," 417.

29. Connolly, "A Narrative," 417–19; Force, *American Archives*, ser. 4, 4:508; Connolly, "A Narrative," 420.

30. Force, *American Archives*, ser. 4, 4: 615; Walter R. Hoberg, "Early History of Colonel Alexander McKee," *PMHB* 58 (1934): 30–35.

31. Hazard, *Pennsylvania Archives*, ser. 1, 4: 703; Force, *American Archives*, ser. 4, 4: 958–59, 1563, 1666.

32. Connolly, "A Narrative," 62.

33. William W. Hening, ed., *The Statutes at Large: Being a Collection of All the Laws of Virginia, from the First Session of Legislature in the Year 1619*, 13 vols. (New York: Franklin Press, 1819–1823), 11: 321; T. L. Montgomery, ed., *Pennsylvania Archives*, ser. 6, 15 vols. (Harrisburg, PA: C. E. Hughinbaugh, 1907), 13: 10–11, 13–15, 22, 27.

34. W. C. Ford, ed., *Journals of Continental Congress*, 18 vols. (Washington, DC: Government Printing Office, 1905–1910), 4: 239, 257.

35. Force, *American Archives*, ser. 4, 6: 784, 1667, 1674; Force, *American Archives*, ser. 5, 3 vols. (Washington, DC: Government Printing Office, 1853), 3: 777.

36. Force, *American Archives*, ser. 5, 3:1606; Hazard, *Pennsylvania Archives*, ser. 1, 5: 101, 130–31; Connolly, "A Narrative," 64–70, 155–58; Force, *American Archives*, ser. 4, 5: 1122; J. B. Linn and William Egle, eds., *Pennsylvania Archives*, ser. 2, 19 vols. (Harrisburg, PA: Theo Fenn, 1879), 1: 719; *Colonial Records*, 16 vols. (Harrisburg, PA: Theo Fenn, 1852–1853), 11: 196, 229; Ford, ed., *Journals of Continental Congress*, 7: 229, 9:1004, 12: 1102, 1136.

37. Connolly, "A Narrative," 159–62.

38. Ford, *Journals of Continental Congress*, 14: 514, 623, 825, 825–26, 990, 15: 1170, 1231; Connolly, "A Narrative," 165–66.

39. Connolly, "A Narrative," 167; Williams, "Fort Pitt and the Revolution," 435, 436–39.

40. Connolly, "A Narrative," 13: 281–83, 284–85, 286.

41. Ibid., 286; Percy B. Caley, "The Life Adventures of Lieutenant-Colonel John Connolly: The Story of a Tory," *WPHM* 11 (1928): 23, n. 13.

42. Claude H. Van Tyne, *The Loyalists in the American Revolution* (Gloucester, MA: P. Smith, 1959), 299–302; Clarence M. Burton, "John Connolly: A Tory of the

Revolution," *American Antiquarian Society,* new series, 20 (1909): 95; "Deposition of John Connolly," Papers of the American Loyalist Claims Commission, Audit Office (AO) 13/134, Public Record Office, Great Britain (PRO); AO 12/109:102, Records of the American Loyalist Claims Commission, PRO.

43. Burton, "John Connolly," 99; Wilbur H. Siebert, "Kentucky's Struggle with Its Loyalist Proprietors," *The Mississippi Valley Historical Review* 7 (1920): 122–23; Caley, "The Life Adventures," 248–49; William Vincent Byars, ed., *B. and M. Gratz: Merchants in Philadelphia, 1754–1798* (Jefferson City, MO: Hugh Stephens, 1916), 18.

44. Caley, "The Life Adventures," 251; Burton, "John Connolly," 100, n. 89.

45. "John Connolly to James Ewing," June 25, 1798, MG 23 I20, vol. 1, James Ewing Fonds, National Archives of Canada, Ottawa, Ontario.

46. "John Connolly to James Ewing," July 30, 1800, MG 23 I20, vol. 1, James Ewing Fonds, National Archives of Canada; Burton, "John Connolly," 105.

CHAPTER 7

From Revolutionary to Traitor

The American Career of Herman Zedtwitz

Eugene R. Fingerhut

Herman Zedtwitz was an officer in the Continental army. While serving valiantly in the Canadian campaign of 1775, he suffered a severe rupture of an internal organ, was promoted from major to lieutenant colonel because of his efforts and his wound, and received a payment in Continental dollars for his services. Subsequently, suffering from the severe injury that left him unable to perform normal physical activity, he felt ignored and slighted by the Americans. He then initiated a correspondence with the British to recover a debt, which he claimed the Crown owed him for services he had rendered before the Revolution. The letter was intercepted. He was tried for treason and imprisoned by the Americans; his physical condition worsened, and he became mentally impaired. He alleged that conspirators had mercilessly tortured him. In this tormented state, he tried to flee to the British in New York City.[1] His journey from Patriotism to Loyalism is surely bizarre, and his plight underscores how difficult it is to make easy generalizations about who the Loyalists were or why they sided as they did.

In the turmoil of the Revolutionary War allegiance was not always firm; men changed sides for many reasons. For example, late in the war Ethan Allen opened negotiations with the British to keep Vermont an independently governed colony, after he had fought valiantly for the American cause. Men such as Herman Zedtwitz became a Loyalist because of personal pique and desire for repayment of a debt that he claimed the British owed him for previous service. His story is an example, too, of those Americans who felt they were not amply rewarded by the Continental government for the hardships they endured. Thus Zedtwitz put personal problems above the interests of the cause for which he had been fighting. Zedtwitz's story has another significance: the

179

impact of incarceration in wartime. The effect of his imprisonment destroyed him physically and mentally. He alleged that conspirators had mercilessly tortured him. Finally and ironically, when Congress took pity and offered to release him, he was too decrepit to leave his jail.

I

Zedtwitz claimed to have been a Prussian cavalry officer who had fought against France in the Seven Years' War and become acquainted with a British nobleman, the Marquis of Granby. Zedtwitz asserted that when Britain's dispute with Spain over the Falkland Islands threatened to become a war in 1770, the Marquis asked him to raise a contingent of riflemen, for which he was to be paid £24 per man. But Granby died nine days after Zedtwitz arrived in London, burdened by a debt of over £2,000 that he had incurred in attempting to raise these soldiers. When the international crisis subsided, all that he received were letters of recommendation addressed to two colonial governors.[2] Zedtwitz became obsessed with this debt, and its repayment came to be of overwhelming importance in his life.

Soon thereafter he migrated to New York City with his wife and children. On April 29, 1773, he notified the budding virtuosi of the city that "Harman Zedtwitz, Intending to settle in this city proposes to teach a certain number of gentlemen the violin, having been a pupil of several of the most eminent masters now in London and Germany."[3] However, few gentlemen were interested in taking lessons from him, and he was soon seeking a new enterprise.

On November 8, he unsuccessfully petitioned the City Council for appointment as sole inspector of chimneys. Two months later he advertised to the public that he had opened a chimney sweep office. Soon he advertised that he would serve everyone who had contracted work from him. He promised to remedy the complaints of those who had suffered poor service and insolence from his chimney sweeps. Zedtwitz cast blame onto others for his own mistakes and problems; this was to be a behaviorial pattern that he exhibited throughout his time in America. Later he accused another officer of cowardice at the battle of Quebec, and when in prison he projected his torments on iniquitous conspirators who tortured him mercilessly. His inability to accept imprisonment for his treasonous act induced him to create villains, who made his life miserable.

His business grew until he could boast of 100 customers, yet his denials of responsibility for customer dissatisfaction became more elaborate. He once publicly explained why fires started in five chimneys that he serviced. Three began because the patrons refused to have their chimneys cleaned when his sweeps visited them. The fourth occurred in the home of Alexander Wallace because his sweep attended the wrong house. The fifth was in the home of Hugh Gaine, the printer of the New York Gazette, whose chimney was so foul that his sweeps could only chip away at the loose flakes. By 1775, Zedtwitz was not only an apparently successful businessman, who counted some of the best people as his customers, but he was a member of the Harmonic Society with the elite of the city. He thus appears to have been a successful immigrant.[4]

II

At this point, the Revolutionary War intervened. On June 27, 1775, Zedtwitz informed the New York Provincial Congress that he was "a German by Birth and hath heretofore served as an officer in the King of Prussia's Army upwards of fourteen years." He volunteered to raise and command a regiment of 600 men "from Paxton and other parts of the province of Pennsylvany." He probably considered that because he was a Prussian he would appeal to Germans living in that province. Although this proposal was rejected, on July 15 the state Committee of Safety appointed him a major in New York's Continental regiment.[5] Zedtwitz's role in the Canadian campaign of 1775 was not as glorious as he would have liked, but it was honorable enough to earn him a promotion.

As General Richard Montgomery's army moved north, Zedtwitz's men took part in the fighting in the Lake Champlain area. However, some Americans leaked information to the British. One historian has asserted, "Among the officers at St. Johns [at the northern tip of the lake], doubtless Major Zedtwitz was not the only budding Judas."[6] This is teleological reasoning, however; whatever he may have become later, at that moment Zedtwitz was an ardent officer in the American military.

On December 16, Zedtwitz participated in General Montgomery's first council of war to plan the attack on Quebec.[7] Unknown is the role that Major Zedtwitz played during the charges through the streets on the stormy snowing night of December 29. In 1778, when he was physically and emotionally weak, Zedtwitz claimed to have been at Montgomery's side in the fatal attack. He also claimed that when the general and his aide were cut down at the head of the attack, he took command, was wounded thereafter, and was carried from the scene of battle. However, other witnesses averred that Deputy Quartermaster Donald Campbell assumed command at Montgomery's death and ordered the retreat.

Zedtwitz's superiors nevertheless agreed that he had fought well. General Wooster commended him, because "in the unfortunate attempt upon Quebec,

[he] fell down a rock, which has brought on a disorder I fear he will never recover from." Several months later American Brigadier General William Alexander, who claimed the title of "Lord Stirling," referred to Zedtwitz as a "brave and good officer, but so disabled by a rupture, occasioned by a fall from a precipice in the attack on Quebec under General Montgomery that he [was now] unfit for active duty." The Continental Congress, with Zedtwitz present, recognized his wounds as being "received by him falling from the walls of Quebec." Wherever he was during the fight, the major received his wounds under honorable circumstances.

However, Zedtwitz's reputation was not unsullied. On August 9, 1776, Captain Thomas Chessman sent a letter to General Washington, claiming that his son was aide-de-camp to General Richard Montgomery in the Canadian invasion. When Quebec was stormed, his son was at Montgomery's side and was killed with his commander in the failed attack. Chessman claimed that Zedtwitz either expropriated or withheld the possessions of his deceased son; he sought Washington's help to regain his son's property. There is no evidence of any action having been taken on this charge.

On March 26, 1776, after Major Zedtwitz had recuperated enough to travel, General Philip Schuyler ordered him to convoy several prisoners to New Jersey and report on the Canadian campaign to the Continental Congress. Schuyler chose him because, "General Wooster has recommended the bearer to me in such terms, that I should not do him justice were I not to introduce him to you." Two weeks later, the major reported to Congress, was awarded "255.6 dollars" for his troubles, and was promoted to lieutenant colonel under Brigadier General Alexander McDougall. Zedtwitz apparently now developed a plan to prove his value to the Americans. Soon after returning to military duty in New York City, he offered to persuade the Hessians to defect from their British allies. Even though Lord Stirling approved the plan, "no use was made of it."[8] At this point Zedtwitz appears to have concluded that he was not only too disabled for active duty and insufficiently compensated for his efforts but was neglected by his superiors.

When he had failed to solve prewar business problems, Zedtwitz had projected blame on others. Now he apparently behaved similarly. On June 18, 1776, Captain John Copp was brought before a court-martial to answer charges that Zedtwitz had made against him. The accuser charged that Copp had assaulted him in an argument resulting from Zedtwitz's allegation that the captain had been too timid in the attack on Quebec. The court decided that Zedtwitz's charges were false, and he publicly apologized. The captain may not have had close contact with Zedtwitz in the battle, but according to the latter cowardice such as Copp's caused the defeat and created the conditions in which Zedtwitz suffered his injury. Once again a villainous incompetent was the cause of trouble in Zedtwitz's world.[9]

After the trial, Zedtwitz seems to have thought more of his own problems than of the American cause. His mind apparently wandered to the great financial wrong that he had suffered. That summer he decided to collect the £2,000 that Great Britain owed him. The debt now became so important to him that he felt justified in sending to William Tryon, the royal governor of New York, information for which £2,000 would be paid.

The act demonstrates a significant weakness in the character of a former Prussian officer, who had served for fourteen years in one of the most formal and disciplined armies of Europe, and who now persuaded himself that he was justified in opening a correspondence with the enemy. Zedtwitz was becoming a traitor to the American cause. His attempt to regain the £2,000 by breaking martial discipline and committing treason violated his military experiences. It marked a turning point in his life, as drastic as in a Greek tragedy. He was on the path to degradation from which there was no return.

In early August 1776, a large British invasion force that had already landed on Staten Island was preparing an assault on Long Island and Manhattan. In the midst of this mounting tension, Lieutenant Colonel Herman Zedtwitz cryptically confided to Lord Stirling that the British "are now come [to New York], my Lord, and I will get my two thousand pounds." Later, Stirling vaguely recalled that Zedtwitz "went on to tell me how, but I paid little attention to the story. He never shew me any letter, nor pointed out any method he intended to take to obtain the two thousand pounds nor have I exchanged a word with him since."[10] Meanwhile, the Continental Congress proposed what Zedtwitz had previously suggested, without formally referring to his suggestion. It ordered that Hessians and "other foreigners" be promised freedom and land if they "quit the British service." Ironically, on August 23, General Washington ordered Zedtwitz to translate the document into German. However, by that day he had already commenced his traitorous activities.

III

On August 21, two days before Washington's order, Zedtwitz had offered to "enrich" Augustus Stein, a German civilian auxiliary with the American army. On August 24, the day after Zedtwitz was ordered to translate the petition, he asked Stein to take a letter to William Tryon, the British governor of New York, who was now on Staten Island. Stein agreed, but instead rushed the missive to higher American authorities. Zedtwitz was immediately apprehended for "holding a treasonous correspondence with, and giving intelligence to, the enemies of the United States." This letter was a catastrophic act by a man who had been an officer in the army of King Frederick II ("The Great"). Other Americans changed sides in the midst of the war because of familial, safety, or monetary concerns. However, few officers with Zedtwitz's military experience did so. When he later recalled his arrest, Zedtwitz remembered that his superior, Brigadier General McDougall, "called me a Traytor and other names unbecoming to a Gentleman." Zedtwitz had been a gentleman in Europe and tried to be one in America, but he had now behaved in a traitorous manner.

On August 25, 1776, at his court-martial for treason, the prosecution opened with Zedtwitz's letter to the royal governor of New York, William Tryon. It tellingly began, "By giving you this intelligence de World will ardenly blame my character, by serving in an armee and giving the Enemy Intelligence, but I apiel to your Eccelency, which knows that I was forced to accepd or to be a ruined man, with my wife and Children, bysides this I begged our Eccellcy's Councell & promised to do all in my power for his majesty, as I luked on myself as a forced man of a Rebellion Mopp."

To further ingratiate himself to the British, the writer also revealed that he had been assigned to translate the proclamation to the Hessians and that once, while he conversed with General Washington, an individual obtained the general's approval of a plan to poison the city's water supply. Next came the motive for his treason. He claimed that he had the friendship of an officer who was willing to supply weekly figures on the strength of the American army. This "interested one" had asked for £4,000 for this information, but Zedtwitz claimed to have persuaded the officer to reduce his price to £2,000 with payment in advance. In order to further impress Governor Tryon with the veracity of the proposition and his sincerity, Zedtwitz informed the governor of his impending promotion to full colonelcy and appointment as commander of three forts along the Hudson River.

The defense consisted of an affidavit that did not deny that this was Zedtwitz's letter, but which explained that his aim was to get back his £2,000. He complained, "This is the cruel fate to be ruined by an English Government for having done it all the service in my power." He had told Stirling of the debt and of his plan to obtain repayment but admitted that after Stirling told him that nothing could be done he wrote the letter.

The defendant next attempted to explain the several parts of the document. "[S]poiling the waters was a mere fallacy . . . as the waters of the city were daily guarded." The story about the informer who could supply information for £2,000 was intended to obtain the money the British government owed him. He excused informing the British of the proclamation to the Hessians, for the public already knew of the appeal. However, he was still not refuting the charge of sending information to the enemy. Lastly, he contended that the news of his new command was a trap to entice and capture Governor Tryon.

In their deliberations, the members of the court disagreed. Zedtwitz's life was spared by the "vote of a militia officer who pretended some scruples of Conscience." The prisoner was cashiered and "rendered incapable of ever holding a commission in the service of the United American States." In addition, the prisoner was confined, probably under orders of General Washington, who reviewed the sentence. Zedtwitz's apparently lenient punishment surprised at least one Continental official. On August 28, three days after the court-martial, Congressman William Hooper commented to William Livingston of New Jersey, "I cannot sufficiently express my horror at the Conduct of Col Zedwitz. There is something very peculiar and misterious in this matter. Pray . . . give me His history as far as it is material & the particulars which attend this infamous transaction." Twelve days later, Hooper again wrote to Livingston, asking how could Zedtwitz be a traitorous criminal and be sentenced only to be "boke by a Court Martial . . . when his charge was so black a dye & yet not deserve death [?] I confess I am at a loss to conjecture."[11]

To Zedtwitz, the decision of the court resulted from the malevolence of General Alexander McDougall. Reflecting on the trial about two years later, Zedtwitz recalled, while he was on duty in New York, McDougall "grew very avers in his Friendship toward me." Zedtwitz complained that when he could not work quickly because his wound reopened, McDougall reported him as dilatory to Washington. Zedtwitz claimed to have performed all his garrison duties, including supervising construction of fortifications in New York Harbor. He also claimed that Washington knew of his value, for he was promoted and put in charge of the Hudson River forts. During the trial, Zedtwitz had complained to the court that his undoing came when his letter to Governor Tryon was intercepted by McDougall, who duped Washington into ordering the arrest.

In the accused's recollection of the trial, McDougall testified against him. The general stated that even before the defendant wrote the incriminating letter, he had doubted Zedtwitz's patriotism and honesty; indeed, 24,000 cartridges for which the colonel was responsible did not appear in the record. Zedtwitz averred that he personally deposited the cartridges in a depot when the teamsters were ill and never received a receipt. However, McDougall had supposedly so impressed the court of Zedtwitz's perfidy that if General Stirling had not spoken on his behalf, then the court would have sentenced him to death. However, the trial record includes none of this testimony. By 1778, when Zedtwitz described his trial, his mental state had deteriorated, so that he probably imagined much of the testimony.

Consistent with Zedtwitz's tendency to blame others, he believed that the villainous McDougall caused his calamity.

During the next three years of his incarceration, Zedtwitz and his wife submitted many petitions for clemency to General Washington and the Continental Congress; all but the last were either rejected or ignored. In these pleas Zedtwitz revealed his suffering. The prisoner's appeals for release, some of which are undated, describe complicated plots and events that cannot be corroborated, so it is impossible to separate what truly happened from what he thought happened. The following sketch attempts to create a comprehendible story from the rambling of a mind that was becoming increasingly disturbed.

Zedtwitz claimed that calamities befell his family soon after he was arrested; his wife could not protect the contents of their home from pillage by New England troops. While being taken to prison he was constantly insulted by a lieutenant who spat in his face, called him a traitor, and had him dragged along the road, even though his wound reopened—a degrading experience for a gentleman.

In October 1776, Zedtwitz was imprisoned at Morristown, New Jersey, and complained to General Washington about his mistreatment. He was locked with twelve men in a foul cell without facilities and suffered from "a stagnation of blood rising from my heart to my throat, and [it] strangles me for want of breath." He pleaded that he certainly would die if he was not granted a parole. To demonstrate his good intentions, he enclosed a plan to get arms from Prussia. If Congress would send him to Europe with two agents of its choice, then he would obtain letters of credit and secure the weapons. All he requested was that his family be supported in his absence, that he receive the "second share" of prizes taken on the ocean, and that upon his return he be permitted to go with his family "to my own country."[12] No evidence exists that Washington acknowledged the plea. The prisoner later claimed he would have died in the Morristown prison that autumn if the jailer had not called for his wife to nurse him. After recovery, Zedtwitz was moved to better facilities, probably because of the intercession of Mrs. Zedtwitz, who worked constantly on her husband's behalf.

The first appeal by Mrs. Zedtwitz to the Continental Congress on November 18, 1776, won an additional $139 for her husband's early services to the American cause. At about this time the prisoner received news that his wife was pregnant and needed money. In spite of his physical problems, the prisoner was probably the father. Zedtwitz's devotion to his family is apparent in his appeals, and his wife's faithfulness to him was obvious; she consistently sought his release.

Because Zedtwitz had only about £50 he sent a letter that sought money from Governor Tryon. He now believed that Tryon was responsible for his troubles, for Zedtwitz claimed to have been imprisoned "on his [Tryon's] account." In his increasingly distorted mind, because he had written the letter to Tryon, he assumed that the governor had received it. The prisoner also wrote to General Sir William Howe from whom he also requested money, because of "my pretensions from the English Government." However, his attempt to send the pleas was foiled by several allegedly evil people who reneged on their promise to carry the letters; Zedtwitz burnt both appeals.[13] He now reached another crisis in his life.

A short time after he destroyed these letters, he claimed he overheard a group of men talking in the next room. They soon manifested themselves and told Zedtwitz that they had an electric machine that projected pain and were going to use it on him. This development marks the emergence of his relationship with a group of conspirators whom no one ever heard or saw. For the next few months, they dominated his life, until he was judged "disordered in his senses."

Who were these men? They seem to have been the creations of a mind that was sliding into illness. Zedtwitz, a former officer in the Prussian army, came from a family of repute and high rank. Raised in a noble or petty noble family, a family that could afford to purchase a commission for him, he may have been accustomed to other people, lower on the social scale, being incompetent and responsible for his problems. Also, hierarchical institutions, such as the army, in which a political pecking order exists, may enhance one's tendency to assign blame for failure to other persons. In such institutions, one may absolve oneself of responsibility by claiming that persons of higher rank either ordered that an action be performed or made incorrect decisions that caused injury. Zedtwitz's emotional predisposition to avoid blame by assigning guilt to others was enhanced by his life experiences. Incompetents of both lower and higher ranks were blamed for his shortcomings. We know that he wrote many petitions telling how the villainy of others drove him to madness.

Zedtwitz claimed that for the next six weeks after he met the conspirators they tortured him mercilessly, leaving him no more than two consecutive hours of rest. He admitted that during this treatment he became a raving skeleton, and that except for his tormentors, the only person he remembered seeing was a minister. The torturers demanded a full confession of all acts committed by the distraught prisoner, or they would cause him such great pain that he would die. He submitted by telling them everything he could remember of his life, back to his childhood. The torture was interrupted when Zedtwitz and his fellow prisoners were transferred to Fredricktown, Maryland. There the torment resumed for about three months, until about August 1777 (an estimate based on the dates of his petitions). The prisoner claimed the torturers then sent him a letter that confided that he had received the shock treatment so his "senses" could be restored. However, they added that he was still in terrible danger because of Washington's and Congress' "privit Instructions to thacke through thier [sic] Electric Instruments entirely away my senses."

Zedtwitz was soon transferred to Winchester, Virginia, where he was paroled, but his peace was short lived, for his tormenters followed him. Supposedly they told him that Washington and Congress would surely order other men to destroy him as soon as they discovered that the electric machine was used to restore, rather than destroy, his senses. The conspirators therefore ordered him to obey their instructions, or he "must inevitably be the most unhappy man in the world." They planned to flee to the British and violently swore that if the prisoner refused to accompany them, they would be "forced for their own security to thacke my life away, or else I mide betray them." After the escape, the party took a circuitous route to Easton, Pennsylvania, where only Zedtwitz was arrested for traveling without a pass. During his confinement there, Sheriff Robert Levers (who also was the county lieutenant) informed Timothy Matlock of the Pennsylvania Executive Council that he witnessed "an Examination taken before me of Herman Zedtwitz—the Honorable Mr. Hancock has since been here and observed, that it has been his opinion this unhappy man was disordered in his senses—[as proven by] two letters wrote by him since his confinement the one intended for General Washington, the other for General Howe, copies I enclose, it is manifest he cannot be in his right mind. I shall be glad to receive the directions of the council relative to this man, he having no wherewith to support himself, and now [is] languishing in prison."

On November 12, 1777, the prisoner sought release based on these two intercepted letters. To Washington he wrote of the conspiratorial work of the villains and of his present degradation in a cell with twenty-five other men and a pitiful diet. In the most humble manner he pleaded, "For the sacke of our Almighty Saviour Jesus Christ, . . . have mercy and grant my discharge, as I am not more able, in any terms whatsoever, to serve" in this war. He also requested that Washington forward to General Howe a message that described the conspirators as "high germans" who would "macke me believe a story to schoking to Relait, touching honorable characters of his Excellency's General Washington . . . and the President [of Congress]." He asked Howe to arrest these men if they appeared in Philadelphia, which the British army had recently invested.[14]

Soon Zedtwitz was transferred to Reading, Pennsylvania. Again, he sought release by writing pleas that described supposed encounters with the electric machine conspirators, who again proposed that he escape with them. About mid-1778, when all hope for release seemed gone, the eldest of the conspirators supposedly called the prisoner to the door of his room. He told Zedtwitz to come to their lodgings for some money. On a rainy night he sneaked out of his cell to get what was promised, but the men forcibly dragged him from their house while his screams for help were drowned by the storm. He was blindfolded, thrown on a horse, and taken about two miles from town to a house where he was interrogated. The captors admitted that they caused his mental disorder and claimed to have been former congressional secret agents who had fallen under suspicion. To allay criticism, they told Congress that in 1776 Zedtwitz informed General Howe of Philadelphia's defenses and how he might conquer the city.

The men now admitted that they had "disordered" his mind by blowing spices up his nose while he slept, and "from this time you never could have you entire senses" had the machine not been used to counteract the effect. To compensate Zedtwitz, the men now offered to secrete him to the British in New York City. There he would board a ship to London with a replica of the machine so that he could earn great sums of money and they could clear their consciences. True to a gentleman's moral code, he refused the offer, for to accept would be to abandon his family. Instead, he pleaded for money. In the face of Zedtwitz's honorable principles, his abductors "Stamped, Swore, and even damned my obstinate Temper" before they threw him into a stable to reconsider their beneficence. After the captors used the machine for several sessions in order to obtain his acquiescence, Zedtwitz escaped his tormentors by tearing some shingles from the roof and climbing out of the building. By 4 a.m. he exhaustedly knocked at the jail door and was readmitted to his cell.[15] In a petition he called on the sheriff and his jailer to affirm his ordeal, but as in his other escapades, no one saw the villains or the events he described.

IV

This was probably the last adventure he had with his conspirators. At this time he wrote long autobiographical pleas to John Hancock and John Jay, which told of his service to America, McDougall's enmity for him, and the machinations of the men who had repeatedly tortured him. Again, his supplications were unanswered. In late 1778, he appealed for his freedom by claiming to have received news that his brother had recently died, and that he had inherited all of his family's Prussian wealth. This he probably learned from his wife, who may have visited him during this confinement, although he did not mention her involvement. Previously he had referred to his genteel status, but now he specifically mentioned his social status as the basis for his release.

By May 9, 1779, after another plea to Congress had been ignored, he seems to have abandoned all hope of receiving a pardon. On that day he was captured near Morristown, "dressed in women's clothing," during an attempted escape to New York City."[16] At this point Zedtwitz had completed his tortured transformation into a Loyalist. With whatever mental acuity he could muster, he now identified his best interests with the British rather than the Americans. Once again his wife interceded, again petitioning on his behalf. She wrote to Congress over her husband's signature, requesting freedom for "Herman Baron Zedtwitz." His attempted escape in May "arose only from a Strong desire of making provision for his unhappy Family who are now reduced to the utmost distress and that he had not even the smallest Intention of doing Injury to the United States." All that he wanted was a suit of clothes and passage to the French West Indies or Europe for himself and his family. This was probably the petition that induced the American Board of War to recommend on July 14, 1779, that Zedtwitz be freed. The board was motivated by the "deplorable condition of his wife and family in consequence of his confinement" and in "consideration of his own unhappy condition." That day Congress directed that passage to the West Indies be provided for the Zedtwitz family.[17]

Nine days later, "Herman Baron Zedtwitz" conveyed his thanks to Congress and ironically requested permission "to remain with my family under confinement during my smale abode in this Country [because] I am so ill in my limbs" and cannot embark on a trip. In three years Zedtwitz had been reduced to an invalid. He probably did not live to leave the United States; in 1781, the tax list for the East Part of the Mulberry Ward in Philadelphia noted that "widow Zedtwitz" was without property and was unassessed.[18]

Thus ended the short American career of Zedtwitz. In describing his tormenters, he appears to have been familiar with one of the scientific fads of his day. In the 1750s, Benjamin Franklin had publicized his electrical experiments to cure paralytics. In 1760, John Wesley, the founder of Methodism, wrote *The disideratum: Or, Electricity Made Plain and Useful*, in which he extolled electricity as an excellent treatment for "nervous Cases of every kind." By 1770, many Europeans were shocking each other with their experiments and salon demonstrations. It is possible that before he came to America, Zedtwitz knew of this work because he was member of that society.[19]

His torturers pose a different problem. Were they the creatures of a disturbed and tormented mind? To those who witnessed his examination under Sheriff Levers, the stories of the electric machine and the conspirators appeared to be fantasy. Although he was not an expert on mental illness, John Hancock agreed that Zedtwitz was mad. Did Zedtwitz actually encounter men and in his disturbed mind embroider his encounters into full-blown fantasy? Was his decrepit mental condition at least partially the result of his confinement, even though he was a member of a noble family? To be confined as a common prisoner would certainly be degrading for a member of a noble family. Zedtwitz's emotions and reasoning may have cracked under that humiliation and strain. In his mind, his degradation would have to be the result of conspirators.

The Revolutionary War caused great hardships for Americans; the career of Zedtwitz illustrates one of its less realized deleterious effects. Zedtwitz's story parallelled Benedict Arnold's. Both men were severely wounded at a battle in which they served heroically. Both men thought and (more importantly) felt they were trivially rewarded for their efforts, considering that they were permanently injured and forced to retire from field duty. Both men offered the British information and Hudson Valley forts in return for their rewards. Both men were undone because they entrusted their plans to messengers who did not deliver their proposals. After valiant service in the Canadian campaign, Zedtwitz descended to the depths of mental decrepitude. Unlike Zedtwitz, Arnold was not captured, but his mental collapse was merely postponed. Both Arnold and Zedtwitz died broken men, both financially and in spirit. After valiant service in the Patriot cause, both men paid a high price for their treason.

Notes

1. Herman Zedtwitz has been described as "a fool" bent on "mischief" by Carl Van Doren, *Secret History of the American Revolution* (New York: Viking Press, 1941), 15–17. This conclusion is based on the few documents in Peter Force, ed., *American Archives* (Washington, DC: Government Printing Office, 1837–53), fourth and fifth series. This story of Zedtwitz's career is based primarily on his statements.

2. Ibid., fifth series, 1: 1159; Continental Congress, Papers of the Continental Congress, Mss. Item 78, 24: 675. A note (without attribution) in W. W. Abbott and Dorothy Twohy, eds., *The Papers of George Washington: Revolutionary War Series*, 18 vols. (Charlottesville, VA: University Press of Virginia (1985–2008), 5: 647, claims that Zedtwitz had been a captain in the Prussian army; the *New York Gazette*, April 29, 1773. The vagaries of eighteenth-century spelling render his name Harmon, Herman, Hermann, Zedtwitz, Zedwitz, Zedwiz. The most frequent form, Herman Zedtwitz, is used in this chapter.

3. John D. Camlin, "Nearly Two Centuries of Music," in *The Memorial History of New York*, ed. James Grant Wilson, 4: 166 (New York: New York Historical Company, 1892). For Zedtwitz's other musical activities, see the *New York Gazette: and Weekly Mercury*, April 1, 18, 1774.

4. New York City, Common Council, *Minutes of the Common Council of the City of New York, 1675–1776* (New York: Dodd, Mead, 1905), 8: 454; *New York Gazette*, January 24, April 11, 1774. See also his advertisement for a runaway sweep,

New York Journal: or Weekly Advertiser, March 2, 1775; *New York Gazette*, January 24, April 11, 1774. For the Harmonic Society, see the *New York Gazette*, April 3, 1775. He alone was mentioned by the colonial legislature when it considered on February 28, 1775, a plea from thirty-two persons for naturalization; New York, General Assembly, *Votes and Proceedings of the General Assembly of the Colony of New York*, 1775 (New York: Hugh Gaine, 1775).

    5. Force, *American Archives*, fourth ser., 2: 115; New York State, Secretary of State, *Calendar of Historical Manuscripts Relating to the War of the Revolution* (Albany, NY: Weed, Parsons, 1868), 1: 104; *New York Journal*, July 20, 1775; New York Legislature, *Journals of the Provincial Congress* (Albany, NY: T. Weed, 1842), 1: 80. There is conflicting evidence about Zedtwitz's rank when he was commissioned. Force, *American Archives*, fourth ser., 5: 317, cites the New York Provincial Congress minutes of February 28, 1776, appointing Zedtwitz to the rank of lieutenant colonel in the first New York regiment being organized for Continental service. However, letters (which will be considered later) consider his rank to be that of major when he was returning to Philadelphia from the unsuccessful attack on Canada.

    6. Justin H. Smith, *Our Struggle for the Fourteenth Colony* (New York: G. P. Putnam's Sons, 1907), 1: 421, 445; Christopher Ward, *The War of the Revolution* (New York: Macmillan, 1952), 1: 158, 160; Papers of the Continental Congress, Item 78, 24: 675; *New York Gazette*, August 14, 28, 1775; *Virginia Gazette* (Dixon and Hunter), September 9, 1775.

    7. Smith, *Our Struggle for the Fourteenth Colony*, 2: 116, 143; John Codman II, *Arnold's Expedition to Quebec* (New York: Macmillan, 1902), 179. Smith dismissed Zedtwitz's role in the council. "Lieutenant-Colonel Zedtwitz . . . was destined for a bad end, but did not intend it should be a bullet." In addition to being a misinterpretation of Zedtwitz's career to that point, it is factually incorrect. At this time he was still a major. See Papers of Congress, Item 78, XXIV, 675; Ward, *The War of the Revolution*, 1: 190; Force, *American Archives*, fourth seri., 5: 511, and fifth ser., 1: 645; Continental Congress, *Journals of the Continental Congress* (Washington, DC: Government Printing Office, 1906), 4: 271.

    8. Ibid., 190, 263, 271; Paul H. Smith, ed., *Letters of the Delegates to Congress 1774–1789* (Washington, DC: Library of Congress, 1976–2000, 25 vols.), 3: 494; Force, *American Archives*, fourth ser., 5: 511, 1662, 1665. On February 28, 1776, Zedtwitz had been nominated by the New York Provincial Congress for the rank of lieutenant colonel "for battalions intended to be raised in this colony." However, these letters refer to Major Zedtwitz, ibid., 317; fifth series 1: 1159. Chessman's claim is in *Papers of George Washington, Revolutionary Series*, 5: 647.

    9. Ibid., fourth series, 6: 790. For evidence that this accusation continued to haunt Copp, see New York State, Governor, *Public Papers of George Clinton* (New York and Albany, NY: State of New York, 1899), 3: 722–23, 4: 8, 9, 26, 620, 763, 765.

    10. Force, *American Archives*, fifth ser., 1: 1159. When promoted, Zedtwitz was placed under Brigadier General Alexander McDougall. However, that officer does not appear in the documents that describe Zedtwitz's activities at this time. The lieutenant colonel may have been temporarily assigned to duty under Lord Stirling, with whom he confided the plan to woo the Hessians, because Stirling recommended

noncombat duty for him. Such a reassignment may have resulted from an estrange-
ment between McDougall and his subordinate.

11. Ibid., 1607, fifth ser., 1: 159; John C. Fitzpatrick, ed., *The Writings of
George Washington* (Washington, DC: Government Printing Office, 1932), 5: 464;
Worthington Chauncey Ford, ed., *The Writings of George Washington* (New York:
G. P. Putnam's Sons, 1889), 4: 371; Papers of Congress, Item 78, 24: 677; William
Henshaw, *The Orderly Book of Colonel William Henshaw . . .* (Worcester, MA: A.
Williams, 1948), 228; Dr. James Thatcher, as quoted in Isaac Newton Phelps Stokes,
ed., *The Iconography of Manhattan Island* (New York: R. H. Dodd, 1915), 5: 1003. A
New Yorker reported on August 29 that "the court-martial divided about Zedtwitz and
have sentenced him to be broke; . . . but I do not learn that the sentence has been
confirmed by the General," *Virginia Gazette* (Dixon and Hunter), September 14, 1776.
Hooper's dismay at the decision is in Smith, ed., *Letters of the Delegates to Congress*,
5: 79, and Edmund C. Burnett, ed., *Letters of the Members of the Continental Congress*,
8 vols. (Washington, DC: Carnegie Institute of Washington, 1921–36), 5: 93.

Zedtwitz's career is surveyed, with the trial as the focal point, in two brief
essays. See Lorenzo Sabine, *Biographical Sketches of Loyalists of the American Revolution*,
2 vols. (Boston, MA: Little Brown, 1864), 2: 465–66; Harry Thayer Mahoney and
Marjorie Locke Mahoney, *Gallantry in Action: A Biographic Dictionary of Espionage in
the American Revolutionary War* (Lanham, MD: University Press of America, 1999),
334–35. The Mahoney sketch of fifty lines is based on Sabine's twenty-seven line
overview. Both statements begin with his petition to the New York Provincial Congress in June 1775 and end with his confinement (albeit Sabine cites John Hancock's
viewing of Zedtwitz in prison.)

12. Papers of Congress, Item 78, 24: 677; Force, *American Archives*, fifth ser.,
1: 1217–18.

13. Ibid., 3: 1573,1579; *Journals of Congress*, 6: 958, 972; Papers of Congress,
Item 78, 24: 677–78.

14. Ibid., 678, 679, 681; Samuel Hazard et al., *Pennsylvania Archives* (Harrisburg, PA: J. Severns, 1879–1890), second series, 3: 123–24, and first series, 6: 5.
Levers's letter to Matlock also is in *Papers of George Washington, Revolutionary Series*,
5: 5; Zedtwitz's letters are on pp. 234–35. On pp. 345–46 is a long note that includes
passages of the letter to Howe and a description of Zedtwitz's imprisonment.

15. *Pennsylvania Archives*, first ser., 6:5; ibid., second ser., 3: 123–24. Papers
of Congress, Item 78, 24: 679–81.

16. Ibid., and ibid., 667; Journals of Congress, 13: 93; *New York Gazette*, May
9, 1779; *Virginia Gazette* (Dixon and Hunter), June 5, 1779.

17. *Journals of Congress*, 8: 673; 14: 773; Papers of Congress, Item 41, 10: 737.
This petition bears the date August 25, 1777, but was probably written in late July
1779. In it is a statement that the prisoner "having these 35 months past suffered a
Close Confinement: deserves freedom." Zedtwitz had been imprisoned in late August
1776; the endorsement by Congress states "Philadelphia, June 22, 1779—Read June
26, 1779 & Referred to Bd of War."

Two standard references on European nobility mention the rank of count in
the Zedtwitz family. It was bestowed by Emperor Joseph II on Heinrich Sigmund

von Zedtwitz on March 24, 1766, but was not completed until 1790. None of the heirs was named Herman. See Marquis of Ruvigny, ed., *Titled Nobility of Europe* (London: Burkes Peerage, 1914), 1585; Johann Sievmacher, *Grosses und Allegeines Wappenbuch* (Nurnburg: Verlag der Raspischen Buchhandlung, 1777–1806), 2: part 2, M–Z, "Prussian Nobility," 466. There is no evidence that Herman Zedtwitz inherited the title "Baron" while in prison. If he did, then he died before these European texts could record his status.

18. Papers of Congress, Item 147, 3: 513; Item 78, 24: 687; *Journals of Congress*, 14: 826; *Pennsylvania Archives*, third ser., 15: 648.

19. Carl Van Doren, ed., *Benjamin Franklin's Autobiographical Writings* (New York: Viking Press, 1952), 71–74; John Wesley, quoted in Richard Hunter and Ida MacAline, eds., *Three Hundred Years of Psychiatry, 1535–1860* (London: Oxford University Press, 1963), 420–22; A. Wolf, *A History of Science, Technology, and Philosophy in the 18th Century* (New York: Harper, 1961), 494.

Conclusion

Joseph S. Tiedemann and Eugene R. Fingerhut

This book includes chapters about individuals, regions, and groups of people who became Royalists in the American Revolution. None of the persons considered here belonged to the social or political elites of the Middle Colonies. They were instead people of the common sort: small land holders, middling farmers, and men who craved high status. They included African American Loyalists and the Haudenosaunee (Iroquois), who had unique reasons for giving their allegiance to the Crown, reasons not shared by European American Loyalists. Whatever their race, however, all who sided with Britain saw the Revolution as a means to an end—protection from an implacable enemy, advancement in status, or the satiation of an indefatigable ambition. In this respect they were akin to many Americans, who became Patriots.[1] That is not to say that none of these people was moved by idealism, but that self-interest and idealism often informed one another.

The accounts of John Connolly and Herman Zedtwitz especially remind us that loyalty in the Revolution could be as much the product of egotism and self-interest as of altruism. The first individual was a persistent Loyalist, who repeatedly sought to advance the royal cause on the frontier. Connolly tried unsuccessfully to create a massive Loyalist uprising against the state of Pennsylvania and the United States of America. He vainly planned military campaigns that were to begin in the West and sweep eastward to join the British forces battling along the Atlantic coast. However, this consistent Loyalist, who had risen from his common status to befriend a royal governor, was motivated as much by his craving to achieve wealth and high social status as he was by his devotion to the Crown. His desire for land grants, which he believed he could secure only if royal government survived in Virginia, was as vital to him as the integrity of the empire.

Zedtwitz is another example of a person whose Loyalism was the outgrowth of his own personal needs and not the consequence of an unselfish zeal for the empire. As did Benedict Arnold, Zedtwitz became a Loyalist after he had persuaded himself that the Americans had not adequately recognized or rewarded his efforts on behalf of their cause. After his imprisonment for treason, his fragile psychological condition led to his demise and underscores how emotionally devastating that war could be for some people.

The experiences of Connolly and Zedtwitz make it evident that quite a few Loyalists of the common sort sided with the Crown for parochial and personal reasons. Their allegiance was the product of what they wanted, whether land grants, repayment of a debt, goods to sustain life, or protection against militant and ardent rebels. In contrast, many Loyalists of the aristocratic sort spoke and wrote of their loyalty to British political and economic institutions. They were familiar with British society; some had even been educated in the mother country. Loyalists of the common sort knew little about that world except through secondhand sources such as newspapers and tavern gossip and instead interpreted the Revolution in light of the impact of imperial policies on their own everyday life.

The exploitation of the Revolution for personal gain also may be perceived in the actions of militant slaves in the Hudson Valley. Obviously not all slaves acted to free themselves from bondage; some were impeded by their own individual circumstances, others by family and personal attachments. But the Revolution gave slaves the opportunity to achieve freedom by running away, by openly resisting their masters, and by taking up arms in either cause. The British found their participation in the war essential. Slaves could win freedom by entering British lines and laboring in support of both Loyalist and Regular troops. Some ex-slaves became spies and lurked about American lines to obtain valuable information; several returned to their former masters' domiciles and wreaked havoc in retaliation for their years of enslavement. Flight into British lines was self-emancipation.

The Haudenosaunee (the Iroquois) also used the Revolution to obtain what they wanted: British goods and protection against the ravenous European Americans, who would drive them from their lands. The Haudenosaunee saw Loyalism as a relationship between equals, albeit not between parties of equal military strength. They had not been subjugated by the British but had made treaties of alliance with the Crown. British officials agreed with this interpretation of their relationship. Although the Haudenosaunee were officially neutral in the war because the nations' leaders feared the devastation that the conflict might bring, individual warriors took sides. A large majority allied with the Crown, and in the period 1777–1778 many fought alongside British troops and European American Loyalists in raids on the western New York frontier and in the Wyoming Valley. The Patriots responded in 1779 with devastating campaigns into Haudenosaunee Country. Haudenosaunee villages were destroyed, crops were burned, and women and children were massacred. Many of those who survived the assault fled westward to Niagara and then to Canada, where the Haudenosaunee established a new life.

The experiences of African Americans and the Haudenosaunee demonstrate clearly one way in which European American Loyalists and Whigs were very much alike, and that is in their attitudes toward these two minorities. For example, Loyalist John Connolly was as eager to steal Indian lands as the most rabid Virginia Patriot on the frontier. And blacks continued to be regarded as second-class Americans whether they fled to British lines or supported the Patriots. After the war, white Loyalist refugees did far better than the black or Indian refugees who had sided with the Crown.

The chapters here also highlight the often vicious hostility that existed among the common sort in the Middle States. Although the facts are less well known, conflict in this region could be as fratricidal as it was in Georgia and the Carolinas. Guerrilla warfare in New Jersey, the Delmarva, and the Hudson Valley divided families and sundered communities. Places and groups that had been plagued by civil unrest in the late colonial period tended to endure armed civilian conflict during the Revolution. The careers of "China Clow" and his allies and the militant Loyalism of the counties of eastern New Jersey are noteworthy examples of this tendency. By the last years of the conflict, combat between Loyalist irregulars and revolutionary "militias" in the Delmarva and eastern New Jersey became indiscriminate and slid into brigandage. This irregular warfare promoted lawlessness and tore at the fabric of civil society. Other areas in the Middle States, including Westchester and Charlotte counties in New York, also experienced disruptions very similar to those in New Jersey.[2]

In sum, the chapters in this book provide some of the missing pieces of American history. Although all of the individuals described were adherents of the Crown, their motivations as Loyalists were as diverse as their backgrounds: Quakers, whom many Patriots regarded as de facto Loyalists because of their pacifism and their belief that only God had the responsibility for changing a legally constituted government; land speculators; outlaws; wives trying to cope with a war that was ruining their husbands; escaped black slaves; American Indians; and even an alleged former Prussian cavalry officer. In addition, as historian Wayne Bodle noted in his chapter, events in the world today can be seen in better perspective through "the study of small, local insurgencies and an appreciation of the energy that they drain from conventional struggles," reason enough not to ignore or overlook Loyalists of the ordinary sort.

Notes

1. For an example of one place where this was true for both Loyalists and Whigs, see "Communities in the Midst of the American Revolution: Queens County, New York, 1774–1775," *Journal of Social History* 18 (1984–1985): 57–78.

2. Jacob Judd, "Westchester County," and Paul Huey, "Charlotte County," in *The Other New York: The American Revolution beyond New York City, 1763–1787*, ed. Joseph S. Tiedemann and Eugene R. Fingerhut, 107–26, 199–222 (Albany: State University of New York Press, 2005).

About the Contributors

Wayne Bodle teaches history at Indiana University of Pennsylvania. He is the author of *The Valley Forge Winter: Civilians and Soldiers in War* and *The Fabricated Region: Making the Middle Colonies of British North America*, a work in progress.

A. Glenn Crothers is assistant professor of history at the University of Louisville, director of research at the Filson Historical Society, and coeditor of *Ohio Valley History*. He is the author of numerous articles on economic development in the early national and antebellum South, southern Quakers, and historical pedagogy that have appeared in the *Journal of the Early Republic*, *Business History Review*, *Agricultural History*, and the *Journal of American History*. He is presently completing a book manuscript, *The Quakers of Northern Virginia, 1730–1865: Negotiating Communities and Cultures*.

Eugene R. Fingerhut, Professor Emeritus of history, California State University, Los Angeles, has authored *Survivor: Cadwallader Colden II in Revolutionary America*, "Uses and Abuses of the American Loyalists' Claims: A Critique of Quantitative Analyses," in *The William and Mary Quarterly*, and "Loyalists," in Richard L. Blanco, ed. *The American Revolution, 1775–1783: An Encyclopedia*. He also coedited *The Other New York: The American Revolution beyond New York City, 1763–1787*.

David J. Fowler, formerly director of the David Library of the American Revolution, is currently a project historian with Special Collections, Rutgers University Libraries, New Brunswick, New Jersey. His dissertation, "Egregious Villains," deals with partisan conflict in Revolutionary New Jersey. He authored an essay on social and economic conditions on the home front in *New Jersey in the American Revolution*.

Michael E. Groth is professor of history at Wells College. His research concentrates on slavery and emancipation in New York and the emergence of free African American communities in the Hudson River Valley. In addition to presentations and professional papers on the subject, he has published articles in the *Hudson Valley Regional Review* and *New York History*. He is the author of "Laboring for Freedom in Dutchess County," in Myra Armstead, ed., *Mighty Change, Tall Within: Black Identity in the Hudson Valley*.

Doug MacGregor is a museum educator at Fort Pitt Museum, Pennsylvania Historical and Museum Commission, in Pittsburgh, Pennsylvania. His articles on Western Pennsylvania and Ohio River Valley history have appeared in *Western Pennsylvania History*, *Westmoreland History*, and the *Dictionary of Virginia Biography*.

Joseph S. Tiedemann, professor of history at Loyola Marymount University in Los Angeles, is the author of *Reluctant Revolutionaries: New York City and the Road to Independence, 1763–1776*. His articles on the Middle Colonies have appeared in *Church History*, *Historical Magazine of the Protestant Episcopal Church*, *Journal of American History*, *Journal of Social History*, *New York History*, and *William and Mary Quarterly*. He also was a contributor to and coeditor of *The Other New York: The American Revolution beyond New York City, 1763–1787*.

Robert W. Venables, PhD American history, Vanderbilt 1967, retired from Cornell University, where he taught two large lecture courses—"The Symbols of New York State's Cultural Landscape" and "American Indian Environments." He coedited and contributed two chapters to *American Indian Environments*. His other publications include chapters in *Exiled in the Land of the Free*, *New York in the 21st Century*, *The Treaty of Canandaigua*, *Encyclopedia of American Studies*, and *Indigenous Peoples and Environmental Issues*. He also was a contributor to *The Other New York: The American Revolution beyond New York City, 1763–1787*.

Index